THE
MARINE
FROM
MANATEE

Bill Harllee, (Circa 1919)

THE
MARINE
FROM
MANATEE

A Tradition
Of Rifle Marksmanship

BY JOHN HARLLEE

A Publication of the
National Rifle Association of America

ISBN 0-935998-52-7
Library of Congress Catalog Card Number 84-60717
Printed in the United States

Photographs courtesy the Marine Corps
Historical Center and the Harllee family.

Published by the
National Rifle Association of America
1600 Rhode Island Avenue, N.W.,
Washington, D.C. 20036

George Martin, Executive Director, NRA Publications
Frank A. Engelhardt, Book Service Managing Editor
Michael A. Fay, Production Manager
Harry L. Jaecks, Art Director

Dedicated to the author's wife, Jo-Beth Carden Harllee, in whom the Marine from Manatee saw the fire and the love.

ACKNOWLEDGEMENTS

The author is deeply indebted to Brigadier General E. H. Simmons, U.S.M.C. (Ret), Director of Marine Corps History and Museums, and his staff, particularly Miss Evelyn Englander, Mrs. Pat Morgan, and Mr. Robert V. Acquilina, for their invaluable assistance in research for this book. He would also like to express appreciation to the excellent reference librarians of the Library of Congress, especially Dr. Thomas Mann.

Much gratitude is due to the National Rifle Association, the files of which contain the story of American marksmanship, upon which a large part of this book is based.

Thanks are also due to the Office of the Judge Advocate General of the Navy.

The editing done by the author's wife, Jo-Beth Carden Harllee, was indispensable. Mr. and Mrs. Joseph H. McCann have made valuable suggestions.

However, the author is strictly responsible for any errors of fact and all opinions in this volume.

FOREWORD

Marksmanship has played a major role in winning our wars. Indeed, intensive training in the use of firearms is an integral part of America's military preparedness.

During the last 100 years, the National Rifle Association of America has made substantial, but underpublicized contributions in this important field. In the first third of this century, the NRA had a tremendous assist from Brigadier General William Curry Harllee (Ret.), of the United States Marine Corps, who helped blaze a trail in educating our armed forces on rifle marksmanship.

General Harllee led the crusade to make marksmanship a part of routine troop training for this Nation's military. This is General Harllee's story—a book which chronicles his colorful and eventful life, from his upbringing in South Carolina and at West Point, through his military service in the Philippines, China, Cuba, Mexico and Santo Domingo.

It is the story of an unsung hero in the fight to keep our troops adequately trained in the use of firearms. Whether or not we agree with him on every stand he took, General Harllee's life is an inspiring and informative tale of courage and a story about an original American mind at work.

STROM THURMOND
United States Senate

CONTENTS

INTRODUCTION

This is the story of the Marine from Manatee who, in a very large sense, taught America how to shoot. He also made other contributions to the United States Marine Corps in a colorful and effective manner. The tale of his life along the way is worth telling.

There is no longer any town of Manatee, Florida—it was merged with Bradenton. There are no longer any men like him—he was a man of his times—but his best qualities should be merged with those of Americans of today, even if he did have perhaps a little too much strength, loyalty and conviction.

The beginnings were colorful and full of combat—the Philippine Insurrection, the Boxer Rebellion, the landing at Vera Cruz, the Pacification of Cuba—and a wild youth and the rescue of fair damsels and poker games, tales that will all be told.

But it was all really prologue to Bill Harllee's major contribution to the Marine Corps and America.

For the contribution was in the field of straight shooting.

"Collier's Weekly," which then had the third largest circulation of any American magazine, wrote in its December 28, 1918 issue:

> Because Colonel William C. Harllee had insisted on target practice for over ten years, the Marines were able to shoot two German divisions to pieces and so save the line at Chateau-Thierry last July.

The Literary Digest, then a pillar of American journalism and possibly its most influential organ, said in its April 5, 1919 issue:

> But Major Harllee, by sheer persistency, gradually wore down the opposition and got the ears of those in high authority. It

xiii

was not long before the good shooting of the Marines became a byword at national rifle matches; and we have had numerous eloquent testimonials latterly to the grim effectiveness of this peace-time training. Without it Paris might have been in the grip of the Germans months ago.

It must be stated that the incomparable, suicidal courage of the officers and men of the Fifth and Sixth Marines at Belleau Wood, Chateau Thierry and elsewhere in France, as well as that of the U. S. Army units, is what stopped the Germans.

This man Harllee, William Curry Harllee, not only taught the Marines how to shoot—he was known as "The Father of Rifle Practice in the Marine Corps"—but he "wrote the book" on the subject, both literally and figuratively. He trained over half a million soldiers, sailors, marines, civilians, including some women, to shoot on the fourteen rifle ranges he built for the United States Navy in World War I.

How did it all start?

It started with fireside tales of sharpshooting by the old Confederates.

It got quite an impetus from Will Harllee's friendship with the most famous Texas Ranger of them all, Captain Lee Hall, and especially from the National Rifle Association—then and now the center of knowledge and competition for firearms.

It was encouraged by the Filipinos, Chinese, Mexicans, and even Americans, who shot at Harllee and missed.

It came into full bloom with his flaming dream of making America a nation of marksmen again as it had been at its birth. Even Franklin D. Roosevelt enthused about this.

After "The Great War" our man turned around and constructed a system of education for the Marine Corps that has flourished to this day.

And he continued to fight for what he believed was best for his country, even when it meant fighting the most powerful men in America with no chance of really winning.

Our story starts with his first gun battle.

I
THE FIRST BATTLE—
TEN MEN ATTACK A
THOUSAND—1899

*The Filipinos were the real patriots of
that war,
(The Philippine insurrection).*
—Brigadier General William C. Harllee,
U.S.M.C.(Ret)-1942

November 23, 1899, Thanksgiving Day. The Philippine Insurrection.

The American Corporal, Bill Harllee, spotted a campfire
through the early Philippine jungle night and some movement
200 yards ahead, which might mean an outpost of General
Alejandrinoe's brigade. He told his point of ten men to lie
down while he crawled towards the suspected enemy through
a muddy, water-filled ditch—"muddy glory" was a phrase
much used then. It was a terrible journey, although for once
he was thankful for the protection of his heavy dark blue
uniform shirt. In the slimy darkness—moonrise wasn't until 4
A.M.—he couldn't tell whether he was inching up on some
unsuspecting manapo snake (the bite of which was fatal unless
immediately cauterized) or through some tarantulas or leeches.

But crawl he did, up to 10 yards from the scene of the

1

movement. Sure enough, several armed Filipino Insurrectionists were on guard there. He had to work his way backward through the ditch to return to his men, because it was too narrow to permit turning around. Then he sent the word back a mile to his Company Commander, Captain Fowler. He advised him to halt the company until daylight. The company had been on the march from early morning until midnight with Harllee's advance party scouting a mile ahead for the last two days, and the Americans could not see well enough to attack at night in the Philippine jungle.

In those few watching and waiting hours in the dark, surrounded by thick vegetation with its background of alien sounds, a lot of thoughts passed through the mind of Bill Harllee.

He thought of the "soldiers" he had just observed—men believed by the Americans to be criminals and outlaws—whose "Filipino Revolutionary Government" was reported to have issued an order on February 15, 1899 to massacre all foreign residents of Manila. Men who allegedly tortured, mutilated and killed American prisoners. And yet these "Insurrectos" were so numerous and formidable that our small standing army could not deal with them. Volunteer regiments had to be raised. Harllee remembered how he had agreed with 1st Sergeant S. S. Megill of another company (E) of the 33rd U. S. Volunteers, later a Colonel in the U. S. Army, that they would some day tell each other about how they felt under their first fire. He recalled the tales of the Civil War and the courage of his father and uncles. He thought with remorse of his terrible problems at the Citadel and West Point and his difficulty in controlling himself and his temper. Fighting men were especially honored in the old South of his day and indeed in all America then. He determined that come what may he was going to join his relatives and ancestors as a fighting man.

Just before daylight Captain Fowler came up to see him.

"Did you watch them?" he asked.

"Yes, sir," replied the corporal, "They're still there."

"I want you to make sure of that, Harllee," said Fowler.

"Very well, sir," said Corporal Harllee. He was mad as hell.

He knew they were there. Rifle at the ready, he walked right up the trail this time. To hell with crawling through mud and water! If he had to prove to this damned captain of his that they were there, then he would do it.

He was 15 feet from the fire in the darkness when two Filipinos leaped up and fired away at him. Harllee raised his rifle and cut them down, thanking the Lord he had learned to rapid-fire his Krag in the dark. Other Filipinos jumped up from the fire and ran off into the darkness, leaving their hats behind them.

He was delighted to find that he was not frightened by being fired upon at close range. He might have been concerned about ruining the operation by losing the element of surprise. Not so. Instead a lot of the superb self-confidence he was to show the rest of his life showed up in his next decision. He decided to attack immediately with all ten men of his point and without orders from anyone, although the enemy brigade had been variously estimated at one to two thousand men.

"Don't shoot until I get back!" he shouted as he ran back to join his men, not wanting to get shot accidentally. They ran up to meet him half-way, with their rifles ready. Meanwhile, Captain Fowler had gone back for his company.

"Spread out! Line of skirmishers! Fire at will! Forward!", commanded Bill Harllee. The 10 men swept forward through the jungle into rice paddies. With the gray dawn they could see a little. They saw Filipinos, ducking and running away from them. The outpost Harllee had driven back had the effect of driving back other outposts like dominoes. The Americans fired, Filipinos fell. The firing range was close, often 50 yards.

"Don't give 'em time to get set! Smash 'em!" yelled Harllee as his ten men raced along. The Philippine air was full of the sound of the firing of the Americans' Krags and the Filipinos' Mausers as the Americans charged and the Filipinos retreated.

Harllee knew he was outnumbered, but he also knew the other 55 men of Company F would be coming up before long; and they did, although for 2 hours Harllee was in charge of the firing line. The early morning light and the spiralling mists of the rice paddies helped conceal the fact that he had such a tiny number of men.

"Forward, battalion!" he shouted to imaginary "captains" as a battalion commander would. It worked. They uncovered more Filipinos, who fired as they fled. They thought an American battalion was at their heels! They had 14 pieces of artillery, but only two Nordenfeldt rapid-fire pieces were employed against the Americans.

It was called "The Battle of Mangatarem". It was an odd fight indeed, the American number swelling by ones and twos to a total of some 65 men as Captain Fowler, reaching his company, ordered them forward into action. They dropped blankets and haversacks; dropped everything but rifles, cartridge belts and canteens. Some cast off canteens. After all, Chinese burden bearers in the rear were bringing up rations and more ammunition. The soldiers ran toward the firing. The fastest runner got there first. Some of the company did not catch up with the advance party for several miles.

Harllee felt so good that he started up a song popular then. The Americans smiled, paused a moment, and sang the chorus as they went through the rice paddies:

I'm lookin' fo' you' bully
    Who jus' done come to town.
I've bring along ma' trusty blade
    To carve dat bully down.

Then he sang "There'll Be a Hot Time in the Old Town Tonight." The sharp sound of firing Krag-Jorgensen rifles provided background music. Bill Harlle was "having a ball", in the slang of a later generation.

Finally all of them, those who charged and those who retreated, tumbled into the town of Mangatarem, 3½ miles from their starting point, in the province of Pangasinan, after leaving scores of dead Filipinos strewn in the rice paddies. If the Americans had ever hesitated, the Filipinos could have gotten set and stopped them. They had plenty of courage, but they were surprised and confused.

The Filipinos in Mangatarem tried to get organized as the wild company of 65 crazy Americans came storming out of the

4

rice paddies and the bamboo. But the bewildered Filipinos who the Americans were driving before them transmitted their panic to those in the town. After less than 15 minutes of hot street fighting with bullets, butts and bayonets, the army of General Alejandrinoe ran off into the "bosque." Those 65 Americans had defeated the biggest army the Filipinos had and, miraculously, without losing a man.

The official report on the battle stated later that the company had been advancing for nearly three hours under very heavy fire. However, the Filipinos shot from the hip, or if they sighted they only used the sight on the muzzle, so they fired over the heads of Harllee and most of the forward men into the rear ranks of the Americans.

The American casualities were only one man wounded. This left a deep conviction in Harllee's mind for the rest of his life that the best chance of safety in war lies in instant and audacious action.

Company F of the 33rd U. S. Volunteer (Texas) Infantry Regiment did more than defeat several hundred or a thousand Filipinos and capture a town. They recaptured seven American prisoners and 96 Spanish prisoners, seven of whom were officers, including a lieutenant colonel and two wives of Spanish officers. They captured warehouses filled with rice, coffee, sugar, uniforms, ammunition, dried meat, and dried fish as well as records relating to housing, collections of taxes and voluntary contributions. It was the biggest base of army supplies owned by the Filipinos. General Alejandrinoe himself was captured. The official report later estimated the enemy at 400 to 1000 men. But the Americans realized that when the Filipinos saw that Company F only had sixty-five men who were a long way from supporting forces, they were likely to regroup and attack the Americans.

Accordingly, Captain Fowler sent four men back for reinforcements. For three days Company F held Mangatarem and its population of 3000. All on guard duty, the 65 exhausted men expected any minute to see one or two thousand Filipinos come charging out of the jungle in a counter-attack. Then into Mangatarem came Colonel J. Franklin Bell at the head of two eager battalions of American infantry. Colonel Bell was riding a "caballo grande"—a big American horse. He was dressed in pants, boots and an undershirt with the front torn open. He was a fighter, in fact, he hammered so hard that the Army called him "Ding-Dong Bell." Instantly Colonel Bell ordered an attack on the 2000 or so Filipinos nearby. He told Captain Fowler that Company F could guard Mangatarem and rest.

"Rest, hell!" said Captain Fowler. "We won't stay here. We're going along."

Colonel Bell knew his fighting men.

"All right, Captain Fowler, if you feel that way about it," he said with a smile.

They routed the Filipinos into the hills. Bill Harllee went with Company F of the 33rd Volunteers and the 36th Infantry into the Zambales Mountains and helped win the Battle of San Miguel on November 29, 1899. They captured 15 pieces of artillery.

Harllee marched back into Mangatarem, his feet wrapped in rags. His shoes had literally been marched off his feet. Soldiers' mail came presently. Colonel Bell was promoted to brigadier general for the Battle of Mangatarem. Harllee, who had instigated the battle, also got his reward—nearly two days of sleep. Then, Captain Fowler gave him a pass to Manila. He rode the first railroad train that ran from Dagupan to Manila, 100 miles. It took them 10 days, fighting ambushing Filipinos in the bush all the way. It's a two to three hour run today.

On December 3, 1899, the official report of the Company Commander stated: "Corporal Harllee deserves special mention for bravery". He was the first named of four enlisted men of the company so commended. He was also cited for bravery in the report of General Lloyd Wheaton.

On December 17, 1899, about 3½ weeks after the action, Harllee remembered his promise to write First Sergeant S. C. Megill:

My Dear Friend,
    They couldn't keep such good people in F company on Corregidor Island, so they sent us out on a raid, and I guess you have heard about Mangatarem.

6

I am thoroughly familiar with the snappy pop of the Mauser projectile and found it blended with the long howl or swish of the Remington music to sing a tune more like "Nearer My God To Thee" than anything else; machine guns and shells kept the interest from growing dull.

Still I felt very differently from how I have aways had an idea I would feel. I believe I promised to tell you how I felt under my first fire.

Well, I felt fine and, honor bright, didn't feel panic stricken at all. I was in charge of the firing line on the right of the road and everything went just as smoothly, and even more so, than at drill, for I wasn't disturbed by any orders from anyone else.

I felt highly exhilarated and our whole line was singing "The Bully" and those old roundelays you always liked to hear. In fact, I felt as I have never felt before, an indescribable feeling. I wanted to locate more "hombres" and was eager to press forward. For a long time after the fight it didn't occur to me that it was likely that one of those bullets might hit me. All of our men did well and Scutalario and some of my other old characters distinguished themselves. I promised to tell you how I felt in action but I have failed because I just can't describe it.

But these were the actions and writing of a 22 year old man from the backwoods of Florida and a cotton farm in South Carolina. Two years later, he wrote his uncle (from Manila), "Everyone out here feels like our government made a mistake in taking them (the Philippines)."

There was a U. S. Army song at the turn of the century which was very popular with the soldiers there:

In that land of dopey dreams,
happy peaceful Philippines,
Where the bolo man is hiking night and day
Where the Tagalogs steal and lie
    Where Americans die
There you hear the soldiers sing this evening lay
Damn, damn, damn the Filipinos
Pockmarked khakiac ladrone
Underneath the starry flag
Civilize him with a Krag
And return us to our beloved home.

A third of a century later, after much experience in higher positions but still on the gun barrel end of "Dollar Diplomacy," he came to the realization that the "Insurrectos" were really patriots, not criminals. They had the sympathy of all Filipinos, because they wanted independence. Such a desire must be considered a worthy one by a nation which believes that "just government should have the consent of the governed." Harllee then made speeches against and fought against "Dollar Diplomacy," but that is getting ahead of the story.

After the Battle of Mangatarem, Bill Harllee received a telegram from Colonel Sparkman, his Congressman and good friend, informing him that he had been nominated for a second lieutenancy in the United States Marine Corps and that he would be appointed as such if he could pass the examination in Washington, D. C. So he was ordered back to Washington. Totally unexpected as it was, it looked like the dream come true, despite all the disappointments and detours enroute.

While awaiting transportation, he spent a week in Manila, where Lieutenant J. C. Minus, from the West Point Class of 1899 and a warm friend of Harllee at both the Citadel and the Point, and the other officers in the Classes of '98 and '99 couldn't do enough for him. He got rigged out in "cits" (civilian clothes) with a Dunlap hat and lived at the 20th U. S. Infantry Officers mess, enjoying good food and "glorious beer". He sailed for San Francisco in December of 1899 on the S. S. Conemaugh, a chartered horse transport returning empty.

Harllee heard later that after his lifelong friend Reese Fowler was mustered out of the Volunteer Army, he went to Nicaragua and became a general in the Revolutionary Army. In one of their engagements, the force he was with was shattered and Fowler was wounded in so many places his body looked like a piece of Swiss cheese. He hid out and was rescued by the Marines, later to become a major in the Army of the United States in World War I.

II
BOYHOOD & YOUTH
Tales of the Old Confederates
The Citadel—Chapel Hill—
School Teaching: 1877–1897

*These sentiments define the tie that
binds each mother's son and daughter
to those who gave them birth even unto
the remote antecedents who each in
turn felt for their sons and daughters
the divine devotion which forms the
family tie and stamps family loyalty as
one of the noblest virtues.*
—**William Curry Harllee in "Kinfolks", 1934.**

Television, radio, movies, automobiles and air travel were
unknown to the people of America in the last part of the 19th
century. Only eighteen out of a thousand people in the United
States owned a telephone in 1900. Books were known and
read, but the ancient, word-of-mouth passing down of legends,
stories, beliefs, even history had a powerful effect on youngsters
and adults, as it had had through the millennia.

And in the case of William Curry Harllee, known in his
boyhood as Willy but later known variously through the years

9

as William, Will, Bill, Beau, Bo and the King, as became his many-sided nature, these word-of-mouth transmissions were especially intense. His family history had such an unusual effect on his life that perhaps an abnormal amount of space must be devoted to it.

The name Harllee had been Harley in England. The powerful Earl of Oxford, Robert Harley, after whom Harley street in London was named, was a kinsman. But Peter Harley, an officer in the Royal Navy, supported the Stuart progenitors of the Bonnie Prince Charley and had to flee England when the Hanoverian George came to the throne in 1714. When Peter came to America he had to change his name to Harllee to avoid deportation and execution. His great great grandson William Curry Harllee wrote of him and his descendants:

> The admirable trait of steadfast adherence to principles and people they have supported, without regard to the ascendancy or decline of their fortunes, has characterized this family in America as well as their English prototypes.

Another direct ancestor was the Reverend Richard Bucke, who was shipwrecked on Bermuda in 1609. He then came on to Jamestown to be the second minister there and to officiate at the wedding of John Rolfe and Pocahontas on April 5, 1614. Bucke and his family accompanied them on their trip to England, where Pocahontas was a great success, being presented to the King and Queen as a princess and attracting much favorable comment.

One of Willy's great great great grandfathers was Dr. James Robert Adair, also known as Robin Adair. Adair (1709–1786), whose family was of the Scottish nobility but who had migrated to County Antrim in Ireland, was among many things a scholar; a surgeon; a fighter with the Indians against the French in the French and Indian War; the holder of a record of several incredible escapes from capture by the French; a highly successful diplomat from the English colonies to the Indian tribes, who kept many Indians from lining up with the French in the French and Indian War; author of "Adair's History of the American Indians," a classic on the subject; an amasser of a commercial fortune; and, an explorer and trader from 1730 to

1770 in the area which is now comprised of the southern states between the Atlantic and the Mississippi River. Adair was indeed a legendary character who had hobnobbed with the English nobility in London, but who also was brigade surgeon on the staff of General Francis Marion, the Swamp Fox of South Carolina, one of the world's earliest and most successful guerrillas. He was a lover, husband and father who founded four families, two white and two Indian. In England he married the Lady Caroline Keppel, who wrote "Robin Adair," the ballad about him. Her father was the Earl of Albemarle, Governor of Virginia, although he never came to the colony.

Willy's family on his father's side supported the colonies and fought the English during the American Revolution.

John Waddell Harllee, William's father, had been elected 1st Lieutenant in Company I, Hagood's South Carolina Infantry, Confederate States Army. He fought through the terrible battles in Virginia, Tennessee and Georgia. On May 7, 1864, he was wounded for the second time—his right knee shattered by a minie ball. His brother, Captain Andrew T. Harllee of the 8th South Carolina Volunteer Regiment, Kershaw's Brigade in the same Corps (Longstreet's), heard that he was mortally wounded (fortunately not true) and found him at a field hospital in the hands of two surgeons who were prepared to amputate his right leg above the knee. Although the surgeons urged the necessity of it, John insisted that this leg not be amputated, preferring death to the loss of the limb. Only with the help of Andrew was he able to avoid the amputation.

The surgeons, their personal friends, had finished their medical courses in Paris and had gained much experience after their fine educations. They explained to him that resection of the knee joint, the only alternative, would jeopardize his life. Few such operations had ever proved successful. The doctors bluntly told him he would probably die under the knife. He replied, "I will take the risk. Give me the chloroform and resect." He also implored his brother not to allow them to remove the limb. Against their judgment, the doctors performed the operation and he survived. His leg was shortened about 4 inches, but it did him good service.

Horace, John, John W., Andrew and William (Circa 1881)

He was then promoted to Captain and assigned to duties as Enrolling Officer (in effect Provost Marshal) in his home district at Marion, South Carolina. He was too loyal and honest not to come into savage collision with the "carpetbaggers" and "scalawags" then reconstructing South Carolina. So, in 1868 he moved to Manatee, Florida. He prospered there as a generous, public spirited and highly successful merchant, the top one in his county.

John Waddell Harllee died of yellow fever when Willy was only 10 years old.

It was from Willy's Uncle Andrew Turpin Harllee, who lived until after the Spanish-American War, that he heard most of the tales of the old Confederates which inspired him all his life. Andrew's war record is therefore worth examining.

Andrew Harllee was born on a farm and raised with a hunting rifle. When quite a youth, he went to the Kansas Territory in 1855 and he remained there for a year fighting Free State forces under Ossawatomie John Brown. He was no stranger to the whistle of bullets from Sharps rifles (Beecher's Bibles) when the Civil War began. These were the rifles from which the term "sharpshooter" was derived.

In one fight, at Hickory Point, Andrew and 64 other sharp-shooting Southerners in a blacksmith shop, hotel and grocery were able to hold off an attack of 250 Northerners for 9 daylight hours of firing with a night of non-firing in the middle. The Yankees had cannons and their foes none; but the Southerners assigned a lieutenant to tell them whenever the cannon flashed and upon signal they threw themselves to the ground. The battle wound up as a draw—with each side quitting and keeping what belonged to them. Eighteen Northerners were killed and three Southerners, but oddly enough at the end the Yankees drank with some of the Southerners. Colonel Harvey, the Northern commander, said, "If his opponents had been Missourians, he would have fought until I killed the last one, but when he found out they were brave Carolinians, I would not kill such brave men."

After the fighting in Kansas, Andrew took a government job in Washington for a short while at the behest of his Congressman. A typical letter from Andrew Harllee in that city to his sister, dated November 30, 1859 is quoted in part herewith:

There is no news of any great importance. The members and Senators are pouring in and the city is full of strangers. Congress meets on Monday, and I expect they will have warm times, organizing the House. The fate of the Democracy depends upon the organization of the present Congress. If the Republicans get it they will appoint their committees and manage so as to carry the Presidential election in 1860 then a dissolution of the Union will come. Only one of our members is here yet, Col J. D. Ashmore. He is one of the cleverest men I ever saw. He is going to room with me, his family will not be on. I went with him to see the President the other night and we staid (sic) with the old Hoss an hour and a half.

I went yesterday and traveled around with Miss Clayton, leaving our cards. You may not understand this, I will tell you— it is fashionable here just before the season commences to call on such places as you intend to visit during said season and leave your card, and then you are certain to be invited to all their parties, receptions, etc. Well this was my first experience in card leaving. We went around in a carriage. Called at the door and did not get out but sent in the cards by the servant and then drove on the next place and so on till you get around. Miss Clayton is very fashionable she thinks. I came near puking 3 or 4 times.

Andrew returned to South Carolina in 1860. He enlisted in the Confederate States Army in South Carolina as a Private on April 13, 1861, fought in the First Battle of Manassas, and was elected Captain of Company I, 8th South Carolina Infantry after the severe battles of the Peninsular Campaign. No regiment of the Confederate Army fought in more battles, and Andrew was in them all, except Fredericksburg. The company was shattered in 1862, 1863 and 1864, but replenished by the return of wounded men.

Andrew did not have an easy time in the war. In the Battle of Maryland Heights, near Harper's Ferry, he was severely wounded. All the color bearers and guards had been killed or wounded, and since his company was the color company he snatched the flag with his own hands and was leading the charge when a minie ball pierced his right thigh. He fell but

14

pulled himself up by the flag staff and went hopping on his left 'till another minie ball hit that leg. Then he could go no further. The flag was seized by Colonel Hennegan, and he, too, fell severely wounded. The regiment, thus inspired, pressed on and caused the surrender of Harper's Ferry by the Federal Forces. For a time, Andrew lay exposed to fire by friend and foe, but was finally rescued.

At Gettysburg in 1863 he was again shot in the right thigh. Every man in his company was killed or wounded. He was wounded in the left ankle at Bean Station, Tennessee. In 1864, he was wounded for the fourth time at the Wilderness Battle. This time, a spent ball hit him in the head, but he did not leave his command.

When Johnston's Army surrendered and was paroled at Greensboro, North Carolina, three weeks after Appomattox, Andrew was not captured. With his command, he had cut his way through the enemy lines. He was Chief of Scouts of General Hardee's Corps, which operated before General Sherman's Army in its raid through the Carolinas. This command consisted of veteran officers and men who belonged to organizations which had been demolished under General Early in the Shenandoah Valley and General Hood in Tennessee. They gathered as mounted men to hang on the flanks of and to the rear of Sherman's "bummers" in their raid through the Carolinas. These daring men, most of them officers, made it hazardous for the "bummers" to stay in small detachments encumbered with loot and far from the main bodies of their armies. One recalls how Scarlett O'Hara of "Gone With the Wind" handled one such "bummer" at Tara. Beside the number of Yankee soldiers treated in such a manner, a number were taken prisoner by Andrew.

When Johnston's army surrendered it was not known what might happen to such Confederates as Hardee's scouts: a dreaded military prison or perhaps worse for some. They did not wait to see. They were mounted and not within grasp of Sherman's forces. Andrew Harllee never did surrender.

He became a highly successful farmer near Little Rock, South

15

Carolina after the War; a Trial Justice from 1876 to 1888; and a delegate to the Democratic National Convention in 1884.

Willy's mother's family, the Currys, had accumulated wealth in South Carolina before the Revolution, but they, along with many other Scotsmen and men of wealth in the "low country" (eastern South Carolina), had remained loyal to the King during the Revolution. They had been so proscribed that all their property was confiscated, and they were to be put to death without benefit of clergy if apprehended in South Carolina. So when the British troops left, they had to leave also, and they migrated to the Bahamas. Some of them left the Bahamas in 1834 for Key West where they became prosperous until wrecked by the Civil War, after which several of them, including Willy's mother, moved to Manatee. The Currys who remained in Key West prospered so well that one of them, William Curry, was called "Rich Bill" and was the first millionaire in Florida. His family owned the southernmost house in the United States. The Currys were also owners and masters of vessels which sailed all over the world.

The Curry men were generally quiet and reserved and not given to relating with any gusto stories of their adventures—nautical, wartime or financial.

Willy's uncle, John Curry, with whom he was raised from ages 2 to 7, had been a sea captain, roaming the world for fifteen years, but strange to say he never used intoxicating liquor nor did he use profanity. He was a man of courage, possibly because of, rather than in spite of, these abstinences. When he was captured by the U. S. Navy as a Confederate blockade runner, he refused to sign the oath of allegiance to the United States and escaped.

So much for the family history.

1882. The little five year old boy called Willy burst into the big house on the north bank of Florida's beautiful Manatee River and saw that his nine sisters and brothers were starting to eat guava preserves and homemade cheese on homemade bread.

He shouted, "Hey, Mamma, I want some, too!"

She replied, "Yes, Willy, come here and get it."

But the person he thought was his "Mamma" was not his mother, nor were the other nine children his brothers and sisters.

He had been born on June 13, 1877 in another home on the north bank of the Manatee River. The town was then called Manatee, but it long ago merged with Bradenton, about 40 miles south of Tampa. When he was two years old William's mother, Mary Ellen (Curry) Harllee, had died of typhoid fever. Those were the days before people had "shots" to complain about: They died instead.

Remarkably enough, he did have remembrances of his mother. He wrote half a lifetime later:

My mother died while I was a child, a little over two years old, yet I retain two vivid flashes of memory of her and her appearance—once, after being "dressed up" to accompany her while she patiently persuaded me to return to her after I had broken loose to disport in the deep sand in the street in front of our house, and again, how she gently induced me to submit to a bath after two strong negro nurses, old "Aunts" Sarah and Bella, had failed to subdue me. Of those recollections and the mental picture of her, a serenely sweet and lovely woman, I am certain, for no one else fixed those unimportant and uninteresting occurrences in my mind.

One incident which occurred when Willy was two years old bears telling. He appeared before his mother and his aunt holding forth a snake which he had found in the yard, saying to his startled mother and aunt, "Pretty boy! Pretty boy!". They did not agree and shouted for his father who came in and removed the "pretty boy". Much of the future could be read into this anecdote—a lack of fear; a precociousness; a willfulness; an originality; and great good luck in that the snake did no harm—it was a black snake. These qualities would some day develop into private and unauthorized wars with the great and powerful.

· When Willy's mother died, his father, Captain John Waddell Harllee, took him to the nearby home of his maternal uncle, John William Curry and his wife "Aunt Lizzie," Elizabeth Abagail (Hutchinson) Curry. There he would have a loving foster mother and be brought up with plenty of other children in a religious home. The morning Christian devotional routine was never dispensed with. At the breakfast table his uncle often said grace as long as some preachers pray.

Little Willy did not know that his "Aunt Lizzie" was not his mother until he moved, when he was 7 years old, to attend school among paternal relatives in his father's old South Carolina home near Little Rock. Manatee was then too much a frontier to have good schools. He knew that his "Uncle John" was an uncle because his father lived in Manatee, loved him devotedly and visited him frequently. In any event, Willy was too young to understand all the family relationships. His life was serene and happy.

From age 7 to 10, he lived with his Uncle Andrew and his Aunts Ann Eliza and Harriet Amelia Harllee, as well as a goodly number of young cousins, on a farm near Little Rock, South Carolina. Some idea of his feelings about his South Carolina home can be gained from a quote from him published by TIME Magazine many years later:

> Near Little Rock, on the banks of the Little Pee Dee, in our family cemetery, where to use the words of my beloved kinswoman, Mrs. Hattie Dillon David, for whose father Dillon County was named, the lovely willows and the cypress cast their soft shadows and the dogwood and the plum tree brighten the spot with their wealth of blossom in the springtime, rest three preceding generations of my forefathers.

For a short time in 1887 he returned to Manatee where his father had found a school teacher he could hire to teach Willy and his three older brothers, John, Andrew and Horace (he had no sisters), but on December 20, 1887, his father died of yellow fever in a terrible epidemic. No household in Manatee escaped the dread disease. A shotgun quarantine was established around the town. No assistance came from the outside and no food; such as there was, people shared. Willy contracted the fever, but he recovered and sat up alone at nights with the sick of his household, as did other youths, for the service of all people able to be up and about had to be used.

Then, in 1888, he returned to the home of his uncle and

aunts in South Carolina and remained there until he went to Oak Ridge Institute in North Carolina in 1890.

School teachers in those days did not spare the rod. At the school at Little Rock in South Carolina the "celebrated" Mr. William R. Walker was especially liberal with its use, according to the persons most concerned, and he found occasion to physically chastise young William hundreds of times. One suspects that this may well have been due to a wild and independent spirit on the youngster's part. But Harllee felt in later years that he "became hard boiled and stubborn and impervious to fear of physical pain or danger" as a result of these poundings.

Modern Americans are horrified at such corporal punishment. However, it was not so unusual in those days. In 1883 and 1884, Winston Churchill, at the ages of 9 and 10, attended St. George's School in England where he remembered the floggings administered to students as "exceeding in severity anything that would be tolerated in any of the Reformatories under the Home Office."

Harllee recalled in a speech to his kinsfolk (at the Bethea family reunion when he was 55 years old) what had happened one day in school when he was eleven years old:

Some of you will remember a book we studied called "Venable's Easy Algebra." It was easy in name only. It was concentrated, boiled down essence of pure mathematics.

None of us will ever forget the day we came to a page or so of rules which read like this: "The square of the sum of the two quantities is the square of the first plus twice the product of the first by the second plus the square of the second," and other pieces of mental gymnastics like that.

That was a day of disaster. None of us were quite equal to the task.

I was a little fellow at the foot of the class and hoped that the storm might subside before it reached me. But it did not.

Learning in those years was not a haphazard, hit or miss affair. It was mostly a hit affair, but thorough and perhaps worth the pains and penalties.

Young Willy spent a lot of time with his Uncle Andrew during those years. One day Andrew told his nephew,

"Willy, I learned after the War that the Yankees qualified a man as a sharpshooter if he could make a string (area of target hit) of not over twenty-five inches with five shots at 200 yards at rest and the same string at 100 yards offhand. Now I'm going to show you what a Confederate sharpshooter can still do. There's usually some squirrels in that live oak over yonder. Let's measure off a hundred yards from there."

He did and asked Willy to bring them a couple of chairs. They sat a while until Uncle Andrew finally spotted two squirrels. He jumped up from his chair and bagged the two squirrels with two shots.

"Let's go measure those squirrels, Willy."

They did and they measured about eight inches without their tails.

"What do you reckon they would have made me in the Yankee army, Willy?"

For once, Willy was speechless.

One night by the fire, the youngster asked his uncle, "What made the war last so long and why did the Confederates lose it when they were so brave, Uncle Andrew?"

The reply, "Willy, the Yankees had a lot more men and guns and shot and supplies and they weren't afraid, and they should have won a lot sooner. But we had General Lee and for a couple of years, Old Stonewall, and the best generals all around. And, son, most of them couldn't shoot straight—not like Confederates—and don't forget, you're a Harllee and you've got to be a fighter and a straight shooter!"

Young William never forgot this.

These first thirteen years of his life formed the embryo of the man's character and mind. In South Carolina, as well as in Florida, he was surrounded by love and strength and there was nurtured in him a devotion to his family, not just his immediate family, but anyone kin to him at all. This devotion was strong and deep.

The tales of the Revolutionary War and the Civil War thrilled and inspired young William Harllee (and many another such, for example General George Patton) to be a soldier. This desire lasted all his life. Courage, loyalty and honor, even if these qualities engendered material sacrifices, were the ideals generated in these formative years. His big ambition was to be a soldier. West Point seemed the best place to start. But several years of school remained before he could get there.

After leaving Oak Ridge Institute in 1891, young Harllee attended the South Carolina Military Academy (The Citadel).

How can one describe this old and unique school to those who do not know it: Its hallowed halls and drill ground had emptied to send its fiery youth into the devouring flames of the Civil War. Then a thin stream of later youth had trickled back—slowly growing, as the South recovered. Here was tradition. Here was military discipline of the strictest sort. Here was all that would lure—yet repel—a strong boy fresh from freedom.

Willy Harllee's first roommate at the Citadel was W. E. Woodward, later the successful author of "Meet General Grant" and other books, but then too much of a fun loving character to be a serious influence on Willy.

One of Willy's classmates, who looked awfully good to the officers at the Citadel, but pretty pompous to his peers, undertook to take Willy down a peg or two one day after he had been promoted to corporal. He said late one night:

"As a corporal I couldn't possibly associate with any private who smokes those nasty cigarettes" (which Willy had started doing at far too young an age).

Young Harllee said "All right, corporal, if you'll come to my room after breakfast I'll burn up all my cigarettes." Willy then got some fresh paint the color of his chair, and early the next morning painted a corporal's chevrons on the seat of his chair.

After breakfast the next morning the corporal came in and sat down. Willy quickly burned some cigarettes in a make shift ashtray and immediately told the corporal that he had forgotten to tell him that the Duty Officer wanted to see him. As the corporal left the Duty Officer and passed by his fellow cadets there was a mixture of mirth and consternation at the placement of the corporal's chevrons on our friend's rear end.

The operation was a great success, but alas and alack, the patient died. The corporal knew full well who had done it,

21

and Willy when confronted by the discipline officer could not tell a lie. So, another slug of demerits.

But in spite of the demerits, the boy's high spirits could not be contained for long and the inevitable result was that on February 23, 1893, he left the Citadel with an honorable discharge for too many demerits resulting from such cadet high jinks. After this, how in the world would he ever get to West Point? How would he ever realize his one ambition?

In spite of his problems at the Citadel, he was to say in later years in a speech before the Citadel Club in Washington, D.C., May 17, 1939:

> The reason why we can confidently proclaim the Citadel to be the finest military school in the world is rooted in its history. The Citadel was a military organization before it was a school. In the eighteen thirties when the federal government undertook to lay tribute on all of the people to enrich some of the people, South Carolina began to prepare to make itself—not the whole world—safe for the brand of democracy of the Constitution of the U.S.
>
> So South Carolina maintained a little army to guard its munitions gathered at the Arsenal and The Citadel. Then its great and wise governor, the first John Peter Richardson, wisely decided, that instead of maintaining this force as guards otherwise idle, that this force would have the dignity and usefulness of a school. The history of the Citadel in peace and war has shown us that Gov. Richardson's idea was sound. That idea has guided me in efforts to transform all of the military organizations upon which I have been able to exert any influence into institutions like the Citadel.

Next, he went to the University of North Carolina, entered as a sophomore, and settled down to study and prepare for West Point. After the troubles at the Citadel, he wanted to make sure of making good at West Point and of realizing his dreams. As far as he was concerned, the Citadel had made a mistake in discharging him and he didn't want West Point to make the same mistake. Young Will Harllee had inherited several hundred acres of good farm land, but the price of cotton dropped drastically. So much so that in 1894, he had to withdraw from Chapel Hill after one year due to shortage of money.

He worked on his Frog Creek Farm, near Manatee, Florida.

He became the teacher at Oak Hill, later Parish, Manatee County, Florida, where he had to, in modern parlance, beat up on the big boys himself to preserve discipline. His schoolhouse was a log cabin without windows. His pay was $36 a month and he "boarded around." He slept on a cowhide on the upper floor and pulled up the ladders so curious bobcats couldn't get at him. South Florida was a rough and ready frontier then. Six months later he signed on as an oiler in the 124° F temperature of the engine room of the steamship Mascotte on the Tampa-Havana run.

Then he taught school again at Seminole, Florida, where he met Professor Ludwig W. Buccholz, a fine German scholar who became superintendent of education before he could even speak English!

Teaching on the frontier then had its amusing aspects. Pads of paper and notebook were not as available then as now. Slates were used and it was the custom of the children to spit on the slates and wipe them clean with their sleeves. Will Harllee got erasers for his students, but they had to be shaken out frequently and their use entailed more work than the older method. With typical directness, he solved the problem in sanitation by simply breaking any slate he saw spat upon. Then he had the new problem of irate parents who had to buy new slates. He enlisted the educational services of the family doctor who explained the sanitary hazards of "spat upon" slates to the parents which solved that problem.

In 1896, Harllee was studying like the devil at the professor's teachers school in Clearwater. In 1897 he went to Tallahassee, the capital of Florida and took a competitive examination for West Point. He won big. So the old dream now looked possible. Yet he wanted to make sure he could master what West Point demanded. He had saved money for more schooling. He went back to Chapel Hill, played football and studied at the University of North Carolina again in 1896; then taught at Persimmon School (later Harllee School) in 1897 to save more money. Teaching laid firm groundwork for his later major contributions to the U. S. Marine Corps.

On to West Point!

III
WEST POINT 1897–1899

He had ability and untold energy,
and was absolutely fearless and cool
under exciting times, and a willpower
that made him stick.
—Classmate and Roommate Brigadier General
Beverly Browne, Front Royal, Virginia,
December 13, 1944

He was a very colorful character.
—Classmate F. W. Clarke, Carmel, California,
December 17, 1944

About the most picturesque figure
amongst us—always colorful, serious
after all.
—Classmate W. T. Tidball, December 21, 1944

June 19, 1897 was a beautiful, sunshiny day and a great day
for young Harllee, the realization of all his heart's desires. He
was admitted to the U. S. Military Academy at West Point,
New York on that date. It was the custom then that even close
friends there called each other by their last names.

"The Long Gray Line" not only wore the right color uniform
as far as he was concerned, but it came from the institution

25

which had nurtured a pantheon of Confederate heroes led by General Robert E. Lee as well as one of the United States heroes led by General U. S. Grant.

Harllee had enjoyed the trip from Charleston to New York by the steamer "Algonquin," a customary way to travel then. He brought Mark Twain's "The Gilded Age" for reading matter. He wrote his Uncle Andrew,

> I met several ladies from Charleston, and they had no male escort, so I had to hustle around to a lively tune to find out all they wanted to know and to see to their baggage.

He was six feet tall then, 167 pounds. That was big for those days, when the average American soldier weighed in at 148 pounds and was five feet eight inches tall. The young ladies noticed his shock of blond hair parted in the middle, light blue eyes, and strong face dominated by a large straight nose and firm chin. They were not averse to his attentions, then or later, and they commented favorably on his manners, which were those of a southern gentleman.

But life in "Beast Barracks," the first summer at West Point, was no bed of roses. Young Harllee wrote his Aunt Amelia shortly after admission:

> The main feature in a plebe's (freshman's) life is being ultra respectful to upper classmen and taking anything from them. They think it is unbecoming to speak respectfully to a plebe and every time we see one it is "Brace up; shoulders back; more yet; more yet; do you understand what I say; drag your chin in; straighten your arms; hold your head up; suck up your belly; more yet; what's your name? Where are you from? You're the slouchiest man in the Corps," etc., etc., ad libitum.
>
> They abuse us all terribly, but we are all treated alike, and every one of us is the slouchiest man in the Corps.
>
> They have interesting exercises called "Choo-Choos," "Wooden Willys," "Footballs" and "Eagles". They are horrible things, and plebes shudder when they are attending.

For "Choo-Choos" a plebe laid down on his back and worked arms and legs like a train locomotive.

In "Wooden Willies" the plebe took a rifle, held it up to the firing position, dropped it down to the ready position and kept repeating until ordered to stop, as was the case in all these exercises.

For "Footballs" he was on his back and swung his legs up at right angles to his body without bending his knees several dozen, maybe even a hundred, times.

For "Eagles" the plebe stood on his toes with his arms extended, dropped to a sitting position, then rose part way while operating his arms like wings, then fell back to the sitting position, rose again and kept repeating the procedure as long as the upper classman thought he could.

Many other "interesting exercises" were then in use for plebes at West Point, including "Sitting on the Bayonet"— which meant a sitting position with the point of a bayonet under him, and "Qualifying"—which meant eating a big mess of prunes, sometimes over a hundred, or a soup plate full of molasses at one sitting.

Another sample of life at West Point in those days is embodied in the following excerpt from another letter he wrote to his Aunt Amelia:

> When next you write cut off a big square of "Take No Dust" tobacco and wrap it up securely and mail it in your letter. I can't bear the strain much longer. I found an old cigarette stump this P.M., and chewed the tobacco in it. I shall not smoke any more, the punishment is too severe.

Most men chewed tobacco in those days. Smoking by cadets was not allowed at West Point. But there were, of course, some lighter moments:

> Lots of boys have had to recite newspaper articles about themselves. Some as long as two columns, and pat themselves on the chest and say 'Ah! Ah! This is I! Behold me! etc.' It is great.

On July 4, 1897, Harllee and three classmates celebrated by smuggling in some ice cream and had a party in the nearby woods. The regular food at West Point in those days was so unpalatable that many cadets would sneak out to Highland Falls to get appetizing food as well as liquor, even at the risk of plenty of demerits if caught.

Ultimately though, a very serious moment had to come. Cadet William Curry Harllee was relaxing one day that summer in his tent when the committee of yearling (second year) cadets arrived. "Mr. Harllee," the yearling said to him, "I am sorry to inform you that our class has met and decided to call you out. Will you please name your seconds?"

Harllee's reaction was one of exultation. He was the first of his class to be challenged! He considered it an honor. Although his frame was big, he was, at age 20, lean and spare. But he had realized his ambition to be at the institution which had produced so many of America's fighting men, and he was to have his chance to prove himself as such.

He had gained this chance very easily. In "Beast Barracks", where the incoming plebes were quartered, his room was subject to inspection at any time by the yearlings.

"Brace, Mister!" was how it began. The plebes threw their shoulders back and arched out their chests. They "sucked in their stomachs" and held in their chins. They stood very still, not knowing what to expect.

"Mister, how'd you like to have your face smashed?" That then followed.

Most plebes replied carefully: "I wouldn't like it, sir!"

Harllee had said: "Immaterial, sir!"

That was the wrong answer. He was then considered a "B.J. plebe," which meant he had to be taken down a few pegs. The means for this was a fight with a selected yearling.

Battery Knox traditionally provided the ring for these fights. It had a gun emplacement, half-way up a hill, where the muzzles of two ancient muzzle loading cannon, placed there to command the Hudson River against the British by George Washington, still looked down upon the mighty river. The green lawn behind the guns, where Continental cannoneers had stood, happened to form a sort of a prize ring. To get there without being seen by duty personnel, the cadets had to remove the iron grating from the rear window of a washroom at the top of the cliff, worm their way through and then jump down to the greensward. An hour before reveille that morning, Cadet Harllee and his two seconds faced a yearling and his seconds. The plebe and yearling had never faced each other before. The fight was completely impersonal. A referee, a timekeeper and sentries to guard against surprise by the West Point authorities: all cadets were ready.

The two stripped to the waist and stood in trousers, shoes and socks. It was against the West Point Code to match men with more than 10 pounds difference in weight. Harllee saw that the code had not been followed. The yearling outweighed him by over 20 pounds. He was a West Point football varsity lineman and a well known West Point boxer and slugger.

He had won all his fights with knockouts in the first two rounds. But Bill Harllee would never have dreamt of complaining. The instructions were quiet and matter-of-fact. Two minute rounds. Two minute rests. To the finish. With bare fists. The yearlings were going to show this "B.J. plebe" with his "Immaterial, Sir!" what it meant to defy custom at the "Point."

The bell was sounded by hitting a gun with a stick. Plebe and yearling raised their fists and advanced on each other.

Harllee hit his opponent with the hardest blow of which he was capable. The yearling laughed and came on in. Twice in the first round he knocked the plebe flat. Each time Harllee picked himself up and attacked, clenched fists swinging.

It lasted eight rounds before the yearling finished him off. Time and again he had knocked the plebe flat before the final knockout mercifully came. This time Harllee couldn't get up. He was unconscious.

Not a cadet who had seen him repeatedly get up and charge, blood flowing from his face and fists pumping, doubted the knockout (it had been known for men to fake knockouts to prevent further damage to themselves). When buckets of cold water would not bring Harllee back to consciousness, they carried him to the cadet hospital with more than a little concern for him.

The doctor had to stitch up five long, deep cuts opened up by his opponents fists. Bill Harllee wore the scars for the rest of his life. They kept him in the hospital for two weeks before they considered him sufficiently well to return to duty. But strangely, Harllee was not unhappy. He had been the first

29

plebe called out. He had lasted eight rounds against a knockout slugger more than 20 pounds heavier; the first man at West Point to do that. He had won the respect of his fellow cadets, all of them. And he proceeded to learn how to box.

This formal "calling out" of plebes resulted in forty such fights between June 1897 and January 1901, of which plebes won only four. The brutal custom was eliminated in 1901.

During the last century and the first part of this one, hazing was very rough at West Point. Oscar L. Booz entered the Academy on June 28, 1898; had a particularly hard time with it, including being "called out" for a fight like Harllee's; resigned in September 1898; and died a year and a half later of tubercular laryngitis. A doctor on October 19, 1898 had found him in "an exhausted condition—some profound depression of the system". His family was convinced upon his death that his throat condition was directly traceable to continuous dosage of tabasco sauce, of which he was forced to drink a whole bottle in one two week period.

John Edward Breth, a classmate of Harllee's, was found deficient in mathematics in January 1899 and died in October of 1899 of typhoid pneumonia. His family contended that hazing had wrecked his nervous system and left him vulnerable to typhoid. This case resulted in bad national publicity for West Point and led to a Congressional investigation, which in turn resulted in considerable moderation of the practice. Some of the violent physical exercises and the forced eating of obnoxious foods or foreign substances were dropped. Through the years, there were several investigations and hazing continued to be moderated, though not completely eliminated. The great majority of the alumni and cadets strongly felt that hazing, if handled right, was conducive to good discipline and to toughening the cadets.

Even as late as Eisenhower's time (1911–1915) it was still so tough that his first roommate "would put his head down and weep" and left West Point after only a few weeks.

Plebe Harllee, however, did not have any trouble with hazing after his fight.

He entered his yearling year at West Point a happy young

man. He had done extremely well in the January plebe examinations which ended the West Point career of many cadets. He played football as a guard, weighing 197 pounds. He was full of high spirits, ate nourishing if unappetizing food, and he gained strength from cadet exercise. However, his disciplinary troubles prevented him from having the privilege of playing in the intercollegiate games except for the one with Stevens Institute, which West Point won 18 to 4.

In those days, most of the faculty at West Point considered football a frivolous diversion detracting from the cadets training. The Point did not have a football team until 1890.

Helmets were an innovation not completely accepted. Football players in most colleges had been growing enormous shocks of hair to cushion the impact of collisions. There was no forward pass. Football then used the "tackles back" and "guards back" modification of Harvard's "flying wedge" and Princeton's "V". The latter two produced bone crushing impacts with ten men moving back and forming hard running wedges or Vs to protect the ball carrier. The mass momentum created could only be stopped by head-on smashing confrontation. This created such horrendous results that momentum mass plays were outlawed in 1894. However, the new rules did not go far enough. The "guards back" and "tackles back" evasions of these rules were outlawed in 1906 when wholesale changes of the rules were made. As late as 1905 nineteen young men were killed playing football in one year, including a West Pointer, who died the day after a game on October 30, 1905. All this created such a public uproar that football was abolished in a number of colleges. President Theodore Roosevelt took a hand in the matter, and reform rules were adopted in the White House in 1906.

There was no question about the popularity of college football then, but neither was there any question about its excessive brutality and doubtful ethics. Some of the top schools had professional roughnecks on their teams who paid no attention to academic requirements.

But Bill Harllee suffered no ill effects, except the psychological disturbance of not being allowed to play in most of the games because of disciplinary problems. Despite these problems he was a cadet drillmaster (in large part because of his experience at the Citadel) and a leader in the class of 1901. He loved it all, as only a boy could love it whose earliest memory was reading Captain Charles King's "Cadet Days" and hoping that some day he might enter that glamorous life. He was disappointed only in how little marksmanship training the Point conducted.

But discipline was his problem. As his classmates wrote in a reunion book twenty-seven years later, "his free and untamed spirit did not vibrate in harmony with the Tactical Department." The brass-bound, hide-wrapped old-timers who ruled West Point had no sense of humor at cadet high spirits. "Skins" were demerits. If the authorities didn't like a cadet's sense of humor, they could hand him "skins" for such vague things as "unmilitary bearing."

One of the "Tacs", as the officers on duty at West Point in those days were called, was known always to read the orders handed to him at morning formation without looking them over. He had come down very hard on Harllee, who decided to strike back, even though such a game would be one-sided. He inserted a paper in the sheaf handed to the "Tac", who, when he came to it, duly read to the assembled Corps of Cadets:

> All cadets desiring a transfer of duty away from West Point for Colonel Albert L. Mills (the Superintendent) . . .

and then he caught himself and glared down the suppressed laughter of the cadets. Of course, such stunts did not endear Harllee to either Colonel Mills or the "Tacs".

Then there was a "Tac" who apparently had a sadistic streak. He had found a large number of cadets deficient in mathematics and he had them dismissed from West Point. Included in this number was a roommate of Harllee's who had been a county superintendent of education at age 22 in Wisconsin. According to their classmates, the "Tac" had boasted in officers' homes that he would find Harllee deficient in discipline. By the time the "Tac" was relieved of command of Company A on August

32

19, 1898, Harllee had 121 demerits; if he had 125 on or before December 31, 1898 he would be discharged. He then got 3 more demerits for erasing at the blackboard without permission while working on a problem in descriptive geometry. The rule he had broken was rarely enforced because it was a nuisance to the instructors, especially in descriptive geometry, and most cadets didn't ask permission to erase.

With six weeks to go and only 1 demerit away from the fateful 125, Harllee spent one night with a sock full of snow around his neck and a towel full of snow around his chest, hoping to get pneumonia or at least a bad enough cold so he would be admitted to the hospital where it was not so easy to give out demerits.

It didn't work! The next day he never felt better. But later on, he managed to get in the hospital with influenza and stay there until January 1, 1899. He had no trouble with his examinations. As he put it, he could learn the subjects much better studying in the hospital without what he regarded as interference from the "instructors."

Such was the life of discipline and instruction in those days at West Point under Superintendent Mills. But it welded together Harllee's classmates into lifelong friendships, and it developed a certain hardihood.

Winston Churchill, then a Second Lieutenant and a graduate of Sandhurst, visited West Point in 1895. According to William Manchester in "The Last Lion—Winston Churchill—Visions of Glory 1874–1932," Churchill wrote a letter to his brother Jack as follows, "To Jack he wrote that West Point discipline was so strict as to be 'positively disgraceful'."

Today's West Point is a far cry from those days. The tactical officers strive to become leaders in the best modern sense, rather than trying to develop obedience through fear. Military smartness is still very much in order, but time devoted to the old close order drill, once considered so essential to blind obedience, has been tremendously reduced.

The official report of one of Harllee's last offenses reads as follows:

The first summer at West Point. Beverly Browne and Bill Harllee stand by for inspection.

January 21, 1899

Special Orders, No. 17

I. For 'Arranging for the taking of a photograph of those Cadets who received one hundred and twenty demerits, or more, during the Academic half year just passed, by producing the publication (on the 8th instant) of a notice to the Battalion of Cadets inviting the Cadets concerned to assemble for the purpose named, Cadet William C. Harllee, 3d Class, will be confined to Cadet barracks, the area of barracks and the gymnasium until May 1, 1899, and will serve punishment tours during that period as follows: One on every Wednesday; and on Saturdays, from ten minutes after inspection until ten minutes before retreat.'

Facts which are a matter of mortification . . . and sorrow to every high and right minded Cadet should be buried, not perpetuated.

The principles which form the corner stone of the success of this Academy are violated by the sentiments giving rise to the commission of the offense here condemned.

By order of Colonel Mills:

(Signed by) Samuel C. Hazzard
2d Lieutenant 1st Artillery, Adjutant

Brigadier General Beverly Browne wrote of him in later years:

Harllee was my roommate from January to May or June '98, and I knew him about as intimately as anyone could at that time. He had been to the Citadel, Charleston, S. C., and had an understanding of discipline or the unyielding rules of it entirely beyond most of us. Yet he was obsessed to get around those rules—to break it off in the tacs in a big way. His studies didn't require too much of his time, as he had no ambition in that line to more than "pass"—so he schemed and planned in all manner of ways to do extraordinary and undisciplined things, and still not quite be found on discipline.

Near the end of Harllee's West Point days, Lieutenant "Black Jack" Pershing (later Commanding General of the A.E.F. in World War I) moved slowly down the Company A line. He was alternately grim and jovial. He stopped before a tall, thick chested, formidable looking young man in the cadet ranks. His spirit sensed a kindred soul. He smiled sardonically and said.

"You don't give a damn—do you, Harllee?"

And Harllee answered, "No, sir."

But he did give a damn. He wanted more than anything to graduate from West Point—he just couldn't seem to find it in him to miss any of the fun, licit or illicit. Perhaps that is why his classmates liked him so much.

In the end young Harllee was "honorably discharged for deficiencies in discipline," effective July 30, 1899. Needless to say, he was convinced all his life that the Superintendent, Colonel Mills, was an impossible tyrant.

Although the alleged incident happened after Harllee's time at West Point, the following quotation from Thomas J. Fleming's excellent book, "West Point: The Men and Times of the United

States Military Academy" concerning Colonel Mills (still Superintendent in the winter of 1900–01) is of interest:

Colonel Clifford Cabel Early of the class of 1905, speaking at a West Point Society Founders' Day dinner at Fort McPherson, Georgia, on March 15, 1957, recalled: "In the winter of 1900–1901 there was, believe it or not, a mutiny at West Point. Although I entered West Point only a few months later, the matter was never discussed or talked about by the upperclassmen, and I never knew what it was about. I don't think it was planned or premeditated but developed spontaneously on the spur of the moment. The Corps, or a large part of it, on being dismissed in the evening after being marched back from the mess hall, swarmed out on the parade ground. They tore the old saluting gun loose from its moorings and dragged it across the parade ground to in front of the superintendent's quarters where they pointed the gun toward the supe's house . . . As a result of the escapade, five or six first classmen were dismissed from West Point. . . The class of 1902 graduated only 54. Five or six other upperclassmen were suspended a year."

When Harllee broke tradition by watching as sole spectator at the evening parade immediately after his release, his class also broke tradition by giving him a salute. This assuaged a little the shattering disappointment of perhaps too strong and willful, too independent a character. But would he ever be able to have a career in the profession of arms he so cherished?

IV
WASHINGTON, D.C.
WITH THE FAMOUS
TEXAS RANGER—1899

I can hardly believe a young man could be discharged for such trivial offenses.
—President McKinley

To hell with that, said Texas Ranger Captain Lee Hall, who then grabbed him by the arm and propelled him into the bar.

When young Harllee was discharged from West Point, he did not propose to take it lying down, nor did he ever take any blow in that manner. He proceeded to Washington and met with his Congressman, Colonel Sparkman, Senator-elect Taliferro, Senator Mallory and Congressman Bob Davis, all of Florida. They were friends of his family and they comprised the complete Florida Congressional delegation. He had lists of the reports for which he had received his demerits, which they took first to Assistant Secretary of War Meikeljohn, who told

37

them he believed the young man could be readmitted in the next West Point class below, as was often done. They next took him to President McKinley. The President stated, as had Meikeljohn, that he could hardly believe a young man could be discharged for such trivial offenses. He caused an inquiry to be made, but Colonel Mills, the Superintendent, said it would be a serious blow to the discipline of the Military Academy if Harllee were returned there.

Harllee remarked that Colonel Mills himself had, as a cadet, been found guilty of a worse infraction of West Point regulations, enough to result in him being suspended without pay, but that he was permitted to join the next lower class. Harllee said that if he had to, he would be glad to settle for that, but Mills prevailed and he was not reinstated.

Then the young man had to consider such alternatives as the proposition to go copper mining in Mexico or to take a berth on a survey ship that was about to sail from Washington, D. C. to Alaska via the Straits of Magellan and San Francisco.

But before he decided on one of these, Congress provided for the raising of ten regiments of U. S. Volunteers to be sent to the Philippines to suppress an insurrection there (later on it provided for fourteen more regiments).

Each state delegation was permitted to submit a slate for the appointment of a quota of officers. The Florida Delegation put young Harllee on their slate as a first lieutenant and took it to President McKinley who approved it and said that he considered it a happy solution to his case and that he had also appointed Harllee's classmate, George M. Lee, son of General Fitzhugh Lee, a first lieutenant of Volunteers.

He waited for his appointment, but it never came. He went to see General H. C. Corbin, the Adjutant General of the Army. The General told Harllee that although his name was on the Florida slate, he would not be appointed if he could prevent it (the General had been briefed by Colonel Mills) and that he had personally taken the matter up with President McKinley.

Young Harllee then asked General Corbin if he had any objection to his enlisting in the Volunteer Army, and if so would he still pursue him and prevent his advancement. The

General said no and that he would be pleased to see him enlist and would help him. He then instructed telegrams to be sent to the colonels of three regiments recommending Harllee as a sergeant major.

Harllee returned to his favorite hangout, the Metropolitan Hotel on Pennsylvania Avenue and 6th Street, Northwest, and there met Godfrey Reese Fowler of Texas, who had been a Captain in the Second Texas Regiment in the Spanish American War in 1898. Fowler and Harllee were friends and had already discussed plans to go to San Francisco and enlist there in an effort to get to the Philippines before the war might be over. Fowler told him that he had just received his appointment as Captain in the 33rd U. S. Volunteer Infantry, which was to be organized at San Antonio, Texas. Fowler asked him to go along with him as his First Sergeant.

Harllee then went to General Corbin where he learned that two of the colonels had telegraphed him that they would appoint him sergeant major, but he told General Corbin that he preferred to go with Captain Fowler as First Sergeant and asked him to prepare an order authorizing his enlistment in Washington and his transfer to the 33rd Infantry at San Antonio. He enlisted as a private in the same building, now at Fort McNair, where Mrs. Surratt was hung just after the Civil War, and got his ticket to Texas. He was to be promoted to first sergeant as soon as the red tape could be taken care of.

One day in the sidewalk chairs of the Metropolitan Hotel where young Harllee, like many others, was lounging and wishing he had enough money for a drink, a rough looking customer with a couple of grinning sidekicks passed by and tapped the youngster on the shoulder and said,

"I hear you got kicked out of West Point."

Replied Harllee,

"I was honorably discharged after two years there. That puts me two years ahead of you."

In those days, West Point was considered by many to be a hotbed of un-American aristocracy and the habitat of pampered pets with political influence.

The older man said,

"What do you do at West Point beside wear fancy uniforms and parade around like a bunch of chorus girls?"

The former cadet could not control his hot temper and rejoined,

"We learn not be obnoxious bastards like you are trying to be."

With that the other man let go with a short left jab and what was intended as a powerful round house right, but Harllee, who expected a punch after calling the man a bastard, and who remembered well his lessons after his awful fight at West Point, ducked the right and like a flash launched his own one two punch. Before too long he had his opponent flat on the sidewalk. Captain Lee Hall, the famous Texas Ranger, watched the fight and with a smile told the younger man, "You're all right, kid."

The next day Harllee received some money from home and suggested to Hall that they repair to the bar. Hall said, "Fine, but let's stock up on some good Duke's tobacco first. You'll never get out of that bar with any money."

The Metropolitan was the favorite rendezvous for large numbers of impecunious but friendly commission seekers. Many more men had wanted to get in action in the Spanish-American War than were able to do so. There were 20,000 applications for the 101 appointments that could be made to the office of second lieutenant for the Philippine Insurrection. The martial spirit of the times was well expressed by the following campaign song of 1898:

Come along and get your musket
For there's going to be a fight.
Uncle Sam has pressed the button
And we think he's in the right.
Well, well, well
We'll give the Spaniards hell
We'll give 'em shot and shell
When they try to break that Texas wall
There'll be a hot time in the old town tonight,
My baby.

Captain Lee Hall was the very epitome of the Texas cowboy

and lawman that has fascinated not only America but the whole world for a century. There were thousands of outlaws in the Texas of the 1870's and 1880's. Colonel E. M. House, principal adviser to President Woodrow Wilson, said of Hall, (February 23, 1929):

> In my opinion Captain Lee Hall and Captain Bill McDonald were the greatest of all Texas Rangers and that is high praise.

In one trial alone, Hall had captured 420 of the offenders, most of them murderers. He made many of his arrests alone and disarmed.

One of his obituaries stated:

> He did more to rid Texas of desperadoes and establish law and order than any officer in Texas ever had. He had made more bad men lay down their guns and delivered more desperadoes and outlaws into the custody of the courts and used his own gun less than any officer in Texas.

But the significance of Lee Hall to William Harllee was his marksmanship, the field in which Harllee was to render great service. Hall not only taught him all about shooting, but also how to teach other people. The following is quoted from Dora Neill Raymond's "Captain Lee Hall of Texas":

> The chief characteristic of the anecdotes related of Captain Hall was emphasis on his ability to make arrests without the use of firearms. One story told of his going alone to the retreat of six train robbers, arresting them at pistol's point, and marching them thirty miles to jail through a district eager for their rescue.
>
> At target practice he showed good reason for the preference of his antogonists for peaceable arrest. It was recounted that Hall once used as his range two rows of figures, each the size and shape of a man. He galloped through the lane they formed, reins in teeth and a pistol in each hand. Only when the figures were shot in the heart region was a bull's eye claimed. The score was surprisingly high and the publicity it gained assisted Hall to increase his number of peaceable arrests. Helped by his training, his company broke the record at the Presidio for marksmanship. This was fact. It could not compete with the deeds that imagination added to the very real prowess and daring of Lee Hall.

The 50 year old Ranger, the inspiration for some of O. Henry's stories—O. Henry had spent a year with him—and for some of Frederic Remington's paintings, took a liking to the 22 year old Florida youth. He sensed and liked the fighter in the younger man. There was endless talk about such matters as "wheeling two heavy Colts in the deadly border roll."

When they met again in Texas, Hall had received a first lieutenant's commision, a rank way below that he should have had, and Harllee was an enlisted man. Hall invited Harllee to the best bar in town at the old Menger Hotel in San Antonio. The invitee said,

"We can't do that now. You're an officer and I'm an enlisted man."

Hall replied, "To hell with that!" and grabbing Harllee by the arm, propelled him into the bar. They talked long hours about "shooting irons," and Hall took Harllee out to practice shooting.

Before going to San Antonio, Harllee and Captain Fowler, had entrained together in Washington in July of 1899 for Texas, where the regiment was being organized. They stopped off in New Orleans long enough to visit and have a party with Henry W. Robinson, one of the city's leading attorneys, whose brother, Gordon Robinson, had been one of Harllee's roommates at West Point.

So the fired West Pointer was on his way to be a soldier and do some real fighting after all. If he fought well enough he could expect advancement and a career. If not—well, he never thought of that.

V
WITH THE 33RD U. S. (TEXAS) VOLUNTEERS
The Sharpshooters in Action: 1899–1900

*He may be a little brown brother to
Willie Taft,
But he ain't no kin of mine—*
—From a U. S. soldiers' song, Philippines—
Circa 1900

The natives are hardy and more intelligent than you would suppose—patriotic, and able to live on nothing.
—Corporal William C. Harllee, Corregidor Island
November 9, 1899

Private William Curry Harllee started his Army career on K.P.—specializing in peeling potatoes. The 33rd U. S. Volunteer Infantry, known as the 33rd Texas Volunteers, was a group of very rough men, who looked more like pirates or bushwackers than Army recruits. That was the state they were in when Captain Fowler and Private Harllee stepped off the train at San

43

Antonio. They had slept in turns in the same Pullman berth from Washington because of a shortage of cash. In those days, they were not paid for their transportation in advance. Captain Fowler was sent out instantly on recruiting duty. Private Harllee reported in to a wild bunch of Texans, Arizonans, Missourians, Arkansans; farmers, mountaineers, cowboys, miners; some in rags, some in overalls, some barefooted. Uniforms had not yet been issued to them. Bill Harllee was dressed in the $100 suit of a Fifth Avenue, New York, tailor; the $15 shoes and the derby hat which he had received at West Point just before he left. They had been issued for the summer furlough he just missed. A tough guy named Hartmann, who was at the moment in charge, gave him a contemptuous look.

"Dude," he said, "peel spuds." Harllee was hardly very enthusiastic about this order or the manner in which it was given, but it was an order, so he reported to the mess tent and started peeling potatoes. He had been a cadet drillmaster at West Point and knew the drill regulations by heart, but he was then drilled by the cook, formerly of a cavalry regiment in the old regular army. He had left the service 10 years before and he knew the drills by ancient cavalry foot drill regulations. But Private Harllee kept his mouth shut and obeyed orders. Nobody knew he ever even saw West Point.

Captain Fowler returned and found his friend peeling potatoes, blew his stack and immediately promoted Harllee to lance-sergeant, the first, last and only lance-sergeant in military history, since there isn't any such rank or rating. But it kept him from peeling more potatoes. Hartmann planned revenge on what he called "that squirt with the dude clothes and the pull." Hartmann told some of his hard-bitten old cronies to watch him show the newcomer up.

Hartmann had 50 men to drill. Lance-Sergeant Harllee was one of the file-closers. Hartmann fell them in, right dressed the line and had the 20 men at the right of line separated into a rather quizzical looking lump.

"Now, Lance-Sergeant Harllee," said Hartmann, "you drill that squad." And he relaxed with his friends, to watch the dude make a fool of himself.

Lance-Sergeant Harllee stepped out as rigid and precise as a model West Point cadet. He mustered up his very best drillmaster voice.

"Fall in!" he commanded the squad, which looked like a meeting of hooligans. He had to push some of them into position with his hands, which he did with some force.

"Right dress!" He had to push some more. He did it impassively. "Front!" At last he got them in a military line. He eyed them up and down.

"You expect to stand like that and be mistaken for soldiers?" he asked with grim humor. Then he began to issue commands like a machine gun.

"Heels together! Toes at an angle of 60 degrees! Body erect! Lean slightly forward at the hips! Draw up your stomachs! Little fingers opposite the seams of your trousers! Palms slightly to the front! Elbows close to the body! Head erect! Chin drawn in! Eyes fixed 15 paces to the front, looking neither to right nor left! Stand up like soldiers!"

Then, he put them through the same squad drill that he had drilled cadets at West Point, and who later wore generals' stars.

Hartmann was astounded. So were his friends. This dude was drilling them like a regular army officer! After it was all over, Hartmann asked Lance-Sergeant Harllee.

"Where did you learn that?"

"In the book," said Harllee. "It's all in the book."

Hartmann looked over the 197 pound, six foot figure. With difficulty he refrained from saying; "You're a liar, big boy; what outfit did you desert from?"

What he did say was, "Let's be friends, soldier." Nobody heard anything more about "the squirt in dude clothes with the pull."

They organized at last with Harllee rising through corporal and sergeant to first sergeant in Company F, under Captain Fowler.

As a first sergeant in those days you had to either have "command presence" or be able to physically enforce orders, or perhaps both.

45

The volunteer soldiers of that day were anything but docile and cared little for military punctilio. They deserted if they felt like it. Before the days of fingerprinting, deserting and rejoining another outfit under a different name was not too difficult. When the U. S. Marine Corps instituted fingerprinting about 1907 it uncovered over one hundred deserters, fraudulent enlistees and dishonorably discharged men.

Examples of the "handling of personnel," as it would be called later, and of deserters, were recounted in the following excerpt of a letter from Harllee to Carl Musgrave, a comrade from Company F of the 33rd, dated March 16, 1936:

> I learned years later that Hartmann had deserted from the Marine Corps.
> I have no unkind feeling towards Hartmann. He was of the old type of "rough neck" soldiers of times gone by who are out of place in the preparation of young soldiers for war today. My conflicts with him did me no injury and enlarged my experience and taught me lessons which have later served me well.
> One of the guard was a corporal named Scott. He was quite drunk and when the adjutant marched the guard off Scott tried to take charge of it and created considerable disorder. I put him in one of the tents which we designated as the "Guard House" and put an Arkansas man on guard over him. He tried to break away. I then borrowed a pistol from the lieutenant and told the sentinel to shoot Scott if he attempted to leave again. Scott had been a soldier in a troop commanded by Col. Hare in the Seventh Cavalry and held in contempt the new soldiers and especially the new sergeant. Next morning he was penitent.
> Our company F got its 106 recruits in a couple of days. It was a task to get them in shape so that they could be marched to meals. I learned a lot about how to drill a big bunch of recruits, and what I learned has been a big help to me since then. The only man I had who had had any previous experience in drilling was a man named Allen. He was a deserter from the Sixth Infantry, and an ex-English soldier and as tough as they come. He was not afraid in action. He deserted from the 33rd and went as a lieutenant with the Filipinos. I do not know what finally became of him.

The 33rd sailed for Manila from San Francisco on the United States Army Transport Sheridan on September 28, 1899.

It was an awful voyage. The primary food was hardtack and

"slum," meat and vegetables dumped into a steam cooker and steamed into a gooey, stringy mess. It tasted like rotten eggs. Drinking water was distilled from salty Pacific Ocean water. It dripped from the condenser, hot, and the men stood in line to fill their cups with it. Someone up higher who didn't have to stand in these lines had issued an order to the effect that men weren't allowed to take a cup away to cool. Armed sentries stood by the condenser and made them drink it hot, on the spot. The combination of the food and such water made men sick.

Nevertheless, as Harllee wrote home on October 6, 1899:

> But we are still living, and even manage to enjoy ourselves a little. The band gives concerts every evening and our company (F) has an orchestra and some fine poker and craps, a pleasant pastime. You would be surprised to see how these people gamble. Men drawing $15.60 a month sit down and raise each other $25.00 and play poker without any limit. Every deck except the promenade deck is literally covered with all the gambling devices known to the world. Even Chinese games are run by way of variety. We stay three or four days in Honolulu and I have but 95 cents, but on that I am going to see all I can.

Young Harllee's comments on Honolulu, written October 11, 1899, are interesting in light of the fact that all his life he had a fierce devotion to Florida and South Carolina:

> I will tell you about Honolulu. If you have any idea that it is a second rate city, or that its people are undesirable for American citizenship, disabuse yourself of that opinion. I have never seen a more beautiful city. Its houses are almost all mansions and even those who are not of the wealthy class live in pretty houses with large and well kept yards. Its vegetation is the same as Florida only it is more luxuriant. No place in Florida can compare with Honolulu. Its sanitation is perfect. Its people all speak English, and the natives are intelligent, and well behaved, and courteous, and all speak English. No country in the world has a better government.
>
> Its weather is perfect. The rains beyond the mountains keep the soil from becoming dry, and the days and nights are ahead of anything Florida can boast of. Honolulu has only 30 or 40 thousand people. Native produce is cheap. Imported stuff is not cheap. But wages are higher than anywhere else I have ever been.

The 33rd reached Manila Bay October 23, 1899. Harllee had been in some trouble about sleeping on deck instead of below deck without authorization. With plenty of room in the fresh air on deck he saw no sense in adding to the crowding in the hot, fetid, sickening air below decks. But he was busted from first sergeant to corporal.

Once again, as so often in the past, it looked like he just wasn't destined to have a successful military career, despite his desire to fight and confidence that he could do so. He just couldn't be bothered with senseless regulations, a terrible handicap in a military service.

But Captain Fowler, who knew him best and who hadn't been the one to bust him, still had plenty of faith in him and assigned him to be in charge of the advance scouting party, or point, of the company.

Bill Harllee lost 30 pounds in that one month voyage, what with the bad, skimpy food, heat and rough seas. When they landed to march, Company F would stagger 100 yards, and then halt for a rest.

His letter home of November 9, describes what happend for the next few days:

> Between General (Arthur) McArthur's army and Manila there are bands who are always threatening the city. It takes several regiments to keep them out, and they are actually operating within a mile of the city and make it very interesting for the pickets. At times hundreds of them may be seen from our lines and no one ventures outside the lines. Even inside everybody has to be armed. In the city it is unsafe to travel unarmed.
>
> We did picket duty with our regiment just outside of Manila for a few days, and it furnished us all the excitement we were looking for, and all night long there was continual firing. Each regiment covers about a mile, and each company has its cantonment a few hundred yards from the next and a few hundred yards behind the outside posts of sentries. In the company camps or cantonments the men live in tents or bamboo shacks, or any shelter they can get, and do not remove their clothing at night, and have their rifles beside them. The ground is low and wet, and even now it rains every day, and the mud sticks to the feet until they become three times their natural size. Water has to be brought out from town with a water

buffalo cart and a Chinaman and a soldier for a guard. The Filipinos hate the Chinos who work for our soldiers and butcher them unceremoniously if there is not a guard along.

Bamboo is the sole building material. They make pillars for their houses, floors, roofs, doors, and windows, and all out of it. Some of the houses of the wealthy look like deserted palmetto shacks, but most of them are far more humble and remind me more of chicken coops than anything else.

The people dress very unassumingly and some do not dress at all, particularly the small children. Boys and girls loaf around looking perfectly happy without a vestige of clothing on them.

Then Company F was assigned to guard Corregidor Island, the Gibraltar of the Philippines. The rest of the regiment was landed at Lingayen. It fought in the historic battle at San Fabian. Captain Fowler was sore as a boil that his company alone had missed that fight.

Harllee wrote home (November 15, 1899) concerning the above battle:

Our regiment, which is in Gen'l. Wheaton's Brigade and in the northern part of the island, has been in an engagement. The paper says that the fight lasted two hours and that Maj. John A. Logan, Jr. and six enlisted men were killed and thirteen men and one officer wounded; that the enemy lost about one hundred killed and many wounded, and prisoners, and that it was one of the most stubborn stands the insurgents have ever made, and that they never fled until our men were within twenty feet of them. No other troops except the 33rd participated, and Gen'l. Wheaton has complimented Col. Hare and his regiment for their splendid charge.

With regard to the 33rd, James Henderson Blount, in his authoritative book "The American Occupation of the Philippines 1898–1912" wrote:

The 33rd Volunteer Infantry, Colonel Luther R. Hare, Commanding, made more reputation than any of the twenty-five regiments of the volunteer army of 1899, except, possibly Colonel J. Franklin Bell's regiment, the 36th. This is no reflection on the rest. These two were lucky enough to have more opportunities, however, Colonel Hare, like Colonel Bell, proved himself a superb soldier, his field officers, especially Major March (Peyton C. March, later General and Chief of Staff of the Army) were

49

particularly indefatigable; and his men were mostly Texans, accustomed to handling a rifle with effect.

Bill Harllee marvelled at the Texans' sharpshooting and never forgot it. But returning to the situation then at Corregidor, it was well described in his letter home of Nov. 9, 1899:

Corregidor is exactly in the middle of the mouth of the bay and there are narrow channels on both sides of it. It contains about 400 acres and consists of two high rocky hills with a sort of a low isthmus between them. A little village of about a hundred bamboo shacks is on this isthmus as is a hospital for soldiers and officers. Our barracks are up on the side of the hill, and are built of bamboo—even the rafters are of bamboo. Old Wash Norman would think it was a big lie if you were to tell him that the fishing poles in this country grow big enough to make rafters and the frames for houses as big as the Kentyre Church. There is not a nail used in building; they tie the joists together with strips cut out of bamboo when it is green.

Our duties here are to guard this island. On both shores the Filipinos are in control and often bodies of them can be seen with the glasses. Big bayous and swamps separate the land nearest us from Manila and our forces have never operated in the country nearest us, except that occasionally the gun boats lay off and shell their villages within a couple of miles of us. The insurgents could run us off the island and murder our sick in the hospitals and get away with all the stores if we were the only protection. The gun boats and cruisers patrol the island at night and the ships in the bay keep their search lights busy, and they would help us make it extremely uncomfortable if parties should try to land from the insurgents' country.

I have never seen a moment when I was sorry I came over and am perfectly contented and hope to come out all right in the soldiers profession.

I can go to Manila almost any time, and I am in the hands of good friends there. All the boys I have met have opened their quarters to me whenever I want to come to the city, and I find myself as much at home there as I would in Palmetto (across the Manatee River from Manatee, Florida).

I forgot to tell you that Dewey tore up this island considerably when he passed it and disabled the old Spanish guns without ever stopping. When they settle down this will be the most important artillery station here. Properly defended no ship could enter the bay.

Then Company F was ordered to San Fabian, after the fighting was all over, and General Lloyd Wheaton sent them out to Lingayen on a scouting reconnaissance. Corporal Harllee was back to 197 pounds now, just 22 years old. He led a point of 10 men to draw Filipino fire. There were no Filipino soldiers at Lingayen. But word came that they were in Aguilar. On to Aguilar.

Captain Lee Hall and his Macabee Scouts passed Harllee on the march. Hall passed his canteen to the younger man. It was filled with "vino" which Hall drank "neat" (straight) on his way to further fame. "Vino" was a violently intoxicating and cheap native drink. Bill Harllee nearly choked on a swallow of it and it brought huge tears to his eyes, but he considered it an honor to drink straight from the canteen of this celebrated man.

General S. B. M. Young later recommended Hall for a brevet promotion, citing him:

> For gallantry and meritorious service in action at Aringay, Province of Union, Luzon, P.I., Nov. 19, 1899, where with great gallantry and good judgment, he led his company forward in the dark, waded the river under a strong fire from a superior and intrenched hostile force and materially assisted in demoralizing and completely routing the enemy and capturing the works and the town . . .

Back to Bill Harllee. Not a single Filipino soldier at Aguilar. His men were hungry. He found a native cow and a native cook. In his Spanish, then fragmentary, he ordered the Filipino cook: "Kill that cow!" and the deed was done. His men ate.

Captain Fowler and the rest of the company came up. They had gone as far as their orders carried them. But—

"We're going on till we find some Gugus," said Captain Fowler.

"They'll court-martial you sure as shooting," said Harllee.

"I don't care if they do," said Reese Fowler. "Think I'm going to have those sons in the rest of the regiment kid us about being the regimental non-combatants?"

Then ensued the Battle of Mangatarem, already recounted.

51

VI
JOINING THE U. S.
MARINES—1900

There isn't a job on top of the earth
the beggar don't know nor do.
—Rudyard Kipling

I decided when I left West Point that
I wouldn't go back to Florida or South
Carolina until I got a commission.
The Marine officers are the "swel-
lest" in the U. S. Service, and the
enlisted men are the most carefully se-
lected and present a fine appearance.
—William C. Harllee, Feb. 20, 1900

The trip from Manila to San Francisco during December of 1899 and January of 1900 through winter storms on the old horse transport, Conemaugh, was punctuated by a great celebration in Nagasaki that the Japanese Chief of Police never forgot and by another memorable party in lovely Honolulu.

Upon arrival in San Francisco, Corporal Harllee went to the office of Major General William R. Shafter, the big hero of the Battle of Santiago, Cuba, who had led his troops in a horse and buggy. Shafter's adjutant-general, a superannuated old Colonel demanded:

"Where are your staff returns?" Bill Harllee had never heard of staff returns which were a soldier's complete personal service record. He told the colonel so.

"You'll stay here till they come," said the bad tempered old adjutant-general.

"I'd stay here till I rotted, then," said Harllee. "My outfit's still back in the bosque, sir. The first sergeant who took my place doesn't know what a staff return is any more than I did before you told me. They'll never come."

"That's enough from you," shouted the adjutant-general. "Get out of this office!"

Harllee started for the door to Major General Shafter's inner office. An armed sentry tossed him out. The following day he sneaked past the sentry into General Shafter's office.

He had just started to tell his story when the furious adjutant-general came roaring in and told Bill Harllee to get out.

"I think, Colonel," said Major General Shafter, "I would like to hear what this soldier has to say."

The adjutant-general, a colonel in the regular army, subsided. Harllee told his story to Major General Shafter.

"Fix up this soldier's transportation to Washington, Colonel," said Major General Shafter casually.

A colonel carries out a major general's orders. But the colonel got even. Months later, as a U. S. Marine officer, Harllee found that his transportation had been charged against him on the colonel's order; it was deducted from his pay!

But that day in San Francisco he was happy. He celebrated again, not neglecting the Barbary Coast. He climbed on the transcontinental train and headed to Washington with $1.65 in his pocket. He lived on $1.50 and landed in Washington with 15 cents. He spent that for a sack of tobacco, a book of cigarette papers and a street car ride. Then he found an American Plan hotel which would give him credit and wrote home for money from his farms.

He passed his examination for second lieutenant in the U. S. Marine Corps on Feb. 2, 1900, at the head of a class of 20 candidates, each of whom, including him, had been nominated by his Senator or Congressman. He received his commission on February 17, 1900. His pay was $1,400 a year. It seemed a fortune. And above all, he had at last realized his dream to be an officer with a lifetime of service to Uncle Sam ahead of him—and perhaps being "a soldier of the sea" would be better than being just a soldier.

He bought a complete outfit of tailored uniforms and civilian clothes. The quality of this apparel can be attested to by the fact that a formal white tie suit, or "tails", has lasted from his purchase of it in 1903 until this writing in excellent shape, meanwhile having been worn on appropriate occasions by his son and grandson! It is now being saved for use by his great-grandson.

Like most officers of that day, he dressed well and would have totally disdained ready-made clothes. His tailor was Heiberger in Washington, D. C. It was a peculiar custom of those times to consider tailors as bankers and personal friends. Harllee allotted fifty dollars a month, a huge portion of his pay, to Heiberger, who kept some for his own bill and paid Harllee's insurance premiums and other bills. This was particularly useful later when the Marine was in China, the Philippines, and other foreign stations before the advent of air mail and electronic payments.

But back in 1900, as soon as his uniforms were ready, Bill Harllee went home to South Carolina to see the family and impress them with his new finery. When he walked into the house in his blue uniform, his Uncle Robert Z. Harllee got up and took a good look at his nephew.

"Son," said Uncle Bob, "you look like a regular Yankee officer!"

Uncle Bob left the room. But a little later he was back, carrying in his hands the sword he had worn all the way through the Civil War as a Confederate captain.

"Here, son," he said to Second Lieutenant William Curry Harllee of the United States Marine Corps, "You wear this. The South is part of the United States now, and this sword will bring you luck, as it did me." Bill belted it on and kept it with him the rest of his life.

He had been ordered to report to the Marine Barracks at the

Taken in 1900 at Marine Barracks, New York, N.Y. L to R Standing: Thomas Holcomb; Theo. Backstrom; Sidney W. Brewster; Eli T. Fryer; Wm H. Pritchett. L to R Sitting: Rufus H. Lane; Hugh Matthew; John C. Beaumont; William C. Harllee. All attained the rank of General or Colonel during their careers.

Navy Yard in Washington for further assignment, which in his case, was to the Marine Barracks at the Navy Yard in Brooklyn, New York.

He had a little extra time before reporting in, so he went up to West Point and spent a few hours with his classmates. They welcomed him warmly and thought it was a huge joke on the "Tacs" and the Superintendent of West Point that he had received a commission in February of 1900 whereas he wouldn't have had one until June of 1901 if they hadn't tossed him out of West Point.

His tour in New York was too pleasant and easy to last longer than three months. He called it "the best post in our service." He had elegant quarters there, two bedrooms and a bathroom, a parlor, a dining room, a kitchen and a large hall. The rooms were carpeted and furnished in good shape. He told his friends coming up there that he could entertain them in style.

There were nine second lieutenants there then and they ran a mess (dining room) together and lived inexpensively but very well. They had two black women for cooks and servants.

He was assigned, among other duties, to be the judge advocate (prosecuting attorney) of the general court martial. As such, he tried 14 cases and gained valuable military legal experience which would stand him in good stead later on, particularly when he became the accused in a monster case in 1922.

But the people of the Middle Kingdom on the other side of the world were stirring. The Chinese did not like the depredations the Europeans and Japanese were making upon them any more than the Filipinos had liked the Spanish or even the Americans to govern them at that time. There were many Americans in China and in those days the United States felt obliged and able to protect its citizens overseas.

So the 5th Battalion of Marines was ordered from the U. S. to the Far East, the New York contingent to entrain on Sunday June 24, 1900. The eight original officers to go were rather an interesting group: Major William P. Biddle, Commanding; Captains Wendell C. Neville and F. J. Moses; and Lieutenants C. C. Carpenter, S. A. W. Patterson, J. J. Muir, D. W. Blake and Harllee. Biddle and Neville were to become Commandants of the Marine Corps.

According to Harllee, Moses was a martinet of renown. Patterson graduated from the U. S. Naval Academy in 1882, but he had served for years in the Old Revenue Cutter Service (now Coast Guard) and had transferred in 1898 to the Marine Corps. Although almost old enough to be the father of the other young second lieutenants, he withstood the extreme rigors of the coming campaign in China better than a lot of the youngsters. Blake, a Cornell graduate, had also served in the Revenue Cutter Service.

Before he left New York, Harllee typically wrote to his Aunt Amelia:

> I hope you will improve in health. I want you to pick out a place in the mountains or springs to go about the first of July and try to get away from home a little while. I shall be able to

give you a trip and would enjoy it more than wasting it on myself here.

He wrote this on his twenty third birthday.

He embarked aboard the U. S. Army Transport Grant in San Francisco on June 30, 1900, headed for Nagasaki. But before they reached the Golden Gate the engines broke down and the ship turned back and anchored near the dock until a casting could be made. The Grant left again on July 3, 1900 under a clear blue sky, and as usual the band played the national airs, but much to Harllee's dismay the band did not play "Dixie," as it had when the 33rd Texas sailed.

There were aboard two companies of Marines, eight troops of the Sixth Cavalry, over three hundred recruits, and some signal and hospital corpsmen, with officers of all descriptions. Several officers had their wives and children aboard, and there were quite a number of trained women nurses.

Harllee had had plenty of money in New York and had brought along a "gramophone" (record player) from there. They were quite rare then, the recording industry having just started. It afforded much amusement for both officers and men. Even the General (Adna Chaffee, later Chief of Staff of the Army) liked it, and one major listened to it by the hour, even though there was not much of a selection of music. Harllee liked such songs as "There'll Be a Hot Time in the Old Town Tonight" and "Sweet Adeline", but he had not purchased the popular "Marching Through Georgia".

The Grant took the great circle route, which was the shortest distance to Japan. This route goes far north, near the Aleutians, so the travellers had a cold July. The New York Journal reported the Grant sunk and lost, and it was two days before this error was corrected.

They arrived safely in Nagasaki on July 24, 1900 after a pleasant trip through the beautiful Inland Sea of Japan. There they learned that there was a real war going on in China—and plenty of it. In the West it was called the Boxer Rebellion. They heard that the Ninth Infantry of the U. S. Army had sustained fifty percent casualties, killed or wounded, among the men who were engaged in the fight at Tientsin. Such rumors abounded, almost all of them false. One of the false ones was that the heroic Marine Captain John Twiggs Myers and his whole detachment of Marines in Peking had been killed. But Harllee looked forward to the forthcoming combat as a great opportunity to serve with troops of almost all the great nations of the world and to gain invaluable experience.

The Grant arrived at Chefoo, China, on July 27, 1900.

VII
FIGHTING THE FISTS
OF RIGHTEOUS
HARMONY
Boxer Rebellion in China, 1900

*20,000 troops of the United States,
Russia, Japan, Germany, Great Britain, France, Italy and Austria-Hun-
gary fought together as never before or
since to rescue their compatriots from
the Boxers in an ocean of 350,000
Chinese—but, oh, what unholy reasons
created the need for this rescue and
what a terrible orgy ended it!*
(anon)

August 2, 1900. Chinese corpses meandered down the surface
of the filthy Pei-Ho River. Newly promoted First Lieutenant
William Curry Harllee of the United States Marine Corps
worked his way upstream under a broiling sun, first on an
iron barge being towed to Taku alongside the old USS MON-
OCACY, an ancient side wheeler, and then on a tug to Tientsin.
Chinese snipers on the river banks took pot shots at him, but

he was happy anyway. This was what he had wanted. He was going to join the Allies on the march to Peking!

He had been adjutant to Major Biddle, then Commanding the Fifth Battalion and shortly to command the Marine Regiment. There had not previously been adjutants in the Marine Corps, and Biddle didn't know what to do with him, so he was ordered to take some equipment and supplies in the barge up to Tientsin and report to Captain Dunlap's Company C in Major Littleton W. T. Waller's First Battalion, Young's Brigade, Major General Adna R. Chaffee's Division. These were all men renowned or to be renowned for exceptional courage. Dunlap with the Marines in France in World War 1; Young of the Army personally leading scouts in the Philippine Insurrection; Chaffee of the Army in the Civil War and on the frontier; and Waller throughout his career. Harllee had heard that Waller "celebrated" continuously except on the march or in action, but he was splendid in both of those activities. He was one of the Corps' greatest fighting leaders.

Tientsin had been taken by the Allies a week before. Herbert Hoover, then a young mining engineer who had been working in the interior of China, and his wife had both played heroic roles there. He had planned the defenses in Tientsin and every night had slipped out of the barricades under fire to bring back from the municipal water plant the only purified water they could get. Mrs. Hoover had pedaled her bicycle around the city to her volunteer hospital work and to her supervision of the dairy herd, despite sniper fire which once punctured her tires.

Tom Mix, the cowboy movie star of the 1920's, was wounded there while serving as an American infantryman.

Henry Luce, the co-founder of TIME, Inc., came there at that time as a child with his Presbyterian missionary family.

What with two future Chiefs of Staff of the Army (Chaffee and Summerall) there, it was quite an American celebrity and celebrity-to-be parade, especially to take place so far from home.

On August 4, 1900, the Allies started for Peking—18,600 Americans, British, French, Italians, Russians, Japanese, Germans and Austro-Hungarians. Not only a lot of nationalities, but a fantastic conglomeration of military and naval personnel, such as never seen before in one campaign. They included not only infantry, artillery, cavalry, sailors and marines from the eight most powerful nations in the world but a pages long list of colonial and other special troops such as the Bengal Lancers, the Italian Bersaglieri, Cossacks, Indian sappers and miners, and German See Battalions. Also on the march were the Royal Welch Fusiliers, which Regiment had attacked Bunker Hill and fought at Yorktown in our Revolution, but which regiment in China in 1900 after the Boxer Rebellion had received a silver cup from friendly and admiring Americans. The Welch Fusiliers in turn gave the Americans a silver cup with reciprocal admiration.

The Allies left behind them looted Tientsin, a city of one million population. They plunged into possibly the most hellish 10 day march that so many troops had ever encountered to that time in recorded military history. They fought Chinese continually—there were 350 million of them and most of them then sympathized with the Boxers. The Boxers trained their men in "the martial arts," but it didn't do them much good.

They had been able to convince their recruits that they were invulnerable. They used such stunts as lining up the new men a few feet away from a Boxer with a gun; pouring small iron balls into the gun and then distracting the gullible peasants with wild gestures during which they would shake the iron balls out of the gun. Finally, when they fired at the amazed recruits there would be fire and smoke but the targeted men would remain unharmed.

The Allies won the battles of Pei-Tsang and Yang-Tsun. The Boxers had modern field pieces which they fired accurately and men fighting with Harllee were killed and wounded.

The Allied artillery was inferior to that of the Chinese, who also had machine guns and smokeless powder. Many of them had been trained by Europeans, and they were definitely the most formidable Oriental military force to face Europeans up to that date.

The Allied marchers sickened from scanty rations and polluted water full of alkali. Wells had been poisoned with dead men. Bill Harllee ate green corn and squash and chewed corn stalks for thirst.

Men, many unaccustomed to taking care of themselves in the field, were given a can of corned beef, a can of salmon, and all the hardtack they could stuff in their haversacks. Six men can live for a day on one two-pound can of corned beef. Green soldiers each opened a can, ate all they could and threw the rest away. Suffering beggared description. They had to march through the suffocating heat of midday choked with dust. Temperatures rose as high as 110° F. They marched with heavy packs through fields of millet and and of "sorghos," Chinese corn as high as a mounted horseman's head. They lay down in treeless country under the blazing sun in a futile effort to get some rest. At night they could not sleep in the airless cornfields with their myriads of mosquitoes and midges. Their lips were so dry and their tongues so swollen they could hardly talk. Harllee saw one man who had suffered such agonies from the unbearable heat and dust and broiling sun that he had become a raving lunatic. With his tongue parched and frightfully distorted features, he made gestures to his companions to shoot him because he could bear the pain no longer. Although the Pei-Ho River was full of dead bodies, men and horses drank from it. Half the men couldn't keep up during the day, but would catch up at night by the light of the burning villages. Sergeant Frank Keeler, U.S.M.C., wrote in his diary that at 3 P.M on August 7, "two-thirds of the command were missing." Young Lieutenant Harllee was able, by tremendous effort, to keep up day and night, but he saw Allied soldiers fall and die in convulsions, stricken by heat, dysentery and typhoid. He wrote that he would have welcomed being wounded in the Battle of Yang-Tsun.

Yet, strangely enough the Americans had a brass band on the march—the only band present.

From that march, Harllee carried unforgettable memories of two great leaders of fighting men. General Chaffee, tall, iron-jawed, soldierly, was one of the last of America's generals to be in the front line as much as his men. No staying at headquarters far to the rear for this man. He was "up front," binoculars to his eyes, bullets whistling around him.

Ten miles from Peking, Major Waller and his Marines camped on a filthy flat piled high with Chinese fertilizer. The stench of that, and of rotting Chinese dead, was so nauseating that men gagged. A trim orderly came to the Major with the message,

"The General's compliments, sir, and he invites the Major to move his bedding roll up the hill and spend the night there."

Waller was in trousers and an undershirt, his shirt and blouse off, washing his face in some muddy water in a rubber wash basin. With a characteristic gesture, he reached down and took a double handed grip on the waist band of his trousers, and pulled them taut. He thrust out his chest, and held his head high. In his stentorian, parade ground voice, he said.

"Present my compliments to the General and tell him that Major Waller will stay with his men."

In their close quarters, the Marines heard those words amid the filth and the stench and knew afresh that here was the kind of a commanding officer they would follow to hell and back.

On the night of August 13 Harllee reached Tung Chow, a large city a dozen or more miles from Peking. The Japanese ahead had already captured it and heaped up the dead in piles and looted the city. Harllee and his Marines were allowed to march at night for the first time to avoid the terrible heat but as luck would have it the rain came down hard, and he tested to see if he could see his hand in front of his face. He couldn't. His column got lost and countermarched three times and finally wound up at 4:00 A.M. a mile or so from Peking, having marched twenty miles that night. They flopped down and had no trouble sleeping without any cover. At 7:00 A.M. they marched again and joined the Allies at the walls of Peking, where further battle awaited them. They relieved the legations, participating in a race between nations to rescue their compatriots, who had been besieged there for 55 days.

Their fears about what had happened or might happen to their fellow countrymen in Peking were fueled by the torture

U.S. Marines move up and into position in preparation for the attack on the Chien Mien (Royal) Gate of Peking, in the Tartar Wall, August 1900

and massacre of white people in China by the Boxers. These feelings ran so high that Bill Harllee witnessed an incredible incident in which a Chinese soldier in uniform was taken prisoner by a Marine and turned over to the Japanese. The man was dragged off, knocked about, punched, kicked and taken under a railroad bridge. A French soldier appeared and shot the Chinese soldier in the face with his pistol and then shot him again. A Japanese soldier then stamped on him. His clothes were torn off him as the Allied soldiers tried to find the charm the Boxers reputedly possessed. It took him an hour to die in agony. This performance was extremely painful to Harllee and the other Americans.

August·15. Lieutenant Harllee was with his men on top of the Chien Mien (Royal) Gate of Peking, in the Tartar Wall, which was 40 feet high and 40 feet thick. He was directing effective fire on Chinese on an inner wall. Below him, Lieutenant Charles P. Summerall was directing fire at a heavy timber gate, studded and braced with iron. Summerall ceased firing, calmly walked forward under heavy Chinese fire, peeped through a crack in the gate, and marked with chalk where the

The Marines assault the Chien Mien Gate of Peking. Typical of the action seen by Bill Harllee in combat during the Boxer Rebellion.

braces on the other side of the gate were so that his gunners could have better targets. They then proceeded to demolish the gate.

Close to Harllee on the Chien Mien Gate, Captain Henry F. Reilly, a beloved American army officer, who was born in Ireland and who was one of the outstanding artillerymen of his time, was directing the shelling of the inner gates with thorite shells when a huge bullet from a Chinese jingal (a rifle 7 to to 10 feet long fired by two or three men), tore through his jaw and throat, killing him instantly. Reilly's men, who had hoisted the gun to the top of the wall, laid him out of the way, covered him with a blanket, and resumed firing their gun with tears in their eyes, hard-boiled though they were. Harllee went on directing his men's rifle fire. Despite Reilly's death, he did notice that the Chinese rifle marksmanship did not compare with the American.

The Allied assault swept through Peking that day. The Allied troops, including Bill Harllee, poured in through gates broken up by artillery fire.

Nothing could shock Harllee now. He had slept in the fields alongside dead Chinese. Some of these Chinese had been beheaded and their heads had been tied by their pigtails to cornstalks. There were too many dead Chinese to bury, and he had seen dogs and hogs feed on dead Chinese until they were almost too fat to run.

Now one of the last really great looting orgies in the history of the world was on. The "spoils of war" was the name of an old tradition in both Europe and Asia. Although President McKinley forbade it, it would have been quite difficult to find any European or American or Japanese, including civilians, who didn't do it—or at least who didn't purchase at real rock bottom bargain prices looted material. Even some of the women and missionaries participated. There were sables, tapestry, gold, silver, jewelry, old porcelain, Ningpo and other silks, lacquerware, bronze, and untold other valuables of all kinds, particularly in the "Forbidden City" of Peking.

The Chinese joined in the looting and coolies were wearing mandarin robes. Harllee reported that although the Allied orders were to shoot Chinese looters, the Chinamen all looted anyway. Allied soldiers threw furs over mud and burned others just for the hell of it. The only problem for Allied soldiers and officers was how to carry the loot—there was more than they could carry.

One of Harllee's West Point classmates was to retain a memory of "Harllee nonchalantly leading a long mule train laden down with loot in Peking in 1900." He had found, among other items, all the silver bullion a horse could carry.

He was billeted in the Palace of the Eighth Prince of the Manchu dynasty. It was quite a dynasty, decadent though it had become. It was dominated by the remarkable Empress Tzu Hsi almost all of the years from 1861 until the time of her death at 74 years of age in 1908. She was from time to time Empress, Dowager Empress, and Regent, but always more powerful than the Emperor. When Peking fell to the Allies, she had the Emperor's favorite concubine murdered by having her thrown down a well because she became impatient with her. The court of Suzy (as the Americans called her) included 3,000 eunuchs, and she did not move from one part of her palace to another without 26 eunuchs in attendance. But she was also reputed to have had lovers, among them General Jung Lu, in her earlier days. Jung Lu is considered by many historians to have been her best adviser.

Back in the Palace of the Eighth Prince, Chinese coolies, glad to be safe as American officer's servants, waited on Harllee and hauled him around in a ricksha. Chinese women, some not lacking at all in beauty, sought his protection.

A once rich Chinese merchant who by his own choice was Harllee's No. 1 boy, bought him some big lumps of carved gray jade, pointing at them with upraised thumb and the word: "Hau!", which means "Good" in Chinese. He tossed some of the Marine lieutenant's souvenirs in the trash with down-pointed thumb and "Bow-hau!", which means "No good." Later, in the Cavite Navy Yard, Nam Sing, the famous Chinese tailor who made Admiral Dewey's clothes, offered Harllee $500 for a lump of that carved jade big as his fist, and he learned that it was worth thousands of dollars.

There was anarchy and chaos in Peking for days after the allied troops entered. The Empress fled Peking and there was no Chinese government. There was rape and murder, usually by bayonet, as well as pillage and plunder. However, such American troops as needed restraint were restrained from rape and murder by their officers. Harllee was assigned late in August of 1900 to be the defense counsel of Stephen Dwyer, accused of both these offenses. It was a job he didn't relish, but after investigation, he believed that the man was not guilty. Dwyer was found guilty by the court and sentenced to be shot. The reviewing authority mitigated the sentence to life imprisonment. When the Judge Advocate General of the Navy back in Washington reviewed the case, he disapproved the conviction on the same grounds that Harllee had used for the defense and released Dwyer.

One evening soon after the sack of Peking had begun, Bill Harllee was taking the air near the Palace when he noticed a very uneven contest. A German soldier was in full pursuit of a dirty, but dainty Chinese maiden. He had the handicap of being full of beer, but she had the much bigger handicap of bound feet and a background of an overly sheltered life. Bill Harllee had been waging a deadly fight with the Chinese Boxers only a few days earlier, but he never liked to see the helpless picked on and had been brought up under a code of chivalry which made it unthinkable to attack women. The German was a big boy, armed and obviously most excited. The Marine instantly recalled his football days at West Point, and the tackled German was so surprised by such an unheard of tactic that he was quickly disarmed by his fast moving opponent.

As near as Bill Harllee could make out the name of the girl he had rescued sounded vaguely like "Summer Crystal." In any event it was August and she was as delicate and beautiful as a piece of fine crystal, so he decided on that name for her. He learned through a missionary interpreter that she was a princess and had been lost and left behind in the terrible confusion of the battle when her family and friends had fled Peking. Some women had committed suicide by jumping from the city wall, but she had hidden for several days. She had ventured forth that night for some water when the German noticed her. His attitude was somewhat exemplified by the Kaiser who sent German troops out to China when the German Ambassador was assassinated with the injunction to so treat the Chinese that they would not look another German in the eye for two hundred years. But Harllee of course, would have taken the same action no matter what nationality the soldier.

When cleaned up, rested, and refurbished with a minimum of feminine aids to beauty, Summer Crystal turned out to be a real charmer. Somehow the young Marine found himself in her company whenever off duty, learning about China. She learned more than enough English to say "American man nice. Don't go away." But after the August moon and the September moon, which most romantically waxed and waned, the bugler blew, and he had to march away. But to him she would always remain more than a fair sample of the oldest and biggest civilization on earth.

The Marines of that day and time were not too given to church-going and at least some of the missionaries were not too averse to "liberating" some unclaimed Chinese valuables, as the phrase went in a much later war. This is not to say that the missionaries and their families were not courageous, strong, and sincerely dedicated to spreading the gospel to save heathen souls, because they were, and hundreds of them faced death bravely in the Boxer Rebellion. Unfortunately they were hated by the Boxers; there was just too much cultural difference.

The Reverend Gilbert Reid was one of the most famous missionaries because he was also a correspondent and a chronicler of the Boxer Rebellion. His wife was a South Carolinian, and the young Marine officer knew him and accompanied him on some of his expeditions during the sack of Peking, because the Reverend Reid knew his way around town and knew what was where. On one occasion, the Reverend came to preach to the Marines, and Harllee was directed to have a place prepared for him. Only one other person beside him arrived for the services, so Reverend Reid decided the two of them could do without his eloquence on that particular occasion, but he remained for tiffin, the word

A U.S. Marine relief party prepare to march out during the Boxer Rebellion, Peking, 1900. (Slide taken by Mrs. Morgan S. (Anna Graham) Woodward, guest of U.S. Minister Couger).

in use in the Far East for lunch as well as for tea. He then found material for a convert in Summer Crystal.

A sad 1st Lieutenant Harllee left Peking on October 1, 1900. He then went to Tientsin and sailed for Cavite in the Philippines aboard the transport Indiana. He had had a unique opportunity to judge European and Japanese soldiers. To most objective observers, it appeared that the Japanese had been the most aggressive and effective. They had certainly taken the most casualties. It is curious that in the years before World War II they were so badly underestimated by Westerners despite the high positions of many of those who had observed them so closely in China.

Of course the Japanese had about 10,000 men in the relief column and the Americans only about 2,000, and the Japanese had already fought the Chinese in the war of 1894–1895.

Some of Bill Harllee's comments in a letter written August 3, 1900, in Tientsin, China, follow:

The British native Hindu soldiers are the finest looking soldiers to be seen. They are tall, erect and as military in their bearing as West Point cadets. They salute all officers most punctiliously and are said to be inferior in courage to no soldiers in the world.

The French are the dirtiest and filthiest soldiers here. They are the only ones who have shirked in the least.

The Russians are also a dirty looking lot, but they are brave. They are very cruel to the Chinese and murder and ravage without end. As I came up the river I could see no Chinamen on the Russian side and thousands on the Jap side where they had flocked to get away from Russian soldiers.

The Japs had confidence in their general and when things looked gloomy and other officers wanted to give up the job of taking Tientsin the Japs said that not one of his men should leave that field alive unless they went forward and that if every other force deserted him he would take it alone, and proposed to blow up the wall or gates. One of his companies advanced for that purpose. The time fuse went out and every man in the company volunteered to relight it, which of course was certain death and one was picked for it and touched it off and was blown into atoms and the gate blown up. Only twenty of that eighty returned alive and all the officers were killed.

Sunday morning we are going to have the biggest fight of recent years—the Chinese have seven lines of trenches about ten miles from here and have all sorts of artillery and rapid fire guns—and the worst of it is that the artillery is along the line the Americans are to fight.

A British officer who was an observer in the Civil War in the U. S. and in the Boer War in South Africa says that the fighting here is fiercer than he has ever seen. The Boxers are a fanatic people who are deluded to believe that if they are killed they will come to life again the next day, and they won't run.

Young Harllee also wrote to his worried relatives:

I have heard old soldiers say that they always had some premonition the days before they were wounded. I feel like I am going to pull through safely and even if I should get hit I have about three chances in four of being only wounded, so I don't worry about it.

In the house I live in (in Tientsin) there is a Chinese who was educated in the States and is a Yale man—he is as entertaining a man as I ever talked to and in fact he is a gentleman.

When Bill Harllee had an opportunity to reflect upon it, he realized that the actions of the European powers and Japan in the latter half of the last century in China were almost totally reprehensible. Four of the many items in the peace terms after the Boxer Rebellion are illustrative of this:

1. The Taku forts (guarding the river to Tientsin) were to be razed.

2. A sentence of death was to be pronounced on any Chinese member of an anti-foreign society.

3. The Chinese Foreign Office was to greatly improve its facilities for receiving foreign diplomats.

4. A Manchu prince was to head a party to go to Berlin to apologize to the Kaiser for the murder of the German Ambassador, Baron von Ketteler.

But the American role was limited to rescuing Americans; we had no territory in China. As was the case in the Philippine Insurrection, the fighting men were carrying out orders which they at the time had every reason to think were reasonable. Furthermore, the United States gave its share of the huge indemnity exacted from China ($335,000,000) to a fund which educated thousands of Chinese students in the United States for almost half a century—until Mao came into power. Despite the Korean and Vietnamese Wars, this helped to nurture roots of Chinese-American friendship which still existed as late as 1979, when the author visited China.

VIII
BACK TO THE PHILIPPINES—THE GRAND OLD GAME OF POKER: 1900–1903

They will never drink and sing and gamble together as we did in years gone by.
—Col. Wm. C. Harllee, in letter to Col. Julius Turrill January 15, 1939

Harllee arrived at Cavite on October 24, 1900. It was located about 12 miles from Manila and was the most important naval station in the Philippines.

The U. S. Marine Corps then had only 201 officers and 6,062 men, the number of people in a small town, and many of them were pretty well known to each other, at least by reputation. During his first duty in Brooklyn, the young lieutenant had been greatly assisted in his training of recruits (there were no recruit training depots then) and most of his other assignments by a grizzled and seasoned old Marine corporal named John Killilea. The youngster felt quite grateful to the older man. When he found Killilea in another company in the Philippines, he got him transferred to his own company, Company C. Killilea was typical of some of the best enlisted Marines of that day, a real Irishman, born in Ireland, hard drinking, ready for a fight or frolic, superb in action, and steadfast in devotion to the officers he liked. There were also many Germans, born in Germany, as well as some from a number of other foreign countries, who made excellent Marines in those days. As late as 1895, one quarter of the enlisted men of the Marine Corps were aliens.

As privates they were paid only $15.60 a month, and as first sergeants only $33.00, but few of them were married and they figured all they really needed money for was tobacco, and beer or liquor on paydays. They were quite a bargain for the United States Government. They were not provided with what would today be considered adequate barracks, recreational facilities, care for dependents, very good food, or the post exchanges with numerous satellite facilities of later years. But the living standards of the times were lower and the Marines were happy and proud to wear the globe and anchor.

From 1799 until 1947, twenty cents a month was deducted from the pay of all Marine officers and men for hospital expenses—perhaps the earliest and cheapest known form of health insurance.

Unfortunately, Bill Harllee did not keep a diary of his eventful early years. The reason can probably be attributed to "Old Colonel Henry Clay Cochrane." He was a notable type indeed and he had performed heroically in the Civil War, in Egypt in 1882 with a force of 70 Marines, and elsewhere. He had accompanied President Lincoln to Gettysburg for the Address. But Colonel Frederic M. Wise and Meigs O. Frost wrote in "A Marine Tells It To You" about Cochrane, "Cordially hated by officers and men alike." Harllee wrote that "the odium in which was held the copious notes Colonel Cochrane kept daily—which were known as the 'son of a bitch book'—kept many Marine officers of that time from keeping diaries." However, Harllee wrote plenty of letters which have survived.

The Marine Corps then had, as it has had in so many other years of its proud history, plenty of colorful officers as well as

A touch of Wild West Frontier days is in evidence from this photo of a U.S. Marine Infantry Company in the Philippines, 1901.

enlisted men. One such in the Philippines in 1901 was Colonel Mancil C. (Old Manse) Goodrill, Brigade Commander at Cavite. The story was that he announced to his assembled officers that he never let anything interfere with his drinking. He had been orderly to General U. S. Grant in the Civil War and thus appreciated the merits of good whiskey. Drinking was a very popular pastime then and there among first class fighting men. Another colonel said,

"Maybe a man who doesn't drink can be trusted, but he's got to prove it to me."

In later years Harllee liked to recall that the Marines of those days drank like the cowboys in the bars of the old Wild West movies. They poured a glass half full or more of bourbon whiskey and drank it neat. To use ice, a mix, or hors d'oeuvres would have been considered effeminate.

Bill Harllee built the first good post exchange the Marines had in the Philippines and made it a pleasant place for the men. He fed the whole post so well that the men were not wretched for lack of good food. Philippine diet and cooking were quite different from what Americans were used to.

Harllee and Killilea and many others in the company naturally thought it was the most efficient company and worked harder and accomplished more than any company in the Islands. The older Irishman and the young lieutenant had also been together on the terrible march from Tientsin to Peking and were both proud of not having straggled or fallen out.

From February 24 until July 10, 1901, Harllee was stationed at Pollock in Mindanao, a relatively pleasant and cool station, from which he sent many boxes of "Perfecto" cigars home to family and friends, although to those in the Tampa area, they must have seemed like coals to Newcastle.

His mail from Pollock was postmarked at Zamboanga, celebrated by Americans in the song from the Song Book of the Military Order of the Carabao, which began:

Oh, the monkeys have no tails in Zamboanga!
Oh, the monkeys have no tails in Zamboanga!
    Oh, the monkeys have no tails,
    They've been bitten off by whales;
Oh, the monkeys have no tails in Zamboanga!

Oh, the birdies have no feet in Marivales!
Oh, the birdies have no feet in Marivales!
    Oh, the birdies have no feet,
    They've been burned off by the heat;
Oh, the birdies have no feet in Marivales!

There's a virgin on the Island of Cebu!
There's a virgin on the Island of Cebu!
    There's a virgin, so they say,
    She'll be six months old today;
There's a virgin on the Island of Cebu!

One evening Harllee said to his close friend from the Citadel, West Point and the Manila days of 1899, Lt. J. C. Minus of the Army:

"Let's go see a cockfight."

Minus replied, "What in the hell do you want to see such a miserable affair for?"

Harllee answered, "They are the natives' greatest diversion, and we've never even seen one. Besides, maybe we can make some money."

So, they went to a large bamboo building with a thatched roof, a little outside Manila, and found a hundred natives gathered therein, some with fighting cocks under their arms. It was really a gigantic gambling den, although rather a bloody one. As the two young Americans pushed up to the front row, two cocks, each armed with four inch long steel spurs, were about to be placed in the cockpit by their owners.

When the proprietor announced that the contest was about to begin, dollars poured into the ring. They were Mexican dollars, more or less the coin of the realm, because the Spanish had had almost all the Philippine exports sent to Mexico to be paid for in Mexican currency.

Harllee saw one fighter with more gray (the Confederate uniform color) in his feathers than the other, and on a hunch he and Minus, also a sentimental Southerner, both tossed all they had with them (about eighty-four dollars Mexican or 42 dollars U. S.) into the ring.

The fight was fast and furious and lo and behold the non-gray cock was killed. The two young men took their money and left. Once was enough. They later asked some Filipino friends how cheating was prevented when each man tossed some money into the ring and took it and an equal amount out for himself if he won, but could easily simply grab more than he had thrown in. They were told that in the hundred or so of these gambling pits around Manila only one exception to this honesty had been known—and that the offender had instantly been hacked to pieces by knives.

The Philippine Islands had an exotic beauty and were full of flowers and fruit—coconuts, pineapples, lemons, oranges, bananas, guavas, mangoes, and natural resources. The Filipinos were by nature friendly.

But he experienced most of the bad features of the Philippines in those days, too. The heat and humidity in the Islands was debilitating even to a young man from way down south in southern Florida. There was a rainy season for four months, starting in June. There were typhoons, with winds stronger than the hurricanes from the Caribbean. When Harllee was in Pollock, a typhoon came up without any warning and blew down the buildings and trees. At Parang-Pasang, two miles away, there was no storm at all, and they didn't know there was one in Pollock until they looked over and couldn't see the buildings or trees. Tornadoes and earthquakes also furnished some excitement.

There was a lack of public sanitation in most areas. Cholera raged from time to time among the Filipinos, although fortunately the Americans didn't seem to get it. There was dysentery, beri-beri, typhoid and "swamp fever." During the period of 1898–1900 the Army's hospital admission rates for dysentery in the Philippines were 3½ times those of the worst American-occupied areas in World War II and the death rate 50 times higher. There seemed to be millions of mosquitoes and stinging flies everywhere. Even the fish, fowl, and flesh to be eaten seemed to have different taste in the Philippines, one which had to be acquired. And then again, those were the days before Americans wore clothing best suited for tropical weather; before the wonderful advances in medicine, vitamins, and nutrition made later in this century. Doctors advised even young men to do nothing except try to keep cool and not to exert themselves mentally or physically. Many Americans sent out there had breakdowns, alcoholic and otherwise, and had to be sent home. Major Biddle told Harllee:

"I would rather be a second lieutenant in the States than a major out here."

Judge James Henderson Blount, an heroic American volunteer officer in the Insurrection and then a United States judge in the Philippines, had to resign on Janaury 25, 1905 because of ill health, and he believed that his health was wrecked for the rest of his life by these conditions. Nevertheless, he wrote a masterpiece on our early involvement with the Islands, "The American Occupation of the Philippines 1898–1912."

Harllee managed to be in reasonable health when he left the Islands after a two year and four month tour, having recovered from hemorrhaging of the bowels and loss of weight, down to 167 pounds.

Bill Harllee and his Marine comrades march into the intense heat and oppressive humidity of the mosquito infested jungle in the Philippines.

In June of 1901, Lt. Minus was sitting on the rail of a Philippine steamer and fell backwards into the sea. It happened that the steamer had a small boat in tow and from this small boat a line dragged in the water. Minus gathered this rope as it was passing and managed to hang onto it for over an hour before he was rescued.

Such were the vicissitudes of life in the Philippines.

But in September of 1901, disaster befell Bill Harllee. When recovering from a severe sickness, the hot tempered young Marine officer became involved in a violent altercation with a Filipino, who, of course, came off second best. This sort of thing had not been too uncommon then. For instance, one night in July, 1888, Bowman Henry McCalla, Commanding Officer of the USS ENTERPRISE, under provocation, struck a drunk, unruly, and disrespectful fireman, inflicting a small scalp wound. The press sensationalized the story, and he was suspended from duty for three years. He later proved himself a brilliant tactician and a courageous and decisive leader in the Spanish-American War, the Philippine Insurrection and the

81

Boxer Rebellion. He wound up as Rear Admiral B. H. McCalla, U.S.N., with several international awards and commendations.

Baron von Ketteler, the German minister to China whose murder preceded the Chinese attack on the Legations in Peking, had thrashed two Boxers with a cane, although one of them had been brandishing a large knife.

In any event, it was certainly not conducive to good Filipino-American relations for Americans to hit Filipinos. Harllee was given a general court martial for assault and battery. He was convicted and sentenced to a public reprimand, six months suspension from duty, and a loss of half his pay for six months. He was refused permission to spend this time in the United States.

Poker was then "the grand old game" of the armed forces, the "Wild West," the South, and much of the rest of America. In Austin, Texas, the home of his future bride, there had been a legendary poker game which lasted from 1853 to 1870. With time on his hands, Harllee decided to study the game. He bought a ten cent paperback book on poker, Henry T. Winter-blossom's "The Game of Draw Poker." He mastered the laws of chance therein and played draw poker, nothing wild, steadily every night except Sunday at the Army Navy Club in Manila.

The Club was constructed around a large patio or courtyard, open to the sky and filled with trees, coconut palms and many tropical plants, including a wide variety of orchids. The club-house included a bar, a men's dining room, a ladies' dining room, a pool and billiard room, and a well-patronized game room. The Club was the center of the social life of Manila.

Harllee played a limit poker game—a dollar Mex or fifty cents U.S. He and his fellow players did not want to play a game for higher stakes—they felt it was likely to ruin someone. He found that few people knew anything about the relative chances—and since he did and had the ability to use the knowledge—he could and did win. He and the serious players of that day would have looked with great scorn on "deuces wild," "jokers," "spit in the ocean," and other such games which the ladies liked but which the men didn't like and which they thought caused "the grand old game" later on to about peter out.

But one night a traveling English Guards captain, George Rose, breezed into the Club and asked to join the game. He was welcomed, but he became quite unhappy about what he called the ridiculously small stakes. He kept ragging the Americans about it all evening. His remarks ran along the lines of,

"I've heard about the 'Wild West' in America. You boys must come from the *mild* West."

Finally, he declaimed, "By jove, I've played real poker in America—in New York actually—and this isn't it at all. Why, you don't even have enough money on the table for a respectable table stakes game. Isn't there anyplace around here where I can get in a real game?"

The Americans looked at each other. Harllee, although his ancestry was mainly English dating back to the 17th and 18th centuries, was never an Anglophile and was proud of his Revolutionary forbears. He considered himself an American, not an English-American. He had enjoyed the company of British officers during Boxer Rebellion days and admired them, but he lacked enthusiasm about the way some Englishmen pretended to look down on what they called their colonial cousins. The other Yanks, mostly Marine officers, basically felt the same way, and Harllee knew it, so he decided to suggest an exception to their limit rule and said,

"Day after tomorrow is pay day. If you're still here, I'll bring my pay and we'll take your money. How about it, gentlemen?"

It was late at night and the others, well stimulated by John Barleycorn, slowly agreed. It seemed to them that *this* Englishman was just a little too much, looking down his long nose at them.

On the appointed date, four U. S. Marine officers; Harllee, Captain Charles J. Hill, and Lieutenants Austin Rogers and J. T. Bootes, came over from Cavite for the evening. They brought their pay plus some other monies to meet the British challenge. Captain Rose had requested permission to bring a friend, Tom Suiter. The Limeys had plenty of cash. They all met at the grand old Army and Navy Club with its view of the bay and tall ceilings and ambience of Victorian elegance.

After drinks in the spacious bar the group had a special payday dinner. The menu selections are worth noting:

Anchovies on toast	Coffee
Salted Almonds	Cadbury's chocolates
Queen's olives	Potato Chips
Consome patti	Roman punch
Frozen oyster cutlets	Roast turkey and cranberry
Petit Pois	sauce
Compote breast of wild	Potato Croquettes
pigeons	Cauliflower
Tenderloin steak bordelaise	Chicken Salad
Cheese	Strawberry jelly

There was plenty of cerveza (beer), coffee, and liqueur and a Filipino string band playing such recent American songs as "A Bird in a Gilded Cage" and "Hello Central, Give Me Heaven" for the dancing pay day celebrants.

The poker players adjourned to the card room. Draw poker, table stakes, was the game, with the ante one dollar Mex or fifty cents in U. S. Filipino waiters kept the players well supplied with liquid refreshments. The cigar smoke would have called for an environmental impact report in a later day.

The game proceeded slowly at first, as the Americans had not been playing this kind of game. But as the evening passed, the betting gradually increased. Bill Harllee was having pretty good luck.

Rose and Harllee were the big winners, but the others still had something left.

Finally, at two o'clock in the morning, the other four players figured they had played enough, and the cards were not running with them that night. Rose wanted one more deal and Harllee was entirely agreeable. The others reluctantly agreed to stay in for one more hand.

The deal resulted in several good hands.

After the ante, Captain Hill opened with $10.00.

Lieutenants Rogers and Bootes folded.

Mr. Suiter raised $20.00.

Harllee, with two queens and two fours, played it cozy and called.

Captain Rose, who was the dealer, raised $40.00.

At the draw of the cards, Hill and Suiter each drew two cards, Harllee, one, and Rose, none.

Harllee drew a queen. This gave him a full house, queens high. Rose didn't draw, so by rights he could be presumed to have an excellent hand—four of a kind, a full house or more likely, a flush or straight. But he had given himself away earlier with some bluffing, and Harllee knew that the chances of his getting four of a kind without a draw were one in 4,165 and of getting a full house were one in 694. He had to think fast— and he knew he could be wrong, but the odds were with his full house.

He looked at Rose and then the others with one of the world's great poker faces, and then out at the beautiful moonlit night. He decided to stay in the game.

Hill and Suiter checked.

Harllee bet $200.00.

Hill, after a lot of thought, decided to fold. Suiter did the same.

Rose raised $400.00, but when he did, Harllee noticed a tic in his eye, which hadn't been there before, and which he figured shouldn't have been there if he had four of a kind or a really good full house or better.

So Harllee raised $340.00, which was all he had.

Rose called. He had 3 jacks and 2 nines.

Harllee won $1,050.00 (the ante going to the Club for drinks, cigars, the room and service) and ordered French champagne for the house. In 1900, the average *annual* wage in the U. S. was $662.48. So ended the table stakes exception to the nightly dollar Mex-fifty cents U. S. limit game. During the six months period of his suspension from duty he won over five thousand dollars. To get an idea of what five thousand dollars in those days would mean today, that was then the salary of a U. S. Senator. One could buy a reasonably good house for that price.

But this more or less concluded his "sowing wild oats," as the expression of that day went. He returned to the United States in March of 1903. He had realized, with lots of ups and downs, his great ambition to be a soldier and soon, in the Paradise of the Pacific, he was to acquire another ambition.

IX
A LIFETIME PASS ON THE FALL RIVER LINE—MARCH 1903

The Major General Commandant desires in this connection to especially commend the conduct of First Lieutenant William C. Harllee
—**April 6, 1903**

Upon his return from the Philippines in February of 1903, Bill Harllee was assigned some leave of absence and some temporary duty at his first and much loved station of the Brooklyn Navy Yard in New York.

He left New York on March 19, 1903, with a detachment of 75 Marines ordered to the Boston Navy Yard on the Fall River Line steamer Plymouth. At midnight that night, in a thick fog, the freighter, City of Taunton, rammed the Plymouth in Long Island Sound, opening a huge space in The Plymouth to the waters of the Sound and exposing a tangled mass of mattresses, boards, blankets, clothing, valises, splintered furniture and detached panelling, criss-crossed with twisted bars of iron.

One passenger was killed in the collision, the only one the Fall River Line ever lost in the ninety years of its service beginning in 1847. Five crewmen were killed.

Harllee had been dreaming he was back on the transcontinental train which had brought him and his Marines back from the Philippines. The train had made many sudden, collision-like stops. But he snapped back when he heard the passengers' cries. He leaped from his bunk, threw on his coat, trousers and shoes, and while wading in water up to his waist, rushed forward to see his men. The men had been sleeping in the forward compartment where the collision occurred and the compartment was filling with water. Shoes, socks, clothing, and haversacks were floating and sinking. The Marines came out in all conditions of dress; some fully clothed, some stark naked, and others in all the stages of undress in between. The bugler brought his bugle out.

"Sound first call!" ordered Harllee, as passengers panicked about him. The stirring notes rang through the night.

"Now sound assembly," Bill ordered. Again the bugle rang out a comforting sound.

Marines came running on the plunging deck.

"Fall in!", bellowed Harllee. "Right dress!"

As reported in the press, the Marines "emerged on the deck before the echoes of the crash subsided, assembling with as much precision as if to be reviewed."

The passengers became reassured. They were astounded and then amused by the brawny but embarrassed Marines standing at attention in ranks in the costume usually reserved for much more private occasions.

Harllee reported to the Plymouth's captain: "Sir, we are ready to help you." After the captain had blankets quickly distributed to cover the naked ones, he put all the Marines to work quieting passengers, distributing lifebelts, keeping the crowd away from the scene of the collision and guarding life boats.

The waters of the Sound were calm and that was all that saved the Plymouth. The ship had passed Gull Light and was right in the middle of the Race, where the current rushes hither and yon at great speed. There was no radio on those ships. But by sunrise another steamer came along and towed them into New London.

Friendly passengers gave clothes to the Marines who had kept order and helped to prevent panic. Marines who lost their shoes cut up blankets to cover their feet. Others wore blankets like capes. Those who lost their caps made "dunce-caps" of newspapers to keep their heads warm. Thus they reached New London.

They travelled by train to Boston, and then by trolley car, specially arranged for by long distance phone, to the Boston Navy Yard. When they marched into the yard, they encountered old Colonel Percival C. Pope, Marine Commanding Officer. Harllee's first sergeant was marching with the perfect posture and cadence of a true Marine, but he was dressed in a preacher's Prince Albert coat, golf knickers and loud plaid stockings, patent leather shoes and a pearl-gray derby hat.

"My Lord!", exclaimed Colonel Pope. "What has happened?" He hadn't read the newspapers which were full of the tragedy. Harllee explained.

"I am happy, Lieutenant Harllee," said Colonel Pope, "to learn that this is not a junior officer's idea of humor."

A typical reaction from an old-time colonel. No compliment for good work at sea. The Fall River Line, though, gave Bill Harllee a lifetime pass and paid for everything his men lost. The Commandant of the Marine Corps officially commended Harllee, as well as Captain T. H. Low and four enlisted Marines.

According to the Palmetto (Florida) News of April 2, 1903, the New York American wrote:

> Lt. W. C. Harllee, standing waist deep in water, rallied the eighty Marines who were bound for Boston, under command, (sic), and led the work of quelling the panic. Many were the brave deeds done.

This was a bit overblown. For the Marines, the incident had held more comedy than courage. The Palmetto News of that date carried the headline "Harllee the Hero," but quoted him as saying:

> Really, it did not amount to much. The men were lucky to escape. Everybody on board the ship behaved admirably. The men went to work at once and our Marines made a respectable adjunct to the crew.

Newlyweds Ella Fulmore and Will Harllee

X
THE WEDDING
JULY 30, 1903

He had sent her gifts of rich silk
embroidered coats from China and at
least one of these had gold buttons
—Mrs. Ellen Harllee Vermilye—Circa 1903

Unreconstructed Rebel Will Harllee spent June and July of 1903 way up among the real Yankees in New Hampshire, at the Navy Yard in Portsmouth. On Decoration Day of 1903, before he got to know them, he had to participate in a parade with the Grand Army of the Republic (Northern veterans of the Civil War). He felt that:

They made a pretty sorry bluff at pretending to be patriotic, and their occasions are not near what you would see on a Confederate occasion.

However, that was "tongue in cheek." He later changed his mind and found plenty of New Englanders to admire and with whom to form warm friendships.

The big event of 1903, if not of his life, for "Will Harllee", as his bride was to call him, was his marriage on July 30 to Ella Florence Fulmore of Austin, Texas. The wedding was at the home of her parents, Judge and Mrs. Zachary Taylor Fulmore of 310 West 13th Street, which was within view of the state capital in Austin.

He had met her in 1896 while she was attending Salem Female College in Winston-Salem, North Carolina, where she later graduated. She and her family had visited his family's home in South Carolina while he was there on vacation from the University of North Carolina. Since their first meeting, he had been in correspondence with her.

Ella Fulmore was from a distinguished old Texas family. Sterling Clack Robertson, grandfather of her mother, Luella Robertson, as an "Impresario", brought 600 families with him at his own expense from Tennessee to settle in Texas in 1835, while Texas was still part of Mexico. Robertson, whose great uncle General James Robertson, was a notable Tennessee pioneer and founded Nashville, signed the Texas Declaration of Independence and commanded a company during the Texas war for independence against Mexico. He fought in the Battle of San Jacinto, in which the Mexicans were finally defeated.

Ella's father was a Confederate veteran, a lawyer, judge, chairman of the commission which recodified the state laws of Texas in 1892–1893, author of five books, and holder of many other honors and offices.

In 1903, Will had visited Austin and decided that his memory was right—Ella Fulmore was *the* girl for him.

Will would later include in his work, "Kinfolks", the following description of her, written by his cousin, Mrs. Ellen Harllee (Forsythe) Vermilye:

> Somewhere near the end of the last century I had a glimpse of my first real young lady. I have never since seen any that so completely filled the bill. No girl could really be as beautiful as I remembered her, and my grandmother's old home in Summerville fairly tinkled with her laughter. Her clothes were miracles of loveliness, and I was told that the things she wore when she went out in society in Charleston were even more ravishing, but I don't believe it. Like any other fairy princess, she was supplied with a doting father and had no financial worries. By keeping a blank countenance and my ears attuned to the slightest whisper, I gathered from the grownups that she was beloved of a young man who was a soldier. He had sent her gifts of rich silk embroidered coats from China, and one at least of these had solid gold buttons. I rejoiced when I learned that he had really captured and married her.

Ella Fulmore and Will Harllee were to remain a loyal and devoted couple all their lives.

XI
ON THE BEACH AT
WAIKIKI: 1904-1906

*Honolulu's climate is perfect—it
never rains in the city—in fact, everything seems combined to make the little
city a paradise—everybody seems to
have plenty of money.*
—William C. Harllee—October 11, 1899

Aloha!

On February 1, 1904, the newlyweds sailed for the islands which were then laying a solid foundation for the winning of their proud title, "Paradise of the Pacific." Will Harllee had already placed an enthusiastic stamp of approval on Honolulu after his 95 cent visit there in 1899.

As they approached Honolulu, they first saw Diamond Head from eight miles away. It was so named not because of its shape but because it was once believed that diamonds were to be found there. Next they saw the long lines of foam-crested breakers running towards the beach which were not only to furnish the riders their surf, but which were to become much later one of the staples of spectacular American advertising. Then they noticed as they came closer to the shore that the ocean kept its dark blue color until they were about a mile off shore, when it commenced to pass through all the colors of the marine spectrum.

Back of the city they saw Punchbowl Hill, a low, round extinct crater towering above the mountains in the distance, with fleecy white and gray clouds nestling near the top of the mountains. Down their sides were emerald green arroyos (water courses). They could even detect the sweet fragrance of flowers and fruit in the cool air well offshore.

As they drew closer they could see the coconut groves near the beaches and the lovely little bungalows and cottages amidst the greenery just behind the beach at Waikiki, which was to be their home for much of their stay in Hawaii.

Finally, Hawaiian boys dove for coins, even pennies, as they approached the harbor, which had facilities for a hundred ships of that time, and wharves, mostly of stone, thousands of feet in length with excellent loading and discharging facilities. The weather cooperated that February day in 1904 as it usually did to make Honolulu the mecca for lucky American tourists. There were only a few there then, but later on there would be millions.

What an occasion for newlyweds!

In those days before air travel, plenty of celebrities such as Congressman Nicholas Longworth and his wife (Alice Roosevelt, the President's daughter) stopped off in the port of Honolulu in their ships en route to the Orient.

Mid-Pacific Honolulu had its fascinations, even then. Its oldest and most historic church, built of coral cut from the Honolulu reefs in 1836 by King Kamehameha, had a seating capacity of one thousand and services conducted in Hawaiian. Close by was the Honolulu brewery. Many of the houses in Honolulu could be considered beautiful in architecture as well as in the foliage surrounding them.

The young couple was later to note the picturesque quality of the attractive people—Japanese, Chinese, Hawaiian (Polynesian), Filipino, American, Portuguese, and a smattering of English, Germans and other nationalities. The women still wore Mother Hubbard dresses and the men very light clothing. The peddlers on the streets sold fruit, shells, coral, goldfish, souvenirs from the koa, hua, and candlenut trees, leis of flowers, and silver-colored seeds known as "Job's Tears."

For public transportation Honolulu had electric cars. The streets were of macadamized coral, with sand and black lava stone and were graded well and smooth. Although there were sudden tropical storms which sometimes surprised the new-comers, the climate was salubrious year round.

The Royal Hawaiian Band, organized in 1892, then consisted of 35 musicians and two lady vocalists. From 1874 until the Harllees' arrival there, it had been under the direction of Captain Henry Berger of the 2nd Life Guard Regiment of Berlin, Germany. He was on loan from the Kaiser to Honolulu. The Band played for the public in various parks on Sundays, Mondays, Tuesdays and Thursdays, as well as for steamer arrivals and departures. The vocals of the Band were in both English and Hawaiian. When the newlyweds first heard the band, Madame Alapai, the wife of one of the bandsmen, sang beautifully in a rich soprano voice. The duets were sung by another Hawaiian woman and man, a contralto and tenor.

With regard to the ship departures, friends sometimes placed so many flower "leis" on the departees that they could hardly move. The custom was designed not only to express sorrow at the parting, but to leave such a memory of Hawaii that it would draw the departees back to the shore of Paradise.

The "leis" in those days were made by hand by fifty to a hundred or so men and women on Hotel Street between Fort and Nuuana, using flowers, evergreens, colored tissue paper (for artificial flowers) and seeds and shells (for the necklaces). Some of the workers were quite elderly, but they were all busy most of the time.

The "poi" from the popular song of much later days, "Little Grass Shack in Kealakekua, Hawaii" was frequently eaten by the Harllees with the Hawaiians. It was the national dish there, made from taro, which grew in patches in mud and water. Its root was baked in the ground, then pounded to a paste, pink or blue in color. It was eaten with the fingers from large individual bowls. It could be flavored, of course, and though it was an acquired taste, the couple grew to like it.

First Lieutenant Harllee had the honor of commanding the first detachment of Marines to be permanently stationed in Hawaii, 46 in number. Soon after they landed, however, Captain Albertus W. Catlin, later of Belleau Wood fame in World War I, arrived to take over command. Catlin, when a Brigadier General, authored a book entitled "With the Help of God and a Few Marines," implying you could do anything with such assistance. Harllee dedicated most of his life to validating this belief, as did so many other Marines. Perhaps the title was the grandfather of the recruiting slogan of two-thirds of a century later, "The Marines are looking for a few good men."

But not much was demanded of the Marines in Hawaii for the next 37 years. Life was as pleasant as could be, especially for the Harllees. Yet it was here that he started down the road which would lead to his great contribution to the Marine Corps and America in the field of marksmanship, as already re-counted.

They lived for a while in a two room suite at the Waikiki end of the roof garden floor of the Alexander Young Hotel on Bishop Street, for $25 a month. They even got a 20% discount on dining room and bar bills, with potatoes and coffee free. The hotel was built of granite, four stories in height, with two extra stories at either end. The roof garden covered a third of an acre. Refreshments were served and concerts given there. A fine view of the city could be enjoyed. Dancing was done in the pavilions erected at either end of the roof garden. The hotel was built in 1900 at a cost of $100,000; thoroughly modern, it could accommodate three hundred guests.

Then they lived for about a year in what was reputed to be the biggest residence in Honolulu, Mr. Tenney Peck's house in Manoa Valley, later known as the Cooper house. They got it for $50 a month, including two carriages as well as the 17 rooms of the house. But they were delighted to see Mr. Peck return from Europe because they hadn't counted on the expense and work of mowing the four acres of lush, fast-growing lawn grass and taking care of such a huge house, even with a cook and house maid.

The cook was a Japanese named Nasaki. He sent to Japan for a "picture bride," which was a wife selected from an agent's photo. She came to Honolulu soon after the Harllees did and cheerfully worked in the house. Nasaki was happy all his life with his "picture bride," acquired an attractive home in Honolulu, and produced a son who graduated from high school. They became lifelong friends of the Harllees.

Then they spent their last year in a bungalow on the beach at Waikiki with Mr. Riggs and his wife, Carrie Ah Fong Riggs. The latter was the daughter of a wealthy Chinese merchant and a native Hawaiian (Polynesian) lady. Carrie's parents had fifteen children, including thirteen girls, who were reputed to be the most beautiful on the island. One daughter married a U. S. Naval officer who became a rear admiral, and another married a U. S. Army officer. The Commandant of the U. S. Naval Station in Hawaii then was married to Harriet Ah Fong Riggs.

Harllee's attitude all his life towards his erstwhile national enemies was somewhat unusual. He had vigorously fought the Filipinos with his Krag-Jorgensen rifle, but he later believed they had the right on their side; now the same way with the Chinese, whom he had fought in the Boxer Rebellion, although, of course, he felt that the Americans in the Peking legation had to be rescued. He was thoroughly imbued with the honor of the profession of arms, but he was not misled by the propaganda that so often tries to justify wars. Although almost all white Southerners of his day would in later times be considered extreme racists, he socially consorted with Filipinos, Chinese, Japanese, Polynesians, and in much later days, black Haitians.

He wrote from Honolulu then, "Honolulu is charming in this respect; it's a pleasure to hobnob with Hawaiian royalty and buy it a drink."

Aloha!

XII
THE FATHER OF RIFLE PRACTICE IN THE MARINE CORPS

The battle-proven axiom is that every Marine is first and foremost a rifleman.

William C. Harllee, the man frequently referred to as "Father of Rifle Practice in the Marine Corps", captained the Marine Corps team of 1908.
—from "The History of Marine Corps Competitive Marksmanship" by Col. Robert E. Barde, U.S.M.C.

Only 98 Marines qualified as marksmen.

The U. S. Marine Corps standing fifth (and had never done better) in the National Trophy Rifle Team Match.

True? Not today, not on your life. But true in 1900 and 1904, when First Lieutenant William C. Harllee, U.S.M.C., arrived in Honolulu. In 1901, National Guard teams had to show the Marine rifle team the proper way to use the sling and how to remove the creep from their Krag triggers.

In the same year, an Irish rifle team came to Sea Girt, New Jersey and, with their favorite back position and long beards, defeated all the American teams. There was such interest in rifle shooting in those days that the American press clamored for more and better American rifle teams.

In 1902, the Marine Corps hired a dentist to coach its rifle team.

The Marines had a tradition of shooting well, which went all the way back to musketry from the maintops and mizzentops in the American Revolution. However, except for the Spanish-American War, there had been a slump in Marine Corps' shooting since the Civil War. Needless to say, there never was a slump in the Corps' great fighting spirit. A typical sentiment of the day was expressed by an elderly retired officer.

> The Northern troops with which I served had never fired a shot out of their rifles before we went into our first battle. The ground was covered with bodies in blue and gray, but we won the fight. Grit is more important than marksmanship.

True, but, oh, how much easier to have the grit if you have the marksmanship!

How did Will Harllee fit into all this?

He stood six feet tall at 197 pounds when he arrived in the land of the lotus eaters.

He had done plenty of gambling, drinking and singing. He had committed plenty of indiscretions, too, although at the time *he* always knew that it was the thing to do and that the authorities were dead wrong to chastise him. Nevertheless, it was now a natural time of life for a young man to get more serious. He had realized, with considerable difficulty, his big ambition to get a permanent commission in his country's armed forces.

He pondered on the stories of his father and uncles and many other Southerners about sharpshooting during the Civil War. And he remembered most vividly the startling marksmanship of that famous Texas Ranger, Captain Lee Hall, and the other Texans in the old 33rd Regiment, and how they had run away with the shooting competition at the Presidio in San

Francisco and how they performed in action in the Philippines. He thought of what Lee Hall had taught him.

He talked to the Marines in the Honolulu Detachment and found that they had done very little target shooting and had had no real scientific training in using their rifles or pistols or machine guns. In the Marine Corps this procedure was ordained:

"Take the best position for holding the rifle. Aim it correctly, hold it steadily, and pull the trigger without deranging the aim." A little rudimentary.

The Springfield M1903, known as the Springfield '03, was replacing the Krag-Jorgenson of 1892, improved in 1896, 1898, and 1900 and known as the Krag. The Springfield, a .30 caliber rifle, was such an accurate and otherwise excellent weapon that it was still in use by some Marines, especially snipers, even after 1942. This change of rifles was of great interest to Harllee, because he had fought the Filipino "Insurrectos" with the 5 shot, smokeless powder .30 caliber Krag, but in the Krag the cartridges had to be loaded one at a time from a cartridge box, whereas the Springfield was loaded with stripper clips of five cartridges or rounds of ammunition.

So Harllee decided this was it; that there was great work for somebody—why not him—in helping the Marines to measure up to and top the great old American tradition of marksmanship. So he began to make an intense study of everything about shooting military small arms—rifles, pistols and machine guns. He thought with a smile about the old myth among shooters that you had to have blue eyes to be a good shooter—brown eyes were supposedly affected by light changes and mirages. He had unmistakably light blue eyes.

Back in those days, officers were rarely on the Marine Corps rifle team, the big-time of Marine rifle shooting, as most of them naturally preferred to vacation during the summer rather than spend long hours under a broiling sun. But it was on the rifle team that the most could be learned and then taught to others later. There were exceptions among the officers, of course, notably Harllee's friend, Lieutenant Douglas C. (Mock) McDougal, generally recognized as the best shot in the Corps in 1905 and 1906, and Lieutenant Thomas Holcomb, Jr., later to be Commandant of the Corps and soon to rack up a spectacular shooting record.

Harllee began his own work by reading every book he could find out about and send for on the subject—books like "Modern Rifle Shooting in Peace, War and Sport," by L. R. Tippins of the 2nd V. B. Essex Regiment, British Army. He got a wealth of information from the National Rifle Association. He requested from the Dupont Company, Hercules, and the American Powder Mills of St. Louis all the information they had on powder. He asked Winchester, Savage, Marlin Stevens, Remington, and Springfield Armory for all the information they had on weapons and their parts.

He learned that temperature, barometric pressure and humidity affected the trajectory of the rifle bullet at long ranges. He studied the effects of rifling (twisting of the bullet in the barrel) and rain on the flight of the shots.

He considered the firing positions of the men; the uses of the sling to steady the weapon; and the extremely important problem of nervousness of the shooter in qualification, competitive shooting and combat. He learned about mirages, shifting lights and fishtail winds. He especially studied the sights of the rifles.

His work was to result later in his development of such practical rules as the "square rule" or the "short cut elevation rule":

> At any range the effect of change of sights of 100 yards at that range is the square of the number of hundred yards. Thus, at 600 yards, changing the sights 100 yards produces a change on the target of 36 inches; 800 yards 64 inches, etc. 25 yards change makes, of course, ¼ as much and 50 yards ½ of this.

He brought to these matters all of the tremendous energies that he had earlier spent so often in raising hell—and all of the brains that had stood him #2 in his class at West Point in the first exams, #1 in the exam scores of his February 1900 group in their examinations for commissions in the Marine Corps, and #1 amongst poker players in Manila.

But it was all just academic without a range to fire on—on

which to test every theory and belief thoroughly under various conditions. So, early in 1904 he went to his Commanding Officer, that splendid leader of Marines, Captain Ben H. Fuller, who was later to become Major General Commandant of the Marine Corps. He said,

"Captain, let's build a rifle range here on Oahu. It's the only way we can really start to develop the marksmanship we want."

Captain Fuller replied,

"Fine, Harllee, but we have no funds for such a project. None at all."

Harllee replied,

"I know a deserted cattle ranch we can use for almost no money—it's a perfect area for a range (it was on a mountainside near the area where Schofield Barracks, the huge U. S. Army post was later developed). Our Marines can build the range without hiring any civilians—after all, why can't we? We can live in our tents in this perfect climate, and the Army and the Navy have enough wood, concrete, wire, tools and so forth laying around for the targets, target butts, buildings, phones and anything else we have to have, and you can talk them into letting us borrow it."

Fuller thought a bit and said, "Fine, Harllee, we'll give it a try."

So Harllee built the range by trial and error. The Marines learned carpentry, plumbing, the machinists' trade, concrete laying, earth moving, cooking, sanitation and public health, and all the rest of it as they went along. It was to serve as a forerunner of many a famous rifle range to come.

In the summer of 1904, the range was ready. Harllee was reported to be the first Marine officer in the Corps to qualify as Expert Rifleman, which was then a brand new qualification, to be added to those of Marksman and Sharpshooter. This was the first fruit of his studies and practice.

Captain Fuller was enthusiastic about the range. He sent his son, Ted, to spend the summer on the range with Harllee. One night after dinner, around the campfire, shortly after young Ted Fuller arrived, Harllee mused to him:

"Ted, how much do you know about shooting in America? "From Judges 20:16 comes the first historical record of marksmanship. The verse reads: 'Every one could sling stones at a hair breadth, and not miss.'

"Perhaps the tradition goes back to our mother country, England. From the day when William won the battle of Senlac by means of his sharpshooting archers, the English people rapidly became superior to all others in the use of the bow. Remember Robin Hood and his wonderful feats with the longbow?

"In the great battles of Crecy, Poitiers and Agincourt, the English bowmen were overwhelmingly outnumbered by the French, but in each instance the English yeoman, with his long bow and cloth yard shafts, crushingly defeated the flower of French chivalry and their men at arms.

"Henry VIII was more famous for his wives and his appetite, but during his reign an act was passed which required that shooting butts be erected in every town and that every able-bodied man, not being an ecclesiastic or a judge, should practice with the long bow.

"I could tell you a lot more about England, but let's get to America. In 1621, Stephen Hopkins and Edward Winslow, during a diplomatic venture to the Indians for Governor Bradford of Massachusetts, were asked to have one of their men shoot a crow which was damaging their corn. The Pilgrim unlimbered his trusty matchcock and killed the crow at 80 yards. The Indians much admired this exhibition.

"You know about the American frontiersmen during the French and Indian War and of the Minute Men at Lexington and Concord, but did you know that in colonial Virginia and Massachusetts it was illegal for able-bodied men, except for ministers and high officials, *not* to have arms and ammunition? At the time of our Revolution, there were proportionately more Americans who could handle a musket or a rifle than there were in any other land.

"Outside of Switzerland, individual skill with small arms has never been cultivated on the continent of Europe. The regular armies have always relied upon massed attacks, the

British square, brute strength, cavalry, artillery, and of course plenty of discipline, spit and polish.

"But the American colonists had to use their muskets and their rifles for food and for protection against Indians. They also had great endurance, hardihood, shrewdness, self-reliance and patriotism. Some historians believe they were just about the best *individual* fighters ever. And the keystone of it all was their marksmanship, which the English had lost by the time of our Revolution. It more than made up for the Americans' deficiencies in discipline, equipment, supplies, organization and training.

"There were numerous cases in the Revolution in which the Americans won victories which could only be explained by the superior use of their weapons. For example, take the Battle of Kings Mountain. Less than one thousand American frontier riflemen surrounded a superior force of well-disciplined British troops in a seemingly impregnable position, and in about one hours' time, they attacked and utterly destroyed the entire British force.

"It was such demoralizing defeats as this and the one of Tarleton by Morgan at Cowpens which finally caused Cornwallis to withdraw to Yorktown.

"After the Revolution, military matters in the U.S. were neglected. In the 13 original colonies a higher civilization was driving out the old pioneer life. The cultured American was slowly but surely losing that honorable title of the best Emergency Man in the world—a man who could fight well in a moment's notice, as he had to in the Indian Wars.

"Incidentally, it was the Americans who developed the rifle. The rifle had a grooved bore, a finer sight, and a lighter and smaller bullet. This resulted in longer range and more accuracy. In those Revolutionary days, American boys grew up with a rifle at home. The rifle is the peculiar American weapon and we won our land wars mainly with it, although artillery and cavalry did help.

"In the War of 1812, General Andrew Jackson found Emergency Men among the pioneers in Kentucky and Tennessee. The English officers called these hurriedly collected, undisciplined riflemen 'Backwoods Rabble'. But the earlier English tradition of marksmanship had faded badly. Until 1852, even the Guards in the British Army were allowed only 30 rounds of ammunition for practice every three years.

"When the Battle of New Orleans was over, two thousand of those brave Englishmen, veterans of the Spanish Penisular Campaign in the Napoleonic Wars, were killed, including their commander, General Pakenham. Only 71 Americans were lost. The British charged American cannons, but the deadly rifle fire of the Americans had never been equalled in history.

"In the Mexican War it was the infantrymen's shooting that broke the foe's resistance—the American frontiersman again.

"In the Civil War one of the two big reasons, besides their courage, that the outnumbered and ill-supplied Confederates lasted so incredibly long was because they had a much bigger percentage of marksmen from their hunting and shooting match experience than the Yankees did. The other reason was the problem between the political and military commands of the North. Did you know that after the Battle of Gettysburg, General Meade complained that hundreds of soldiers had failed to fire their rifles because of a lack of training? Furthermore, at the Battle of Gettysburg, Colonel Hiram Berdan's 100 highly selected sharpshooters and 200 riflemen from the Third Maine Regiment delayed Confederate General Longstreet's advance on the west slope of Seminary Ridge long enough so that it may well have turned the tide for the North at this crucial battle!

"But after the Civil War the Army and National Guard gradually went back to emphasis on close order drill, parades, ceremonies, and spit and polish.

"At the beginning of the Franco-Prussian War of 1870, the French Army was considered the biggest and best in Europe because of its appearance and drilling ability. But it was defeated by the German armies, which unlike the French, then sent no unit to a forward position until all its men had been thoroughly schooled in the use of their weapons.

"I've heard that the Marines in action in Korea in 1871 still had muzzle loading muskets and were badly outnumbered by the Koreans, who had excellent repeaters. But the Korean marksmanship was so bad, as was their organization, that the Marines won with their better sharpshooting ability.

"Ted, the important thing now is that the great American tradition has had its ups and downs, and now with so few frontiersmen and Indian wars, it's in a slump."

Ted asked, "Well, what's to be done now?"

Harllee replied,

"It's late and the rest of it is a long story, but I'll tell you this. If the Filipinos had known how to use their Mausers and Remingtons five years ago or if the Chinese could have done better shooting with their Jingals four years ago, I wouldn't be here tonight to tell you.

"But it's time to turn in and wake up early tomorrow and shoot. That's the first thing to do."

The next morning Harllee started instructing all his Marines, using the principles he had learned as a school teacher from that splendid German pedagogue, Professor Buchholz, and from the book "The Seven Laws of Teaching."

Here are the simple rules from those "Seven Laws":

I. Know thoroughly and familiarly the lesson you wish to teach—teach from a full mind and a clear understanding.

II. Gain and keep the attention and interest of the pupils upon the lesson. Do not try to teach without attention.

III. Use words understood in the same way by the pupils and yourself—language clear and vivid to both.

IV. Begin with what is already well known to the pupil upon the subject and with what he has himself experienced—and proceed to the new material by single, easy, and natural steps, letting the known explain the unknown.

V. Stimulate the pupil's own mind to action. Keep his thoughts as much as possible ahead of your expression, placing him in the attitude of a discoverer, an anticipator.

VI. Require the pupil to reproduce in thought the lesson he is learning—thinking it out in its various phases and applications till he can express it in his own language.

VII. Review, review, REVIEW, reproducing the old, deepening its impression with new thought, linking it with added meanings, finding new applications, correcting any false views, and completing the true views.

And so a schoolmaster he became, the very best they ever had in the field of marksmanship.

The results attained by himself and his marines came to the attention of the Big Chief back in Washington, the Commandant of the Corps, and culminated in a decision in 1908 which would change the course of Harllee's life.

Having cut his teeth on the construction of the rifle range, Harllee and a number of his Marines, with Captain Fuller's approval, volunteered to build a temporary magazine for the Hawaii Naval Station. Following completion, they were issued a commendation for their services by the Chief of the Bureau of Ordnance, Navy Department back in Washington.

On April 18 of 1906, the day of the San Francisco earthquake, Harllee left Honolulu for that city. When he arrived, the city was still smoking and was under martial law. For ten days he did humanitarian duty in that stricken city. This included the distribution of food, clothing, and shelter to hundreds of thousands of people, as well as protection of life and property. He marvelled at the indomitable spirit of its citizens, who would rebuild San Francisco to glory and beauty, right on the site of their catastrophe.

He then went to Mare Island, near San Francisco, for a bit of duty; then he was ordered to the Brigadier General Commandant in Washington for a week in June of 1906. General George F. Elliott, a hot-tempered Alabaman and a great fighting Marine, was intensely interested in marksmanship and wanted to know all about what Harllee had done in Hawaii. Would the Commandant order him to the Marine Corps Rifle Team? If so he could start to realize his dream of making the Marines the straightest shooters in the world.

But no, it was apparently not to be. Parts of Harllee's record viewed through unsympathetic eyes might well have stopped the granting of this cherished honor. He was ordered instead to command the Marine Barracks, Port Royal, South Carolina. This subsequently became known as Parris Island, where hundreds of thousands of Marines much later had their boot training. He held this post from June 21, 1906 until September

17, 1906, when he joined the First Provisional Regiment and left with them to "pacify" Cuba.

On July 6, 1906, he was promoted to Captain, to rank from August 30, 1905. He now held the rank his father and Uncle Andrew had in the Civil War, and he was proud to have commanded, even for such a short time, a U. S. Marine Corps post in his beloved adopted state of South Carolina.

XIII
PACIFYING CUBA
1906–1907

Captain Harllee, with a detachment of Marines worked his way up to Camaguey (Cuba)—where a rebel general with 3,000 troops was reported—

The frightened mayor—sent word that the insurgents were shooting up the town and terrorizing the inhabitants. Captain Harllee took twenty-five men and went in to clean it up. . . .
From "With the Help of God and a Few Marines,"—by Brigadier General A. W. Catlin, U.S.M.C.

Camaguey, Cuba was in flames. There was shooting and looting.

Cuba was seething with insurrection. Sugar plantations owned by U.S. financial interests thought they were in danger. The second Cuban Pacification was on.

On September 22, 1906, Captain William Curry Harllee landed at Nuevitas on the northern shore of Cuba, commanding the 165 men of the United States Marine Corps expeditionary force off the USS TACOMA.

He detached 50 men to guard Nuevitas and boarded a train with 25 men for Camaguey and ordered 90 more men to follow as soon as another train could be found. The first greeting he received as he approached Camaguey was the sound of lots of shooting. The rebels were having a great time with their pistols and rifles. Plain citizens were hiding in their boarded up houses. Harllee dug one out.

"The great General, he attacks Camaguey!" cried the Cuban. Then, answering Bill Harllee's questions, he informed the Marine captain as to the location of the great General's camp. Harllee took his force out immediately, ignoring the shooting and positioned it between the town and the Generals camp. In the meantime his other 90 men had arrived. Then he fanned out 30 Marines across the path of the great General's return to his camp, and collected the remaining 85 Marines around himself.

The American public was deeply concerned at that time about the killing of natives which had gone on for so long in the Philippines, and it was strongly desired that Cuba be pacified without firing a hostile shot, if at all possible. Furthermore, at that particular point in history the opposing Cuban factions were mad at each other and not at the United States, so Bill Harllee acted accordingly.

"Men," he said, "there's no need to shoot and kill these poor devils. Don't one of you fire a shot without direct orders. Use the bayonet and the butt. Jab 'em easy with the point. If they're really tough babies, knock 'em over with the butt. Now we're going to spread out and herd these insurrectos into the plaza."

The Marine bugle sang out into the town. Through the streets of Camaguey the Marines drove the Cuban insurrectos as cowboys drive cattle. Not a shot was fired. Marine bayonet points jabbed the seats of Cuban pants. Marine gun butts swung. Insurrectos horsemen were pushed off saddles. Within two hours, 150 insurrecto were driven into the plaza. About 100 of them ran for open country. Harllee smiled. The 50 prisoners remaining were all he needed. Those 50 Cubans were disarmed and stood surrounded by Marines.

"Now we'll hold a census," decided Harllee. The company clerk came forward with his writing materials. Rough Marines picked three insurrectos, kept them apart from each other, and brought one insurrecto out in the open and asked each of the three others: "Como se llama esta hombre?—What's that man's name?" If the three didn't give the same name, all three were spanked publicly with gun barrel staves. Harllee began to get an accurate list of insurrecto names. In the middle of all this, Sergeant John W. Hingle, a six foot powerhouse, came in with a very unhappy Cuban in tow. Sergeant Hingle had been with the 30 Marines between Camaguey and the insurrecto camp.

"I told him to get off his horse when he rode up, Captain," reported Sergeant Hingle, "and he wouldn't. He told me where to go. So I knocked him off the horse with my gun butt. Here he is. I think he's one of their big shots."

The prisoner had now composed himself. He looked angrily at the scene where one Marine was holding a recalcitrant Cuban, and another Marine was whacking him with a barrel stave.

"What are you doing with my men?" he thundered at Captain Harllee.

"These are your men?" Harllee asked.

"They are."

"Who are you?"

"I am the General!" said the prisoner, straightening himself out, and making a monumental effort to impress his captors.

"Lord bless your soul!" said Harllee. "You're the man I'm looking for!"

"I, too, am looking for you," said the General. "I come to warn you. Outside this city I have an army of 2000 men. This very day they attack you. The fight starts soon."

"General," said Harllee, "you're the luckiest Cuban in Cuba."

"Why?" demanded the General.

"Because when the fighting starts, you'll be in a jail with walls so thick no bullet can ever reach you."

"That may be true, and I may be safe, but I fear for you," said the General. "My men attack soon."

"You are mistaken, General," said Harllee. "My men attack soon. At your camp."

"How soon?"

"Right now," said Harllee. "The minute I return from throwing you in jail."

"For God's sake, don't attack. Please let me speak to you privately, Captain," said the General.

"Speak right up right now," said Harllee. "We've got no secrets here."

But the General whispered to Harllee: "There will be no attack. You are ruining my reputation."

Captain Harllee decided to save the General's face in his home town. Hiding his amusement, he arranged for a formal surrender. Under Marine escort the General and four officers of his staff came in and turned in their swords (machetes). The formal surrender was accepted and their weapons were returned. Harllee had coffee and rum made available as refreshments for his prisoners. Then, he set them free before the citizenry on their paroles as officers and gentlemen, with a stirring speech in Spanish in which he praised the courage of a gallant enemy who loved his people so much he saved them unnecessary bloodshed. They cheered him without stint. The insurrection was over in Camaguey and the province of Puerto Principe. Everybody had come out full of honor.

The General asked for contributions, with the approval of the Governor, and Harllee and his Marines were guests of honor at the biggest party in Camaguey's history. And when Harllee and his Marines left, there was a two mile long parade. Every Marine was covered with flowers. They found their railway car stacked with cases of champagne!

Bill Harllee was not the only Marine company commander to have a pleasant episode then in Cuba. According to Dr. Allan Reed Millett, in his excellent book "The Politics of Intervention—The Military Occupation of Cuba—1906–1909", First Lieutenant William P. Upshur wrote his parents of his experience in another part of Cuba, Pinar de Rio:

114

Duty in Pinar de Rio was excellent, the shopping good, the people friendly, and when the Marines left in late October, the town band and color guard, carrying the Cuban and American flags, marched with Upshur's company to the station. Earlier there had been banquets and speeches; at the station a cheering crowd bid the Marines farewell.

Harllee's next job was at Palmira, which was characterized as the "dirtiest hole in Cuba, with the dirtiest mess anyone ever saw." An Insurrecto leader and a chief of police, both of whom straightened themselves out later and became highly esteemed Cuban officials, had made life tough for the young Marine officer Harllee relieved. Palmira, near Cienfuegos, was a town of 5,000 population. Bill Harllee proceeded through town from the railway station and established a camp just outside the town. Then he requested a young sergeant to bring the Palmira chief of police to him. The sergeant returned and reported, "He says he won't come, sir." Captain Harllee recalled his superior's warning him against his hot temper and youthful predilection for personal violence and called in veteran Sergeant John F. Byrnes.

"Sergeant," said Harllee, "I sent a message to the Palmira chief of police that I wanted to see him. He says he won't come."

"He'll come, Captain!" said Sergeant Byrnes. He came, too, with Sergeant Byrnes gripping him with one hand and holding an automatic pistol in the other. Captain Harllee took a good look at the Cuban who had caused so much difficulty.

"I am delighted to have the honor of inviting so distinguished a visitor into my tent," said the Marine officer. The police chief told him to go to hell. Harllee looked at Sergeant Byrnes. The police chief entered the tent with an assist from the Sergeant.

"Permit me the honor of offering a chair to so distinguished a guest," said Captain Harllee. The police chief was not in the mood to accept the offer. The Captain looked again at Sergeant Byrnes. The police chief sat down, again with an assist from the Sergeant.

"It is a privilege and a pleasure to offer so distinguished a visitor a drink of rum," said Captain Harllee. The police chief

115

was still unfriendly. Harllee smiled, poured a Marine mess kit cup full of the powerful liquid, and looked once at Sergeant Byrnes. The Sergeant simply grabbed his nose; closed his nostrils, tilted his head back and poured the rum down his throat.

"Now that you have been received with the courtesy customary among gentlemen, distinguished chief of police," said Captain Harllee, listen to me. Because you thought my predecessor here was under orders not to shoot, you made it very unpleasant for him. You pride yourself that you are a hard man. Listen, hard man! You son of an impossible combination of circumstances, when you see me on the street after this, you stand to one side, you lift your hat, and you keep it lifted until I am 10 paces past you. I was sent here under orders to pacify Palmira, and I give you my word as a captain of United States Marines, Palmira will be pacified if we have to have a police chief's funeral first. Now get out!"

The police chief left with a big frown. He went directly to see his friend, the local Insurrecto general. The next day, the big dark-visaged general, sporting a nickel-plated, pearl-handled .45 caliber pistol, burst into the Marine camp looking for the young captain. Harllee appeared with a friendly smile.

"What the hell do you mean by treating my friend the chief of police as you did, you son of a bitch!" asked the General. His hand was near his pistol butt.

Bill Harllee leaped, knocked the Insurrecto general off his horse, got a hold on the General, and ripped the pearl-handled revolver out of its holster and threw it away. A Marine recovered it.

"You seem to be asking for trouble, my distinguished friend," said Harllee, to the man he was holding helpless. "Listen to me carefully, General. If you deserve your title, you know an officer obeys orders. My orders are to pacify Palmira. I give you my word as an officer that if you start trouble here, you will be the first Cuban to get killed, and I promise myself that pleasure. Now get out!"

And the General did, with speed.

But the Palmira tough guys were not finished yet. The town

116

remained in bad shape. The citizens were still having plenty of problems. The chief of police and the Insurrecto general claimed the Marines were afraid to shoot, and although there was no open conflict, there was a sort of an underworld domination of the town.

A wandering Venezuelan circus visited Palmira. Harllee attended the performance and noticed that almost all the townspeople, both Insurrecto and respectable citizen, were there. When he returned to his camp after the circus, about midnight, he sent for the bugler.

"Sound the call to arms!" he ordered. The bugle call rang through Palmira. The Marines fell in, wondering what was up.

"We'll have a little rifle practice," said Captain Harllee. "You boys haven't had much chance to shoot. Forward, MARCH!"

He marched them into the Plaza. Then as midnight came, 165 rifles flamed into the starlit sky, and orders flowed: "With ball cartridges, LOAD! Volley fire! Fire at will! With counted cartridges, five cartridges, FIRE! Rapid fire!"

The good people of Palmira curfewed themselves. The men in the black hats left town and the area. Without the loss of a single life, Palmira was pacified and stayed pacified, as was the rest of Cuba—for quite a while.

However, Lieutenant Colonel Franklin J. Moses, no friend of Harllee, thought he should be proceeded against for his method of suppressing the insurrection at Palmira. Apparently he objected to the firing of rifles, even though care had been taken to hurt no one. Accordingly Moses took Harllee before General J. Franklin Bell, who was commanding all our forces in Cuba at that time.

Upon presentation to General Bell, Harllee said,

"I am glad to see you again, General."

The reply,

"I can not recall having met you, Captain. Where have you seen me before?"

Harllee,

"At Mangatarem, sir."

The mention of that battle, at which Bell had raced to the rescue of Company F of the 33rd Volunteers, prompted a lively conversation. General Bell waxed into a pleasant mood of reminiscence. They talked over an hour. Finally, Colonel Moses shuffled his feet and cleared his throat and remarked that he had brought Harllee in to report his high handed behavior at Palmira. General Bell smiled at him indulgently and said,

"That will be all right, Colonel. We won't worry about that."

As a veteran of the pacification of the Philippines where the methods used were much rougher than any used by Harllee in Cuba, he was not horrified at the conduct there of the man who had led the attacking point in the Battle of Mangatarem.

Moses then sought action against Harllee by Marine Colonel Littleton W. T. Waller, but that famous fighter wrote Harllee, "In my judgement you had acted with judgement and coolness and zeal, and should receive commendation and not condemnation."

So ended Bill Harllee's only Cuba problem.

After Palmira he was ordered to Camp Columbia in Cuba, a delightful spot indeed.

Finally he was ordered back to Washington to report to Brigadier General Commandant for a few days beginning July 30, 1907. General Elliott wanted to talk some more about marksmanship. The rifle team? No, not at all.

The General ordered Harllee to Chicago to take charge of the Marine Corps Recruiting Office there and run an experimental operation.

XIV
STARTING THE FIRST MARINE CORPS PUBLICITY OFFICE 1907-1908

The United States Marine Corps established a publicity bureau in Chicago in 1907 under Captain William C. Harllee, thus paving the way for todays' large scale public relations programs in our military services.
—From "Effective Public Relations (3rd Edition)" by Scott M. Cutlip and Allen H. Center (Prentice Hall)

Recruiting duty in the old Marine Corps back in 1907 was looked upon as something of a sinecure, particularly for an officer and especially in a big city like Chicago.

But General Elliott wanted to try out something new—publicity. This was years before World War I, in which the fighting record of the Marines started such a torrent of publicity for them. The General wanted to try out his plan in Chicago,

119

the headquarters of the most important recruiting district. So according to Robert George Lindsay in his book, "This High Name—Public Relations in the U.S. Marine Corps":

> In 1907 a publicity bureau—the first of its kind in the Marine Corps—was established at Chicago. This was the first office specifically dedicated to the propagation of recruiting publicity. It was established by Captain William C. Harllee, then in charge of recruiting for the Chicago district.

In those days, hard to believe though it may be, publicity was abhorred by the armed services and newspapermen were shunned as disreputable characters.

The accepted recruiting methods were to put up signs— "Men Wanted for U. S. Marines"—and to comb the barrooms and pool halls. It was considered unethical to associate with newspapermen or have anything to do with their newspapers. But unconventional as always, Harllee strenuously cultivated them, especially Charley Michaelson of Hearst's Chicago Examiner and later the big press agent for the New Deal. A little later Harllee was the second officer in the armed services (after General Leonard Wood) to join the world famous National Press Club in Washington, D.C. (as an associate member).

Soon after he arrived in Chicago, Harllee tossed at Gunnery Sergeant Clarence B. Proctor:

"Sergeant, let's get a story out to the press about a Marine running away with a beautiful blonde with exquisite curls."

The Sergeant replied,

"I don't know of any such, sir."

Harllee retorted,

"Let's make one up. We can get a fake picture and call the Marine 'old Chaw Brannon'!"

Said Proctor, "What's the point, sir?"

Harllee, "Sergeant, you know perfectly well that nobody here has ever even heard of us. We've got to start to change that with this story. We can exploit the address of the office and draw attention to a picture of a hard boiled old-timer in our eye-catching Marine Corps dress uniform. We can start the ball rolling to get some good recruits!"

Proctor, "Aye, aye, sir, if it's an order!"

So the story went out, and Huey Fullerton rewrote it. People began to know the address of the recruiting office. The office was crowded with applicants and the best of them were chosen. With regard to the office, an odd commentary on the time is that the total equipment of the office was one mimeograph machine and one typewriter.

In the meantime, however, Marine Corps Headquarters demanded an investigation of that deserter "Old Chaw Brannon" and following its revelations, Harllee was reproved and directed to cease and desist. But he took the attitude that Huey Fullerton and the newspaper people were not amenable to his discipline, and they merrily carried on.

A little later Harllee told Proctor,

"Let's get out a story with pictures—about a Baptist preacher who joined the Marines because he gets a better salary, considering his food, lodging and clothing. It will call attention to our benefits."

Proctor did and again the applicants poured in. In fact, so many came in that Harllee had to advise some qualified candidates not to enlist because he did not believe they would like the rough old time ways of the service. So many candidates applied that all the Marine Corps recruiting vacancies could have been filled from his district, and he was held to a quota so Marines could be enlisted from other parts of the country and other recruiting stations maintained.

Harllee and Proctor had now broken the ice and pumped out plenty of true stories, for which the press was more than grateful. The reputation of the Corps flourished in the mid-West as more and more people learned of the real exploits of the men who not only sang the Marines' Hymn, but indeed "fought in every clime and place where we could take a gun."

XV
CAPTAIN OF THE MARINE CORPS RIFLE TEAM

The representatives of the Marine Corps at the shooting tournaments held this year carried off a majority of the honors and added several very valuable trophies and prizes to those already held by that branch of the service. The members of this year's team were: Captain W. C. Harllee, team captain—
—From front page, Army and Navy Register, October 31, 1908

1908

June 1, 1908.

"I'm sorry to say that you've got some very black marks in your record, Harllee, a court, suspension from duty, arrest, disrespect for superior officers," said the Commandant, Major General Elliott.

"But," he continued, "you've got some good items in there, too, a commendation for bravery in action, and you just did a bangup job with recruiting and publicity in Chicago. I like what you've learned about shooting. So I'm going to take a chance and make you Captain of the Marine Corps Rifle Team. But God help you if you get in trouble—unless it's somebody else's fault. Will you promise me to do everything possible to keep out of trouble?"

"Yes, General," replied Captain Harllee, "and you won't regret your decision." He never did.

General Elliott, a hero of the Spanish-American War and the Philippine Insurrection, was the last Commandant to command troops in the field as Commandant, which he did in Panama in January and February of 1904. Major General Smedley Butler remembered him as "one of the kindest men in the world" to his juniors. General Holcomb remembered that "the old boy had the worst temper I've ever known." Harllee also had a hot temper, and perhaps that was one reason why the General liked or at least understood him—that plus their common interest in marksmanship.

Harllee didn't have much time to prepare for the National Matches to be held at Camp Perry, Ohio in late July and early August of 1908, but he buckled right down to work with the team at the rifle ranges at Williamsburg, Virginia and at Sea Girt, New Jersey.

The Springfield '03 had been issued to the Marines in 1906, but until 1908 the Krag was still required at the National Matches when the military rifle was specified. Harllee held school on the relatively new Springfield anyway and on the micrometer, which was required to make a small change in elevation accurately on that rifle.

Although he had been reported as the first Marine officer to make expert rifleman, he did not shoot on the team. His duties and responsibilities paralleled those of a football coach.

Years later, General Thomas Holcomb, Jr., who was a member of the 1908 Rifle Team, characterized Harllee as a "born instructor—he could teach on anything." General Holcomb didn't know that Harllee was a self-made instructor, having trained himself among the pedagogues, bobcats, and overgrown schoolboys of south Florida. But is was also true that he had an abundance of natural leadership.

124

School, school, school—shoot, shoot, shoot,—teamwork, teamwork, teamwork. These are what he hammered on. And did he hammer!

Colonel Robert E. Barde wrote in his masterpiece on the subject, "Marine Corps Competitive Marksmanship": "The third fault (after shortages of rifle ranges and practices) lay in the need to have a team captain capable of putting the competitive game on a scientific basis." General Elliott thought Harllee was that man, and Barde wrote that the team "had a firm, competent leader in Captain Harllee."

Beside Holcomb, the 1908 team included Harllee's friend, Mock McDougal, who shot a possible (the maximum possible score—which included a 36 inch target at 1000 yards), and McDougal's partner, First Sergeant John W. Hingle, who had helped Harllee in pacifying and making the Cubans happy in 1907, about which more later. Hingle was to make the 2nd highest score of the 12 Marines in the 1908 National Trophy Rifle Match.

But that's getting ahead of the story. Back to the training in preparation for the National Matches. Captain Harllee absolutely insisted on teamwork. If a shooter learned something new and good, he had to tell his teammates about it. This went against natural personal ambitions and created quite a battle for the team captain to wage. Officers and enlisted men remained separated both on and off the firing line. All this militated against optimum teamwork. However, as shooter Fritz Hartmann of the National Meter Company of Chicago was to say, "I doubt if I ever knew a more forceful man." So, although with great difficulty, Harllee got the job—the building of teamwork—done.

As an example of his modus operandi, he discovered that a first sergeant who had been McDougal's shooting partner (not Hingle), had been using commercial ammunition during practice. This was superior to government ammo and was forbidden during firing for practice scores, as it could not be afforded for all practice, and it gave higher competitive scores, thus giving an unfair advantage to its user.

Harllee confronted the culprit with the facts and by noon of the same day the first sergeant was on his way out of the camp, even though he was a promising shooter. Teamwork was the watchword, and Harllee never had been and never was a man who didn't mean what he said.

So the team was schooled, some thought even too much, and trained and readied for competition. Twelve team members were selected out of forty candidates, and the team reported to Camp Perry, on the shores of Lake Erie in Ohio.

On the lighter side, Harllee made friends with Major Merle Johnson and his Hawaiian National Guard team. The Hawaiians were selected for their ability as entertainers as well as shooters, and the Marines enjoyed many evenings they spent in the Hawaiians' camp. The hula was new to Americans then, and there was a romance to Hawaii which still hasn't washed away. And his honeymoon had been spent there.

One of the most important factors in competitive or qualifying shooting is nervousness, buck fever, or to use the term shooters use, "pressure." It will start before shooting and can last either for one shot or for all shots or for any portion. Experience can combat it, but for many, especially beginners, it is the very devil to control.

Harllee's method of combatting it for his team in 1908 became enough of a legend for Captain Edward C. Crossman to recall it thus in the "American Rifleman" twenty-eight years later:

> To your mind, if you are an old-timer and familiar with the rifle game in its pre-war years—pre-Spanish and pre-World War, may come that tale of Colonel Harllee of the Marine Corps, one of the most brilliant and independent thinkers in the Services, and under whom I once served as Chief Range Officer and Assistant Executive at a National Match, where I had a fine chance to watch the workings of that unconventional mind of his. In charge of one Marine National Match team, he evolved the idea that the way to do away with the "buck" of that tough start of the Team Match—offhand at 200 (sic), and let his men do justice to their real ability, was to take them all out the night before the Team Match, and ply them wisely but not too well with spiritus frumenti and entertainment until the wee sma' hours. Doing this, reasoned Harllee, no worthy Marine could be lying awake shooting millions of rounds offhand and skirmish, and wondering if the dawn would never come. Also, he

would be plumb tired out; too tired for the buck, or snatches, or the general collywobbles that afflict the best of men in the take-off of any hot match.

I forget how the idea panned out, but my memory is that the Leathernecks won that year. Of course, this is no novelty, but that was back in the years when Marine wins were less chronic.

But would this method work? What about hangovers and lack of sleep? Colonel Barde states more officially that the team under Harllee stayed up until between two and three in the morning and slept only four or five hours. Let's let the results speak for themselves.

The Herrick Trophy Match, fired by an eight man team at 800, 900 and 1000 yards, was won by the Marine team over 35 other teams. According to the Army and Navy Register, this was the most important team match of the National Rifle Association. It was the first team match at the National Matches ever won by the Marines. As a result of this victory General Elliott promoted each enlisted man on the team to the next higher rank. Holcomb won the 1,000 yard Tyro Match against 300 distinguished riflemen. In the Hale Match the Marines won five out of the first ten places. At Sea Girt the Marines won the Dryden Trophy, the Briggs Trophy and the Gould Rapid Fire Match, all team events. Marines also won the Spencer Match and the Reading Match. Although they did not win the Leech, Wimbledon, and President's Match, they did make higher standings than they had before.

At the 1908 National Matches, Camp Perry, Ohio, the Marines took fourth place out of 42 teams, with a score of 3117 against the Infantry's winning 3224. Only once before had they done so well—in 1905—but their score of 4360 had been 168 points behind the New York National Guard's winning score of 4528 instead of the 107 points they were behind in 1908. The Marines won six team matches that year.

General Elliott was happy. He and the Marine Band and a battalion of Marines met the team at 3:55 P.M. on September 14, 1908, at the Union (railroad) Station in Washington. According to the Washington Post of the next day:

The 1908 Marine Corps Marksmen. Captain Harllee is in the center near the guidon.

A crowd of several hundred awaited the visitors and greeted them with hearty applause and lusty cheers.

The winning team which broke world's records and "beat everything else in the United States" was organized and led by Captain William C. Harllee, to whom his brother officers gave credit for the remarkable work done.

When Captain McGill had brought companies into battalion formation, the victorious rifle team to the fore, on the barracks parade ground, he read the following letter of commendation from Secretary of the Navy Metcalf:

Navy Department, Washington,
September 14, 1903
The Major General Commandant,
United States Marine Corps

128

"Presented by the U.S. Marine Corps Rifle Team, Season 1908, to Captain William C. Harllee, Team Captain, In Appreciation"

Sir: The department has noted with great satisfaction the excellent work done by the team representing the Marine Corps in the shooting tournaments recently held at Camp Perry, Ohio, and Sea Girt, N.J. The efficiency of a soldier is largely dependent upon his ability to shoot accurately, and the department, therefore, records its appreciation of the work done by this team, which reflected great credit upon the Corps and the service. The result is the more satisfactory when consideration is given to the fact that this team was selected from but a small quota of the Corps on shore duty in the United States.

You will communicate to the officers and enlisted men of the team the department's views as above expressed.

Very respectfully,
V.H. METCALF, Secretary

The Post also reported that in addition to "The Halls of Montezuma", the battalion marched "jauntily," to the "seductive bars of 'Happy Harney.' "

The Washington Post of September 27, 1908, with perhaps a bit of hyperbole, carried this headline on a feature story:

THE U. S. MARINES HAVE THE SHARPEST EYES IN THE WORLD.

On September 15, 1908, Harllee reported in person to Major General Elliott and became his aide-de-camp, as a practical matter his senior line assistant. He was also to remain as Captain of the Marine Corps Rifle Team until after the 1910 matches.

1909

Later in 1908 and in 1909, he began to be interested in the "plum tree" of Washington, where the bureaucrats then and now shake out the best of the plums for themselves, and where the social life has always been interesting.

But he was glad to carry a heavy load of widely varied duties for General Elliott, including acting as detail officer, recommending duty assignments for Marine officers. This was bound to win him enemies, as well as friends.

The Adjutant and Inspector, Quartermaster, and Paymaster of the Marine Corps and their assistants were then permanently stationed in Washington. There was, in the opinion of many, an inevitable tendency on the part of these officers to try to dominate the Corps.

In several instances during Harllee's career when the President or the Secretary of the Navy or Senators and various others wanted to review his official record, Harllee remarked that this cabal was able to put together a melange which omitted some favorable material and included all the raw unfavorable material. Half a century later there were items in his official record of highly controversial material which had been the subject of orders not to include them in the record. All his fitness reports got lost!

But his main concern in 1909 remained the Marine Corps Rifle Team, and for the shooting season from April 27, to September 12 of 1909 he again captained the team.

This year he had eighty candidates report in May. Never before had so many men reported for tryouts, and never before had they reported so early. He wanted plenty of practice—school, shoot, and teamwork—and he believed that those who did not make the team would still benefit the Marine Corps by what they learned. They would spread out through the

The U.S. Marine Corps Rifle Team, 1909. One of the early Bulldog mascots is shown pictured with the Team.

Corps when they returned to their units and act as competent instructors.

Harllee's central idea was not just to do well with the team, but rather to see that all Marines could shoot well—better than any outfit on earth. The team was a means to this end. It not only supplied coaches and instructors throughout the Corps, but it developed methods and equipment through practical use and provided an incentive to the others in the Corps through publicity. Before the widespread availability of radio, television movies, automobiles, and before the great expansion of professional spectator sports, competitive rifle shooting and shooting for sport commanded much publicity and attention.

Harllee's ambition for Marine Corps marksmanship would later expand to all Americans. His dream was to make America again a nation of marksmen as it had been at its inception. This was why he supported the National Rifle Association and its rifle clubs and many thousands of shooters so strongly.

With regard to the armed forces, others believed that rifle, pistol, and machine gun instruction was simply a duty for all company and platoon commanders and their non-commissioned officers, regardless of their training. Harllee believed that only specially and highly trained coaches could efficiently teach men to shoot well. He, in a sense, was helping to usher in the age of specialization. There was tremendous initial opposition to this as there was to much of what he did. Tradition dictated that shooting was just something else for the officers and non-coms to teach the men, but Harllee prevailed, and history proved him right.

At the Ohio Rifle Association Matches held that year at Camp Perry, one Marine won the All-Comers Off-Hand Match, breaking all previous records and another Marine set a world's record in the Catrow Match. Still another Leatherneck won the Wimbledon Match with a "glass eye" (a scope), new in those days.

In the National Matches, the Marine team made a higher score than the last year (3671 against 3117), but the eligibility rules had been changed; instead of only regular service and National Guard teams, any member or club of the National Rifle Association could shoot. In spite of the fact that the Washington Post on May 9, 1909 reported that the Marines were making more thorough preparations than ever before, the team stood ninth. They would have to do better, a lot better, the next year.

ALMOST INVISIBLE IN A TRENCH WHICH TOOK 15 MINUTES TO BUILD

This was the caption under a photo in the May 13, 1909 issue of "Arms and the Man." The preface to the article containing the picture included:

> In a report made by Capt. W. C. Harllee, U.S. Marine Corps, to which this is an introduction, two points are particularly well brought out by means of the text and illustrations. One is that the intrenching tool which he used proved eminently satisfactory in every particular. He found it light, strong, easily portable, and best of all, that it could be used from the lying down position when the blade was turned at right angle to the handle. Of this intrenching tool we may say a word in passing. It is the invention of Gen. George F. Elliott, Commandant of the U.S. Marine Corps, and we believe it is manufactured by the Sub-Target Gun Company of Boston. General Elliott, with an extensive experience in field service, is full of practical ideas upon

the subject of equipment. One of the best of those ideas is exemplified in this tool.

In publishing this very valuable report, which we do at some cost of effort and money, we must take occasion to compliment Captain Harllee upon the clear and incisive way in which he has presented the account of his operations and produced for us his conclusions. No man can read the article without having a better idea of trench building, or lay it down without a new thought of what he would do in an emergency.

Another picture showed how men:

MAY CARRY INTRENCHING TOOL SNUGLY TUCKED IN BELTS

Harllee had never fought in a trench—this was before World War I but he had been giving a lot of thought to his profession.

Now that General Elliott had the team captain he wanted in Harllee and had started Marine Corps-wide competition, he wanted to complete his marksmanship ambitions for the Corps with a Marine Corps rifle range. He knew Harllee had built one in Hawaii, so he allowed him to build the one he wanted at Stump Neck, Maryland, on 1100 acres the Marine Corps owned between the Mattawoman and the Chickamuxent Creeks, a few miles below Indianhead, Maryland, about 30 miles south of Washington, D. C.

In 1916, "Arms and the Man" reported:

The Winthrop Range was built in spite of deeply-grounded opposition. Its construction was begun October 1, 1909, by a detachment of Marines, under the command of Major (then Captain) William C. Harllee, and which included Gunnery Sergeants Hale, Joyce and Lund of the Corps, men who are widely known in the rifle shooting fraternity.

The building of Winthrop was not all fair sailing. On several occasions the Navy Department seriously considered abandoning the post, and dismantling the range. Each time such an agitation was started, however, the friends of rifle shooting were influential enough to prevent such action.

This land had been bought by the government some years earlier after protests by the occupants against the firing of projectiles over them in the tests of ordnance from the nearby proving ground. It was a mosquito infested, wooded peninsula. Somehow, it seems that all rifle ranges were originally mosquito infested. Harllee took two officers and 56 enlisted men to Stump Neck. They all spent the winter of 1909–1910 there in tents fortified with logs and in rough log cabins. By spring the timber had been cleared and used in construction, and the swampy areas had been drained. Carpenters, plumbers, electricians, and machinists had been brought in from the ranks of Marines in East Coast posts. They didn't even request funds they knew were too scarce; Marines did the work and the materials were scrounged up from government supplies as had been done in Hawaii.

All his life Harllee had a curious concern for the taxpayer's money; the huge wastage of federal funds of much later years was neither possible nor desirable as far as he was concerned. With a small saw mill cadged from the Marine Corps quartermaster, they built big mess halls, shooting galleries, officers quarters', an ice plant, an electric light plant and an administration building. They planted a vegetable garden between the firing lines and established a dairy farm. They kept hogs in an old tent and raised ducks, turkeys and some White Orpington chickens. There were other livestock and horses—some Marines were cowboys.

An excellent range was developed. Some of the buildings at Winthrop were taken to the Marine Base at Quantico in 1917 and were still in use 40 years later. Initially, it had 13 short range targets—6 for midrange and 2 for long range—with plenty of room for expansion.

1910

On May 16, 1910, General Elliott opened up the range at Winthrop by firing five bull's eyes at 200 yards.

There was a little skepticism about the bona fides of the General's score, but Harllee assured the press that it was honest and that the General had scored 24 out of 25 at Sea Girt the year before.

The range was named the Winthrop Range in honor of Assistant Secretary of the Navy, Beekman Winthrop, who strongly encouraged marksmanship, and it remained the center of Marine marksmanship until the beginning of World War I.

Thousands of Marines fired on it, and from it generated the Harllee system-trained coaches and instructors who taught the new Marines how to shoot and the older ones how to improve their marksmanship.

On June 29, 1910, Harllee left Winthrop for the National Rifle Matches at Camp Perry, again as Captain of the Marine Corps Rifle Team. At Winthrop, the team had had much more time to practice than ever before. As usual, Harllee checked carefully with his assistant, Captain McDougal, and with his team coach in selecting the 12 men for the team. The choices were good; four out of five new men fired above the previous team average.

At the National Matches, a Marine won the President's Match which was an important event, and he received a letter personally signed by the President of the United States.

In the National Trophy Rifle Team Match, the Marines wound up in 4th place in the 200 yard slow-fire. At 600 yards, they slipped to 11th at mid-range, but fought back to 4th for the long range stage which was fired at 1,000 yards. They took 4th place again in the 200 yard rapid-fire.

In the skirmish run, a "run and shoot" event, the Marines did very well indeed. They tied for 1st place with the Iowa team. They then tied for second place for the entire 43 team National Trophy Rifle Team match. They started to celebrate.

Then all hell broke loose. Second Lieutenant Randolph Coyle of the Marines had watched team member First Lieutenant W. Dulty Smith's first shots on the skirmish run. When he saw them hit the silhouette he involuntarily yelled, "Good wind! Good wind!"

Colonel R. K. Evans, Executive Officer (officer-in-charge) of the Match, ruled it illegal coaching, even though it seemed to almost everybody there that it was a spontaneous exclamation rather than coaching. Colonel Evans threw out the entire score which cost the Marines 1000 points and stood them in 42nd place, one place above Montana the team that didn't bother to fire the difficult skirmish "run and shoot."

That was how the match ended.

The 1910 U.S. Marine Corps Rifle Team at the National Rifle Team Matches, Camp Perry, Ohio. The Team Captain, Bill Harllee, is in the center of the photo.

1910-NATIONAL RIFLE TEAM MATCHES-1910

	Team Score
1st—Infantry	3,186
2nd—U.S. MARINE CORPS	
3rd—U.S. Cavalry	3,115
4th—U.S. Navy	3,111

Members of Marine Team	Score
Gy-Sgt. Peter S. Lune	250
1st Lt. William D. Smith	263
Cpl. George W. Farnham	271
Sgt. William A. Fragner	269
1st-Sgt. Victor H. Czegka	270
Gy-Sgt. Frederick Wahlstrom	262
Cpl. Ernest E. Eiler	258
Cpl. Augustus B. Hale	261
Cpl. Watt G. Higginbotham	258
Cpl. Tom Worsham	264
Cpl. John E. Peterson	265
1st-Sgt. Thomas F. Joyce	245
	3,136

Team Captain: Capt. Wm. C. Harllee

INDIVIDUAL RIFLE MATCH

Place	Name	Medal
6th—Cpl. Ernest E. Eiler		Gold
8th—Cpl. George W. Farnham		Gold
17th—Sgt. William A. Fragner		Silver
24th—Cpl. Joseph L. Renew		Silver
36th—Cpl. Watt G. Higginbotham		Bronze

Held at: Camp Perry, Ohio.

The Cavalryman Cup was donated in 1911 by the 1910 U.S. Marine Corps Rifle Team to be awarded to the high-scoring cavalryman in the President's Match.

136

Colonel Evans said in his report:

> The throwing out of the Marine's score on the occasion was the hardest and most unpleasant duty which has fallen to the lot of the Executive Officer in the course of the four Matches in which he has held this position.

All of Harllee's hopes, as well as those of the rest of the team, were absolutely shattered. It is hard today to realize how important that match was to them. As far as the armed services were concerned, they had lost the Super Bowl without even scoring—and all on a bum rap from the umpire.

It was a time that called for grace under pressure. Harllee and the Marine team said nothing at all and headed for their tents. It was also a time for sportsmanship and self control, and they had it in spades. Harllee had learned how to control his superheated temper.

But it was not really over after all.

First Lieutenant William H. Clopton, Jr., Captain of the Cavalry Team, told Colonel Evans that his team must, as a matter of justice, protest the ruling to the National Board for Promotion of Rifle Practice, which ran the matches. The Cavalry did this in spite of the fact that the disallowance of the Marine score had moved the Cavalry up from third place to second place.

On Monday, September 26, 1910, the National Board for Promotion of Rifle Practice heard both sides and then reversed the Executive Officer's decision. They allowed the Marine skirmish score in its entirety which restored them to second place, the Cavalry becoming third.

At the suggestion of one of the Marine enlisted men and approved by unanimous vote of the team, the $350 second place prize was used to purchase a three foot silver cup. It was then presented to the Cavalry Team as the Cavalryman Cup. Since 1911, it has been awarded annually, with no Cavalry now, to the Army officer or enlisted man firing the highest score in the President's match.

The cup is sterling silver, mounted upon an ebony base, 34½ inches high. The cover is surmounted by the emblem of the U. S. Marine Corps, modeled in full relief. Regulation cavalry sabres and Marine Corps swords, crossed, appear around the upper portion of the cup. Laurel wreaths suspended from the beaks of eagles form the handles. Between an upper border of laurel and a lower decoration of acanthus leaves, encircling the body of the cup, there appears a finely etched group showing a cavalryman at full gallop rescuing a wounded Marine—a scene full of spirited action. On either side is a rifle; underneath the group is etched the name. "The Cavalryman's Cup" and the cavalry flag, enameled in full colors.

As a result of this skirmish incident, the Marine team wallowed almost ever after in good feeling with the other teams. Even Colonel Evans said that the Marine team "deservedly enjoys the reputation of being good soldiers and straight, clean sports."

Although Harllee wanted to make the Marines the straightest shooting outfit in the world—and they were on their way, too, because by the end of 1909 one third of them were marksmen instead of the 1½% in 1900—he was also interested in other Americans shooting straight. He even opened the Marine's armory to the other teams at the National Matches for gun repair.

And in the end the Marines stood two places higher in the National Matches than they ever had—second place. The next year Harllee was to be in charge of the Marine detachment on what he always called the biggest and best battleship afloat, the USS FLORIDA, but his old friend and assistant McDougal was to take the team to first place. The die was cast.

For the rest of 1910 and until July of 1911, Harllee was ordered hither and yon about the Marine Corps and to the Governor of Virginia giving instruction in rifle practice and in the construction of rifle ranges.

In 1910 Harllee wrote his "U. S. Marine Corps Score Book and Rifleman's Instructor," which the Corps used for a quarter of a century and which was credited with materially aiding in improving the marksmanship of Marines. The U. S. Army used the material in Harllee's book, which was also used by England, Cuba and Haiti.

Harllee received enough money from royalties on those sales

of the book to enable him, in 1916, to buy a large house at 1753 Lamont Street, Northwest, in Mt. Pleasant, then a fashionable part of Washington. Through much of his life he received income from rental and sales of his inherited Florida property, which was fortunate, because he always spent so much of his own money getting the job done that his Marine Corps pay could not cover it and his living expenses. But he figured it was spent in a good cause and didn't hesitate to do so. He was never interested in accumulating money.

His "The U. S. Marine Corps Score Book and Rifleman's Instructor" was an early paperback, five inches by four inches in size, with 73 small pages of instructions and 51 pages of scoring sheets, giving it a thickness of $5/16$ of an inch. The size and shape were designed for easy carrying in almost any pocket. Its first two sentences were:

> An effort has been made to make this book easy and clear to the beginner, so that if it is distributed among men they can use it to instruct themselves; and many men anxious to qualify do this without any further attention. But some men are not so diligent, and the book is designed also to be taught in squad or larger schools.

For those interested in what it meant to qualify as a marksman:

The qualification course for the rifle was fired as follows:

SLOW-FIRE

Range	Time Limit	Shots	Target	Position
200	No limit	10	A	Standing
300	do.	10	A	5 Sitting, 5 Kneeling
500	do.	10	B	Prone
600	do.	(x)10	B	Prone with sandbag

(x) Two sighting shots were fired at 600 yards.

RAPID-FIRE

Range	Time Limit	Shots	Target	Position
200	1 minute	10	D	Sitting or kneeling from standing
300	1 minute, 10 seconds	10	D	Prone from standing
500	1 minute, 20 seconds	10	D	Prone

The targets were as follows:

Target A.	Target B.	Target D.
Bull's-eye 10 inches	Bull's-eye 20 inches	Silhouette 19x26 inches
200 and 300 yards	500 and 600 yards	All Ranges
Slow-Fire.	Slow-Fire.	Rapid-Fire.

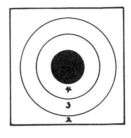
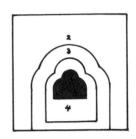

4 ft. x 6 ft.	6 ft. x 6 ft.	6 ft. x 6 ft.

The value of a hit in the bull's-eye of Targets A and B and in the silhouette of Target D was 5.

The rings of all the bull's-eye targets were about nine inches.

The minimum aggregate scores required for qualification were as follows (out of a possible 350):

Expert rifleman—306   Sharpshooter—290   Marksman—240

In the summer of 1911, Bill Harllee got forty days leave and accompanied the Army War College class on its tactical and historical ride over the Civil War battlefields of Virginia. They went on horseback and were followed by a wagon train with tents and equipage. Several days were spent on each battlefield. Having previously been over the fields and having studied them with Confederate veterans, he found himself better informed on the battles than anyone except Lieutenant Colonel (later General) Hunter Liggett, who was in charge of the expedition. In those days, study of the battles was considered excellent professional training by army officers all over the world.

XVI
WITH THE USS FLORIDA: 1911–1914

Over the Bounding Main

On September 11, 1911, Captain Harllee reported to the USS FLORIDA as Commanding Officer of its Marine Detachment. This was a choice assignment. The Florida had just been placed in commission and, as far as her crew was concerned, she was the biggest and best dreadnaught afloat. Also, there was a sentimental angle. Harllee was the first Marine officer to be commissioned directly into the Corps from civil life in Florida. This was done by recommendation of its Congressional delegation.

It was a minor miracle that he got such a plum. Service aboard ship was then considered to be very desirable for Marines—the soldiers of the sea. The Marine ship guards formed important parts of the Marine detachments which "landed and had the situation well in hand" all over the world. This was in the days before there were fleet marine forces and formally organized amphibious forces. A clique in the Navy fought for many years to get Marines off Navy ships and into the Army. At times this clique came close to succeeding. Through several periods of its history, the Marine Corps had to fight for its existence. Its foes, believing Marines should simply be soldiers, and not soldiers of the sea, have been persuasive at times with such mighty personages as Andrew Jackson, Theodore Roosevelt and Harry Truman.

Bill Harllee had many proven friends in Congress through

the years, due to his work in the field of marksmanship and his fighting qualities, and in later years due to his efforts in the field of education and in the matter of our Latin American policy. These included Senator Park Trammel of Florida, Chairman of the Senate Naval Affairs Committee, and Senator Duncan U. Fletcher, of the Military Affairs Committee, also of Florida, as well as Senators Morris Sheppard of Texas, Robert M. La Follette of Wisconsin, Arthur Vandenberg of Michigan, Carl Hayden of Arizona, and Smith W. Brookhart of Iowa. The latter two captained state rifle teams, and Brookhart became President of the National Rifle Association,. Senators Charles McNary of Oregon and Henrik Shipstead of Minnesota also gave evidence of friendship for him, as did a number of Representatives. It was not at all hard for Bill Harllee to convince these men that the Marine Corps should not be abolished or merged with the Army, as its enemies came so perilously close to doing.

It was surprising that Harllee got the USS FLORIDA assignment because Major General William P. Biddle was Commandant, and the official record spoke of "numerous controversies between Major Biddle and Lieutenant Harllee in the Philippines" including "10 days under arrest for disrespect to his commanding officer."

Bill Harllee was never one to "crook the willing hinges of the knee that thrift may follow fawning," to use the elegant Shakesperean phrase he sometimes used instead of "bootlicking" and much more earthy expressions.

It was widely reported that the powerful Senator Boies Penrose of Pennsylvania, the home of Biddle's influential family, had gotten his appointment as Commandant from President Taft. Harllee, the famous Colonel Fritz Wise, and others referred to Biddle as "Sitting Bull" because of his addiction to comfortable chairs. He was a portly gentlemen indeed, but he did emphasize training, and he established the recruit training depots, or "boot camps", so revered by old Marines. But Biddle perhaps recognized that Harllee, though always a rebel, could do a good job and kindly approved the assignment.

The Commanding Officer of the Florida was Captain William R. (Wild Bill) Rush. He was an interesting type of what was called in the Navy a "sundowner" or martinet. He was so strict at weekly personnel inspections that officers and men had to keep special uniforms which were worn on no occasions other than the inspections. He was really a bearcat about haircuts and all other features of personal appearance. He even insisted that men not look at him unpleasantly. However, he had acquitted himself very well in action in the Spanish-American War and would do so again in the 1914 action at Vera Cruz. The officers felt he was tough, but fair.

When Captain Harllee, U.S.M.C. reported for duty to Captain Rush, U.S.N., the latter said,

"Good morning, Harllee. I've heard a lot about you and it's not all good. Don't expect to get away with anything at all on board my ship."

Harllee replied, "Captain Rush, I've heard about you and it's not all good either, but what you have heard about me that's unfavorable must have come from persons who didn't have enough to do except harrass their subordinates. My record will show that I've gotten along famously with busy people. You're going to be very busy running this ship, and I propose to help you. We're not going to have any trouble."

Rush responded, "All right, Harllee, I hope so. We'll certainly give it a try. But remember you're helping and not vice versa."

The Marine Captain did not run into a collision with Captain Rush as he had with that other man known to many as such a martinet, Colonel Mills at West Point. In fact, Harllee got along quite well with Rush and all the other officers on the Florida. Indeed, he liked and admired Rush. He made himself and the Marine Detachment very useful to the ship. They cheerfully coaled ship along with all hands in a terrible three day effort in the middle of a sleet storm in Boston in the winter of 1911–1912. Coaling ship tended to separate the men from the boys in those days; sometimes men were crippled or even killed in accidents when coaling ship.

The Florida Marines won the 17 entry two mile service cutter race in Guantanamo later that winter. They volunteered to run

143

the ships laundry, a pioneering venture then, and successfully did so.

It is not only in modern times that difficulties are experienced with new installations of weapons systems. The Florida, big and new, had 16 five-inch guns, eight on each side. The Marines manned eight of these guns. The bluejacket-manned guns were installed on decks right below the Marine-manned guns. The relative positions of the guns and the light protection afforded were such that the firing of one of the bluejacket guns gave an awful blast to the Marine crew above, members of which had their hair scorched. The pointer's shirt caught afire. Harllee and his Marines nevertheless stood by their guns and shot up most of their ammunition, ten rounds per gun, even though they had to grab and hold a couple of the men.

The concussion from one of the sailor's guns, right below a Marine gun was so strong that it carried away the iron bulkheads (walls) in several places and wrecked the chief of staff's room. Most of the sailors had to leave their guns, and they shot very little of their ammunition.

The only hit on the target was made by a hangfire from a Marine gun. Harllee had adjusted the sights to take into account the changed range of the hangfire. He stood by at the firing of all his guns, but it was several weeks before his ears got back to normal.

This defect in the placing of the guns was corrected later on when the ship went into the Navy Yard for an extensive overhaul.

ITALY—1913

On November 9, 1913 the USS FLORIDA arrived in Naples, Italy, for a three weeks' visit.

Bill Harllee told Dr. Elliott, the ship's medical officer, "Doc, they're offering us ten days leave. Let's see the sights. There are plenty of them in sunny Italy. Beside that, I've got an Italian friend from the Boxer Rebellion up in Rome, and I'm sure he will give us a welcome."

The doctor readily agreed.

They started off in Pompeii. Harllee was prepared for this

144

phenomenon of preservation by having bought earlier, for fifteen cents, Sir Edward Bulwer-Lytton's novel, "The Last Days of Pompeii". He not only read it himself but persuaded six other ships officers to read it so he could discuss it with them.

Nevertheless, he and the doctor were a little taken aback in Pompeii by the guide's emphasis on Roman phallic worship. The Italian pointed out the stone phallus built into the walls of many buildings to ward off evil spirits. Pompeii, of course, had been a pleasure resort for wealthy Romans. Followers of the Egyptian worship of Isis as well as others had conducted fantastic orgies, the depiction of which in murals had been preserved for almost two millennia by the volcanic ash of Vesuvius. The most interesting (or worst) example of this was covered up. Bill Harllee, always allergic to cover-ups, created quite a commotion by removing the cover, but was immediately sorry he had done so, as its eroticism extended to hermaphrodites.

The pair then proceeded to the Eternal City and were fascinated by the remnants of the great Roman civilization which had lasted so long. They noted the curious fact that the height and diameter of the Pantheon were the same—one hundred and forty-two and a half feet. They also marveled at the construction of the drainage for the Forum, built originally on a marshy lake. Although the sewer draining it had been constructed without mortar in ancient times, it still carried the sewage from the Forum into the Tiber.

As a soldier, Bill Harllee was interested in the Rome which, although just a city, had produced the legions of warriors who had conquered the then-known world. As a civilized human being, he admired the Trevi fountain, then described as the finest in the world, and the Trivoli, where the Emperor Hadrian had gathered five thousand of the best works of Greek art.

On the lighter side, Harllee's old friend, Lieutenant Adolfo Cignozzi, decided to celebrate with him and the doctor, very belatedly, Italy's victory in the 1912 Libyan War.

One evening after some of the world's best pasta and wine, Bill Harllee said to the Italian,

"Italy is really great. But if you first step ashore in Naples you get surrounded and badgered for the longest kind of time by the damndest bunch of beggars, pickpockets, guides, touts and pimps I have ever seen and you have a hell of a time getting rid of them. What a putrid first impression of a delightful country! Can't your police do something about this?"

Replied the lieutenant,

"My dear Captain Harllee, the police don't need to do anything about it. If you shake your head or say anything they will think or pretend to think you don't understand. All you need to do is to slowly and lazily move your head upward, as if it is too much trouble to speak. Don't say a thing. Then they will all fall away!"

Rejoined Harllee,

"I can't believe it—it's too easy—but I'll try it out when we return to Naples."

And he did and it worked.

The pair then proceeded to Milan, where Harllee was fascinated to learn that the box immediately above the stage on the fifth tier of the world famous theater, La Scala, was always occupied by blind people. In about 1860, the owner of the box had given her rights to the Archbishop at Milan. The latter had turned over this box to an asylum for the blind on condition that the box should be forever used exclusively by its blind inmates. Oddly enough, the operas of Wagner were the most popular with these blind people, who loved all opera with a passion, probably accentuated by the loss of their sight.

After Milan, the Marine and the doctor happily sampled Florence, Venice and Genoa. They basked in the warmth of friendly Italians and vowed to return some day with their families to sunny Italy, which for so many years attracted world record numbers of tourists.

One evening in Italy, the Florida's paymaster brought a Britisher aboard for poker. He was a novice, and the easiest meat they had ever had in "the grand old game." Everybody cleaned up a big pile of the Limey's money except Harllee, and this despite the fact that, earlier, he had to quit the game for fear of getting a bad reputation as too much of a professional gambler. But this was a special occasion and the gang had insisted he join them. He had no luck with the cards that night until finally he got four fours in one hand and four "girls" in another hand. He bet both hands strong but lost both times.

The Florida poker games were something to see. One of their features was Gus Freudendorf, the super salty old boatswain, who had ham-like hands which were so strong that he could tear up a whole deck of cards at once, which he did whenever he lost a bet.

A Celebration In The Florida's Wine Mess

Life aboard the Florida was such a pleasant experience that Harllee considered himself very fortunate in remaining aboard longer than any other officer "plank-owner"—from September 13, 1911 until November 3, 1914.

Late in 1913 it became apparent that Will and Ella Harllee would have an heir (or heiress). The USS FLORIDA was in the Brooklyn Navy Yard in New York, and they were living in Brooklyn. But their sentiment for the South was such that they were determined that their offspring's place of birth would be south of the Mason Dixon line. Accordingly when the time arrived, which turned out to be a bit early, they rushed down to Washington, D. C., then a Southern city and one they knew well. On January 2, 1914 a son, John Harllee, named after his uncle and grandfather, was born to them. He graduated from the U. S. Naval Academy and followed a career in the Navy and, later, as Chairman of the Federal Maritime Commission. True to the family tradition he married a Texas beauty, Jo Beth Carden, all of whose eligible forbears had fought valiantly under the Stars and Bars.

While Bill Harllee served on the USS FLORIDA, the U. S. Navy still had "wine messes" aboard ship for the officers, although since 1862 alcoholic beverages had been prohibited for enlisted men. The "wine messes' actually served whiskey, rum and gin as well as wine and beer. Southerner Harllee in those days liked to tell people that the famous Confederate ship Shenandoah continued to issue grog to all hands as well as sink Yankee ships long after the Civil War had ended.

The popularity of grog in the old Navy was attested to by Hanson W. Baldwin in his excellent August 1958 article in the Naval Institute Proceedings:

Abolition of spirits would have caused mutiny; aboard the frigate Constellation there used to be a saying, "Blow up the magazines; throw the bread over the side and sink the salt horse—but handle them spirits gentle-like."

The wine messes were very popular with the officers. There was pleasant ship visiting, and fine drinking and eating. But Secretary of the Navy Josephus Daniels, in a move much cursed then, but later almost unanimously approved by U. S. Naval officers, abolished the wine messes effective July 1, 1914.

However, at the time, Daniels was reviled not only by the Navy, but lampooned in the press. According to Hanson Baldwin in the Naval Institute:

A storm of denunciation, abuse, and opprobrium descended upon the Secretary's head. The New York Tribune ran a series of famous cartoons depicting Daniels as "Sir Josephus, Admiral of the U.S.S. Grapejuice fleet." One of the cartoons was accompanied by verses of a parody of an old song, "The Armored Cruiser Squadron"—long sung in the fleet:

Away, away, with sword and drum,
    Here we come, full of rum
Looking for something to put on the bum
    In the Armored Cruiser Squadron.

Josephus Daniels is a goose,
    If he thinks he can induce
Us to drink his damn grape juice
    In the Armored Cruiser Squadron."

On the night of June 30, 1914, much of the United States Fleet was still off Vera Cruz, Mexico, and they buried "King John Barleycorn" with great serio-comic ceremonies, boating from ship to ship to drink up all the alcohol left.

However, when young John Harllee was born on January 2, 1914, the officers of the USS FLORIDA did not know of their impending doom and Bill Harllee, in celebration, gave one of the last great wine mess parties.

XVII
THE ACTION AT VERA CRUZ, MEXICO APRIL 1914

Secretary of the Navy Josephus Daniels issued a letter of commendation to Captain William C. Harllee for "eminent and conspicuous conduct in battle."

Vera Cruz, Mexico. April 21, 1914. U. S. Marines and bluejackets were ordered by the Secretary of the Navy to land from their ships and seize the Custom House! The orders were approved by President Woodrow Wilson at 2:30 A.M. Their mission was to prevent the landing of 100 machine guns and 15 millions of rounds of ammunition destined for the forces of President Huerta of Mexico.

Captain Harllee, commanding the USS FLORIDA Marines, landed about 11:10 A.M., shortly after those Marines from the USS PRAIRIE, who were first to land because they were closer to the wharf.

Before Woodrow Wilson was inaugurated as President of the United States in March of 1913, General Victoriano Huerta had succeeded General Francisco I. Madero as President of Mexico in a coup d'etat which commenced on February 9,

1913. Wilson had for years taken an interest in Mexican affairs. He strongly approved of Madero, who was a reformer, and even more strongly disapproved of Huerta, who was a very tough old soldier of almost pure Indian blood.

President Wilson was determined to drive Huerta out of office since he believed that the General was not sufficiently liberal or democratic. A group called the "Constitutionalists" were in revolt against Huerta, but in the fall of 1913 Huerta's regime was in good shape.

In October of 1913, Wilson sent a squadron of U. S. Naval vessels, including three battleships, the dreadnaughts of their day, to show the flag along the Mexican Gulf Coast. This was where the oil industry was centered, and where thousands of Americans lived.

The ships, including the USS FLORIDA, spent several boring months off Tampico and Vera Cruz, with the men fishing for giant sharks, eating alligator pears and illicitly gambling. Harllee held school and conducted competitions for his men, including rifle and pistol shooting at cans in the water at various distances.

Vera Cruz, where the Florida was stationed beginning January of 1914, was beautiful to view from the sea. The two or three story buildings were painted with various pastel colors. The houses, the green of the palm trees, and the land all blended together with snow-capped Mt. Orizaba, 18,700 feet in altitude and the highest mountain in Mexico, to make a beautiful sight. The deep blue water, hills, white walls, and other mountains in the distance all added to its exotic beauty.

The Americans then had very limited shore leave because of fear of creating an incident. Later they were to find that closeup in Vera Cruz there was dysentery, malaria, and an almost complete lack of public sanitation. Zopilotes (big black vultures) and dogs were relied upon to perform the duties of garbage removal.

At Tampico, Mexico on April 9, 1914, one U. S. Naval officer and eight bluejackets had been removed by Mexican soldiers from a boat flying an American flag alongside a dock. They had been kept under arrest for an hour and a half. The Mexicans had not complied with American demands for an apology to the satisfaction of the United States Government and feelings were running high, so much so that Congress had authorized the President to "use the armed forces of the United States in such ways and to such an extent as may be necessary to obtain from General Huerta and his adherents the fullest recognition of the rights and dignity of the United States."

Returning to April 21, 1914, the ammunition about which President Wilson was concerned was aboard the SS Ypiranga, a German freighter. Germany was not only a sovereign nation, but a superpower of that day, and her ship could not be made subject to American orders in international or Mexican waters.

At nine o'clock on the morning of April 21, while Bill Harllee was still at breakfast, an orderly brought a message from the captain to the executive officer, who was in charge of the landing party, to land immediately. Harllee's Marine detachment was in its boat before ten, but Rear Admiral Craddock of the British ship Essex came aboard and protested against precipitating hostilities until due notice could be given to his non-combatant British subjects to take refuge. The Marines were then the only part of the ship's crew who were embarked in boats. The sailors were not yet ready. Harllee was ordered to disembark his men from the boat to the ship. No sooner was this accomplished than Rear Admiral Frank F. Fletcher, in command of the U. S. forces at Vera Cruz, changed his mind, so the Marines went back into the boat, a motor launch, and proceeded to a wharf. Harllee expected with certainty that they would be fired upon while they were in the boat, but for some unaccountable reason they were not.

The Marines wore the khakis and the peaked campaign hats made well known to later generations by drill instructors. They carried big knapsack rolls on their torsos. These rolls were made famous both in many old Marine Corps pictures and in statues of soldiers.

Captain Harllee and his men landed at 11:10 A.M., shortly after those of the USS PRAIRIE. Still there was no firing. They were ordered to the northern edge of town to protect the electric power plant, which was about 500 yards from the railroad terminal. The latter was the initial stop of most of the

Harllee's USS FLORIDA Marines firing from an outpost in the sand hills near Vera Cruz

American forces after they left the Custom House. The power plant was also the part of Vera Cruz where the Americans expected Mexican reinforcements to show up, if any were sent at all. Harllee and his Marines arrived there and began to have dinner at noon when a fusillade broke out in the town. For a few minutes no bullets came their way, and there was no change in their orders, so he and his men gathered their arms and continued with dinner.

Finally, after the Florida's bluejackets began to cross Calle Emparan, a street about one hundred yards from the Custom House, firing began close aboard. A fusillade of bullets fell among them, but there was still no change of orders for them, so Harllee moved his men inside the cover of a range of sand hills nearby. He informed them that the fire they were receiving was from American forces and that they must not shoot back. He instructed the non-commissioned officers that if anyone attempted to fire to take his gun away from him. In the excitement several of the men tried to shoot, but he and his non-coms took their guns away from them and took the breech blocks out. Bill Harllee had to do this personally in the case of

152

The Marines prepare to leave the sand hills and move through the city to dislodge Mexican resistance.

one corporal. He relieved him from being in charge of his squad and made him stay with him. Not a shot was fired from his line at friendly forces.

He and his men were still ordered to remain at the power plant. They lay under cover of the sand hills the remainder of the day, continuously under fire, heavy at times.

During the first day, twenty sailors who came to the electric light station got on the roof and began to fire into those American forces at the railroad station. Harllee still had his detachment outside of the building under cover of the sand hills there. He left cover and went to the building and made the bluejackets quit firing. He had to manhandle personally some of them and threaten to put their officer under arrest, but he succeeded in preventing them from firing at the Americans who were firing at them in apparent ignorance of *their* identity. He left a sergeant there with orders to see that there was no more firing at friendly American forces , even if they were fired upon by such forces.

At night the firing continued. Harllee and his men stayed in position and established an outpost line to observe both the direction of the city and the opposite direction.

The next morning they were ordered to move to the outer edge of town. They were then ordered to work in towards the waterfront and dislodge the Mexicans firing from the house-tops. These were faulty orders for they thrust them directly in front of hundreds of their own men working out from the waterfront, and they received friendly fire as well as the fire of the Mexicans. The fire of the Mexicans was heavy but not too accurate. And again Harllee would not permit firing in the direction of his own troops, but caused his people to keep buildings between them and the fire of their own men, and he did begin working his men through the part of the city assigned to him.

In the area covered by Harllee's detachment, each house in each block was gone through thoroughly. All the men brought out by the Marines were assembled and informed by Harllee that the Americans were there to help them against an op-pressive government and not to harm them. They were then released. Only in one case was firing resumed after they had been through the premises, and on their next visit they were unable to find any men there. They were well hidden out. It was a particularly bad nest of hostile Mexicans. Bill Harllee's close friend, Captain James C. Breckenridge, and his USS UTAH Marines had gone through it before and had killed several of the armed Mexicans. The survivors opened up again from their hiding place after Harllee had been through there with his men, but finally they were eliminated.

Progress through the city with its hundreds of snipers was very difficult. The Marines had to use posts to batter in doors, and the Mexicans would shoot at them as they were breaking in, but the Marines worked in squads to cover and protect each other. Finally Harllee and his men cleared the part of the city assigned to them.

Presently his detachment, being on the flank, found itself in the line of fire from the five inch guns of the USS CHESTER which just then opened up on the Mexican Naval Academy

154

building. This building housed cadets who had offered much resistance and who had driven off some U. S. Navy companies with a loss of several Americans killed and a large number wounded. The bluejackets had advanced on this building en masse, a poor tactic under the circumstances. The five inch gun fire from the Chester fell directly in front and in rear of Harllee's detachment, so he moved it by the flank into a big ditch or canal to clear the line of fire and then mingled his company with Captain Breckenridge's Marines.

That night they slept in one of the streets of the city. There was desultory firing from housetops all night, but it did very little damage. Harllee and his men had been able to do their job without any fatalities.

Vera Cruz was firmly in American hands by sunrise of April 24. The Mexicans began to hold their funerals then.

On April 25, 1914, reinforcements, including Bill Harllee and his company and considerable additional forces, were ordered to the relief of Major John H. Russell's battalion at a point about ten miles south of Vera Cruz called El Tejar, where the plant was located that supplies water to the city.

This strange incident, pertinent to a later chapter, is reported thus in Lieutenant Colonel Clyde H. Metcalf's "History of the United States Marine Corps":

> There were occasional rumors that Mexican forces were being concentrated in the vicinity to attack Funstons's forces. Most of the reports proved to have no foundation in fact, but one force of undetermined strength appeared at the outpost line of El Tejar and demanded the immediate surrender of Russell's battalion. Russell's calls for reinforcements from Vera Cruz caused considerable excitement, and a column was sent scurrying to the relief of the supposedly beleaguered garrison, only to arrive at El Tejar, after a few hours marching and train ride, to find that the danger of Mexican attack had vanished.

Colonel Frederic M. (Fritz) Wise and Meigs O. Frost in "A Marine Tells It To You" used somewhat more colorful language:

> What had happened, we learned, was that some damned Mexican cattle thief had come in to El Tejar under a flag of truce and demanded that the Marine officer surrender. We marched back again.

155

First Sergeant Major John Quick and Captain Monk Delano help hoist the American flag atop the Hotel Terminal, Vera Cruz.

156

This photograph was taken on April 30, 1914, in Vera Cruz as Marines were marching to return to their ships.
1. Lt. Murray, 2. Major Reed, 3. Capt. Harllee, 4. Capt. Robards
a. Capt. Breckenridge's USS UTAH Marines; b. Capt. Harllee's Company of USS FLORIDA and USS MINNESOTA Marines; c. Capt. Robards USS NEW JERSEY and USS MICHIGAN Marines.

The reinforcements remained there until the 30th of April when they were relieved by another battalion and returned to the ships.

On July 31, 1914, Secretary of the Navy Josephus Daniels issued a letter of commendation to Captain William C. Harllee for "eminent and conspicuous conduct in battle." This was done on the recommendation of Colonel Wendell C. Neville (later Major General Commandant of the Marine Corps), who was in charge of all the Marines ashore during the action at Vera Cruz.

American troops continued to occupy Vera Cruz until November 23, 1914, but of course American attention had long since turned to France.

During the whole Vera Cruz affair, Harllee instructed his men that the motive of the United States Government was not to make war upon the Mexican people but to assist them in

U. S. Marine reinforcements in formation near the railroad terminal with Navy and Marine Corps bands. The Marines and Sailors occupied Vera Cruz until November, 1914.

establishing a truly republican form of government such as would give them the same blessings the people of the United States enjoyed under their government. He received these impressions from Mr. Lind, President Wilson's personal representative, who aboard the ship one evening gave a clear and lucid exposition of President Wilson's views.

Harllee explained that the way to accomplish this beneficent mission was not to shoot wantonly the inhabitants of this unoffending city nor to depredate upon their property, not even to act with cruelty towards their men in arms. These men had a right to defend their land and to repel the invader, and the more courageously they did it the more they were entitled to honorable treatment should they fall into American hands. Harllee added further that brave men were generous and that cruelty to defenseless soldiers or helpless inhabitants was not a quality that distinguished brave men nor added luster to their arms.

His detachment used over fifty first-aid packages in dressing the wounds of Mexicans who were wounded the second day.

Wherever Harllee and his men went, the people were made to understand that they were not there to harm them. The Marines would respect their property, and that they could spare themselves the rigors of occupation by restraining those in their houses from firing upon them, but that if firing was resumed the Marines would be obliged to eliminate all the grown males engaged in such firing.

Harllee reported that to the credit of the U. S. Marines and bluejackets, there was very little looting of the people's effects, and in the great majority of cases the manhood of the Americans made them perform their duty in such a way as to work as little hardship as possible on the inhabitants.

As already indicated, there was some confusion in the Vera Cruz operation.

Jack Sweetman in his masterpiece on the subject from the book, "The Landing at Vera Cruz, 1914," reported a "brisk firefight" between the USS MINNESOTA battalion and a USS NEW HAMPSHIRE outpost. He also reported friendly bullets passing inches over the heads of the USS NEW JERSEY artillerymen. Also hundreds of men (American servicemen) milling about in apparent disorder.

"A Marine Tells It To You" states,

> We learned that most of the American casualities were due to wild shooting by our own people. I heard that doctors in the hospital said that of the nineteen Americans killed at Vera Cruz, thirteen deaths were due to accidental shootings by Americans. I heard a lot of shooting there, but never a shot I knew was Mexican.

Official papers understandably don't normally deal much with accidental shooting of one's men by one's own men. The American casualities at Vera Cruz were reported as 17 killed and 63 wounded. Had Mexican marksmanship been better, American casualities would have been much greater. The Mexican casualities are not known precisely, but estimates varied between 126 killed and 195 wounded and 230 killed and 230 wounded.

To sum up the Vera Cruz situation: although sailors had performed landing forces duties very well in many an earlier action, these particular groups did not seem well organized and trained, nor were they well directed. Their use as soldiers fighting ashore was dying out, and was quite moribund by World War II, when they manned both on the sea and in the air the greatest navy the world has ever known. Modern doctrine provides for fleet Marine forces from amphibious ships to do the fighting ashore, although shipboard Marine detachments might also be called on.

THE POST MORTEM
Military

Harllee considered from a military point of view that the landing at Vera Cruz was very poorly run. He contended that it was directed by Naval officers who were ignorant of any conception of land operations. This type of problem has long since been ironed out by the development through experience and study of joint doctrine between the various armed services, but hard lessons were learned from Vera Cruz.

There were miles of excellent beaches where any number of men could be landed from boats without any confusion, but the boatloads of Marines and bluejackets were sent to the center of the waterfront of the city. That they were not destroyed in the act of landing and before arrival at the wharves was due only to marvelous good fortune. About an hour's notice was served upon the town that the landing was to take place. That was just enough in Harllee's view to forewarn Mexican troops to prepare to resist, but entirely too little for non-combatants to seek refuge. He believed that to land troops in that way was bound to precipitate street fighting and much shooting by the inhabitants. He felt that, of all troops suitable for that most disagreeable form of fighting, sailors not disciplined as soldiers nor trained as such, were the least suitable. It was a hard task for trained and disciplined soldiers. In his opinion the result was that they began to fire indiscriminately.

Even though the shooters from the housetops became persistent, Admiral Fletcher's orders were to seize the Custom

House but not to advance further. In Harllee's view, such orders were silly. A thousand troops were to land to seize a custom house and then remain along the wharves. What was the end of such a situation, he asked? How long should they have hung out on the narrow fringe of the waterfront? What could they do there?

Harllee thought that the useless hanging out along the waterfront emboldened the nondescripts in town to get on their housetops and practice shooting at them. Even then when the shooting started, the officer in command of the landing force, Captain William R. Rush of the Florida, did not have authority to act but had to send word to the Admiral to ask for permission to advance. The Admiral was not on the spot, but on board his flagship. His reply was "No, we are only ordered to seize the Custom House." That impossible situation continued all day. The Americans were firing but could not advance or move out and go after the Mexican shooters, who were firing away from their safe positions.

Harllee believed that the moment troops landed, a column in single file should have been pushed rapidly down each avenue. He figured the vital and commanding positions of the town could have thus been secured in a matter of minutes.

Colonel Buck Neville of the Marines wanted to do this. Harllee felt sure that if it had been done there would have been practically no resistance and what little there was could have been promptly suppressed. Vera Cruz is small in area and could have been quickly and easily covered by the troops at our disposal there, he reasoned.

Then, he believed, few if any of our men would have been shot and the city would have been spared the wholesale killing of its inhabitants which followed as the Mexican shooters accumulated courage and arranged themselves without inter-ference in their housetop positions.

So, thought he, the casualties of both Americans and Mexi-cans were due first to a faulty plan and then to a hesitating and faltering manner of meeting the exigencies which this plan produced.

A Better Plan

Harllee's knowledge of military science and tactics indicated to him that topography around Vera Cruz was ideal for investing it by a line of troops—immediately around the outskirts of the town there were ridges of low sand hills up to ten feet high which completely encircled the town from the beach north to the beach south. This line of investment could have been held, he thought, by 500 men. Ideal landing places existed outside of town where troops could have been landed without confusion or without being intricated in town or involved in hostile fire.

Having surrounded the city, he believed it should have been summoned to capitulate. Upon a refusal, due notice should have been served so that non-combatants could clear out. He felt the United States was rich enough to agree to feed refugees, including Mexicans, who sought shelter behind our lines, and the officer who had ordered it would have held an enviable place in the history of those times. Forty-eight hours, he wrote, was a reasonable time for people to arrange their affairs and clear out.

Then the United States troops could have retired to a line of high sand hills about 100 feet high which enclosed the city and laid about two miles distant from it and the United States ships could have used their splendid armament to bring the city to capitulation. A few minutes of it would have been sufficient and no one would have been injured except Mexican soldiers and citizens who elected to accept the chances. That was the procedure adopted by General Winfield Scott in 1847 and was the procedure adopted by all military men in the reduction of cities, he wrote.

Surprise is a splendid thing against armies afield, but to plunge an unoffending city into such distress as was done was outrageous, in his view. As a matter of fact he had no doubt that General Maas, the Mexican Commander, anticipated such rational proceedings and very properly removed his troops from the city to prevent their becoming involved in its fall. Harllee reported that the only armed people who resisted the

162

landing were non-disciplined troops who were unable to get out quickly enough and citizens who had nondescript firearms. He believed that the most gallant defenders were boys, cadets at their Naval Academy. A number of them died at their posts. They put up a brave defense of their building, used their machine guns effectively, repelled the attack of the troops and succumbed only after their place was wrecked by fire from the five inch guns of the USS CHESTER.

Of course Admiral Fletcher was ordered to seize the Custom House to prevent the landing of the Ypiranga's munitions. But Harllee's view was that there was more than one way to do this and if a proper interpretation of these orders was not possible, modifications could have been requested.

Political

With regard to the political aspect, Harllee strongly felt that the harmless detention of one officer and eight men for an hour and a half did not warrant such an act of war, particularly when the Mexican government relieved its officer in command at Tampico and was willing to meet our original demands for an apology for the Tampico incident. The problem had arisen when the Mexicans required that their 21 gun salute to the American flag be returned gun for gun, which is what Admiral Mayo at Tampico had originally stipulated, but which was over-ridden by the requirement of the United States that compliance with the demands listed below be unconditional!

1. A disavowal and apology to be sent by a member of Mexican General Zaragoza's staff (he was Military Governor of Tampico),
2. Assurance that the officer responsible for the arrest would receive severe punishment,
3. That Zaragoza publicly hoist the American flag and salute it with 21 guns, which salute would be returned by his flagship, and
4. That a reply be made and the gun salute fired within 24 hours from 6:00 P.M. the date of the communication (April 9, 1914).

Harllee also pointed out that our flag was worse violated by Spain in the case of the Virginius, in which she removed men from our ship and shot them. The British flag was violated by the United States in removing Confederate Commissioners from a ship under the British flag. Neither case resulted in an act of war.

The landing at Vera Cruz did not result in the justice, law and order which Wilson had hoped for, but rather in six more years of bloody Mexican internecine struggles. As far as Mexican-American relations are concerned, Jack Sweetman in 1968 in his "The Landing at Vera Cruz, 1914" wrote that "Mexico remembers the landing at Vera Cruz as a kind of a Caribbean Pearl Harbor."

This is the story of the landing at Vera Cruz in 1914. It would seem today to be a very flagrant interference in the affairs of what should have been a friendly and neighboring sovereign nation, the established government of which was not threatening the United States.

However, as far as the U. S. Marines were concerned, Harper's Weekly, Vol. LV, No. 2844, 1912, stated it well:

> There wasn't any fuss about their (the Marines) mobilizing. There never is. Just an order issued and . . . one regiment after another are on their way to Cuba, or Mexico, or the world's end. Where they are going isn't the Marines concern. Their business is to be always ready to go.

It should also be noted that, with regard to the U.S. Navy and Marine Corps officers and men, there was a considerable amount of heroism displayed, particularly in the matter of visually signalling the ships from an exposed position ashore; and, in the matter of shelling the Mexicans with one pounders from three steam launches under the command of Chief Boatswain John McCloy, who continued after being wounded and who had performed heroically in an earlier war. There was also very considerable courage involved in rooting out the snipers and saving wounded Americans.

A curious footnote to history is to be found in Mark Sullivan's book, "Our Times." He reports with regard to President Wilson's 2:30 A.M. message ordering the landing at Vera Cruz:

> Then Wilson went back to bed. Awaking the next morning he sent for the White House chief usher, Irwin Hoover. Still in

his night-shirt, a shaving-brush in one hand, Wilson shook a minatory finger at the usher: "I wish you to give orders that under no circumstances am I ever to be called on the telephone at night." Softening his imperativeness, he added in explanation: "No man aroused from sleep in the middle of the night can have his best judgment about him."

It's a shame to exhume such a dead cat and whirl it around, but it would be hard to think of a better example in this century of why we have a savage problem in our relations with Mexico, and with most of Latin America. It is easy to understand why we have worries about Afghanistan, Poland, and the Persian Gulf, as after all they are neighbors of the Soviet Union. But many Americans do not fully understand why, despite the headway made by Franklin Roosevelt's "Good Neighbor Policy" and John Kennedy's "Alliance for Progress", there is such a deep seated antipathy among so many latinos for the "Colossus of the North."

XVIII
THE GUNS OF
EUROPE—1914

"Never mind whether they know
anything about drill. It doesn't matter
whether they know their right foot from
their left. Teach them how to shoot and
do it quickly".
—Lord Kitchener, Commander of the British
Forces, in his General Orders of Sept. 2, 1914

Late in 1914 Bill Harllee was telling America:

Military experts in all lands and from the earliest times have
made knowledge of weapons and accurate aim the first requisite
of a good soldier.

More battles have been won by good marksmanship than by
any other method.

Lord Roberts, the top English general who finally defeated
the Boers, is urging Englishmen to learn to shoot above all
things else, and has stated that the war will be won by that
army which could shoot the straightest.

Major General McLachlan of the British Army has deplored
the condition of military training such as caused an English
soldier to chase a Hun through No-Man's land with a loaded
rifle in an effort to bayonet him.

Statistics indicate that only one enemy is killed for every
45,000 bullets fired on the battle front now.

It didn't take anything like that to get a man in the Civil War,
even though the soldiers of that war were not trained in

marksmanship. If they had been so trained, or if they had been like the frontiersmen soldiers of the Mexican War the Civil War would probably have been over sooner.

Troops not trained in the use of modern fire arms are subject to panic and will become panic stricken when attacked by determined forces.

The Marines can shoot, but we've got to build rifle ranges and train the Army and the Navy and the civilians of the nation to shoot. It is a healthy outdoor sport and it's the best action we can take towards the goal of preparedness, because the civilians of today may have to be the soldiers of tomorrow. Switzerland, a nation of citizen riflement with none of the disadvantages of militarism of wars, is a good example for us.

Our men must learn to shoot machine guns and pistols . . . all their weapons . . . as well as rifles.

There was plenty of opposition to Harllee's creed—some of it almost insuperable. For example, the Chief of Naval Operations felt with some justice that it was not up to the Navy to teach the Army how to shoot rifles, pistols and machine guns, as the Marine Corps was organizationally under the Navy. But Bill Harllee was convinced that the Army needed plenty of help.

In the fall of 1917, some British and French officers were brought here to train Americans. Their field of instruction included small arms. The National Rifle Association and Harllee protested this procedure. Not only were members of the NRA, who were highly skilled in rifle shooting, being overlooked for this duty, but some of the British believed that it was impractical to teach men marksmanship in time of war. They agreed it might be useful to do so, but thought it took too much time. The French did not think soldiers could be expected to shoot like marksmen in the midst of battle, even if trained. As far as they were concerned their soldiers should follow the fire of their artillery and use their grenades and bayonets on the enemy.

We shall see how wrong the British and French advisors to the U. S. Army were.

Opposition and difficulties were Harllee's meat, however, and the risks to his career was the sauce on the meat. He forged ahead.

XIX
ON BEHALF OF NAVY
MARKSMANSHIP—1915

It is a good little book, and Allah be blest, gotten up by a practical rifleman knowing the ropes and knowing how to explain them to the neophyte. Without doubt the wonderful shooting of the Marines during the last year is due in great measure to such men as Captain Harllee and Captain McDougal and the best of the Marines' knowledge of rifle shooting is wrapped up in the short plain talk of the Firing Regulations of the U. S. Navy for 1915
—Edward C. Crossman in "The Rifleshot," an English shooting journal.

1915. The Marines had become the straightest shooters in the world.

The Navy wanted the services of Captain Bill Harllee who had captained the Marines' team, written their book and developed their system of training. In short, the U. S. Navy bought Harllee's creed for use by the Navy.

There was known to be a strong positive correlation between the physical and temperamental qualifications for rifle shooting and for pointing and training (aiming) of the Navy's big guns. Good eyesight, coordination, and freedom from flinching were the qualities desired. A great deal of ammunition and therefore money could be saved by selecting the best potential big gun pointers and trainers via the small arms route.

So Harllee was ordered to report to Washington, D. C. for duty in charge of the Small Arms Section of the Navy Department's Office of Gunnery Exercises and Engineering Performances, which he did on November 6, 1914. He and Ella established their residence at 1721 Q Street, N.W., in Washington. When he reported to the Director of the Office, Captain Roy Campbell Smith, U.S.N., a fine officer who helped to establish a famous Navy family, he was told that his first job would be to write the Navy book on the subject. It was called "The Navy Small Arms Firing Regulations" and was used until after World War I. Franklin D. Roosevelt, as assistant Secretary of the Navy, signed the order promulgating these regulations.

Ordinarily regulations of almost any kind would be the last reading matter in the world that the average reader would desire to have anything to do with. But as the Army and Navy Journal wrote:

> The regulations prepared under the direction of Captain Harllee are concise and intensely human.

In view of this enthusiam, a few features of the book are worthy of listing:

1. It provided, for the first time, for firing from cover, i.e., parapets or trenches, instead of from sandbags or smooth firing mounds only.

2. It eliminated all differences between regular Navy and naval militia in small arms training.

3. It allowed anyone in the Navy to fire, i.e., chaplains, doctors, paymasters as well as line officers and seamen. For example, the theory was that if a doctor was to be sent to the range in case of an accident, why not let him help out by shooting and eventually teaching others to shoot instead of just standing around waiting for accidents that never happened and for which he would be there anyway if they did happen.

4. Prizes were paid immediately and in accordance with wide open blackboard records instead of waiting until much later when interest had waned and scores were secret and suspect.

5. The marksmens' medals were eliminated and a white target sewed on the blue jackets sleeve substituted. So many men would be making marksmen that the medal could become a laughing stock, but the sleeve mark would be accepted as were other such marks, e.g.. for seaman or fireman. A gold badge was provided, however, for the few really top riflemen.

6. After the shooter became competent, he could fire from any position, e.g. prone, squatting, kneeling on one or both knees or standing.

7. A simple system of individual and team competitions within ships and between ships was set up.

8. The skirmish firing run, from cover to cover, was simplified and made more practical.

9. Machine gun and pistol courses were set up.

Incidentally it is interesting to note that all of the machine guns in use in those days—the Colt Browning, Browning, Benet-Mercier, Lewis, and French Hotchkiss—were invented by Americans.

10. Previous restrictions about types of sights were eliminated. Peeps, open sights, telescopes, and any alterations or substitutions were encouraged to develop competitively for each shooter the best possible sight.

11. The manner of aiming was simplified. The bulls-eye and front sight were to be put in the center of the aperture of the rear sight. This was considered natural by Harllee; several other methods of aiming had been used, such as the top of the front sight touching the bottom of the bulls-eye or held with a white line at six o'clock on the bulls-eye. Interestingly, this is the principal feature with which "Arms and the Man," then the unofficial organ of the National Rifle Association, and later its official organ, disagreed. It otherwise strongly praised the book.

171

Parapet and post shooting included in the course.

Kneeling on right and left knees and squatting.

Harllee's published reply to this dissent was,

I believe that I have had enough experience both on ranges and in service to convince me that the best principle is to let fly at the middle of things. When I or any of my soldiers shoot at a hostile man when we are in a hurry, we think it best to catch him where he will appear all around the front sight. If the front sight lays on him, we will get him sure, provided, of course, we have our sights properly set and we will not get him with our sights improperly set if we aim below him. When you begin to teach men to do anything except to aim directly at what they want to hit and the part they want to hit, they wonder why. They can see no reason for it, and I am frank to say I can see no reason for it.

Above all, the Navy Small Arms Firing Regulations were short—64 pages—and simplified.

An idea of what this pamphlet covered can be gained from a partial list of the Table of Contents:

Cleaning and care of the rifle
Aiming
Sight setting
Holding the rifle
    The sling
    The prone position
    The kneeling position
    The squatting position
    The standing position
    The sitting position
    General principles for firing in all positions.
Kinds of fire
    Slow-fire
    Rapid-fire
    Skirmish
    Changing positions
Firing at ranges longer than the prescribed ranges authorized
Sharpshooter course
    Notes on winds
    Zero of rifle
    The windage rule
    The quarter point rule for changing windage
    The square rule for changing elevation
Expert rifleman course
    The micrometer or vernier
    Weather conditions
    Finding the target
Machine gun course
The pistol course

One of the stories, strictly apocryphal, which went into the legend of the so-called Harllee system, was recounted by Brigadier General L.A. Dessez in his oral history at Marine Corps Headquarters,

> Beau Harllee offered his book free, gratis, to the Navy, but the officer on the small arms desk turned it down. Later, when the Marines were breaking marksmanship records, the Navy wanted it. Harllee said they could have it for a price. I heard it was $25,000.

General Dessez also wrote that Harllee was intensely loyal to the friends he had, which was more than true.

Having written the book, the next item on the agenda for Harllee was to establish a school for Navy small arms coaches, which he knew were absolutely necessary to effective training. He did this at the fine Winthrop Rifle Range, about 30 miles south of Washington, D. C., built by him for the Marine Corps in 1910.

Officers and men were sent to this school from the ships during their Navy yard overhauls, when they could best be spared. A battleship, for example, would send three officers and thirty enlisted men at a time to be trained as instructors and coaches.

The next step to get the Navy on track was to have all its officers and men shoot. In those days most of the U. S. fleet was in the Atlantic and the big rifle range for the Atlantic Fleet was at Guantanamo Bay, Cuba.

Captain Harllee was sent down to Guantanamo (Gitmo, as the Navy called it) early in 1915 to stir up interest in small arms firing in the fleet. The range at Gitmo was then the largest in the world, with 286 targets by 1916.

He first reported to Lieutenant Colonel Ben Fuller, the Fleet Marine Officer. His old friend and boss told him that there probably would be no small arms practice by the fleet on the rifle range ashore because it had been made discretionary with the various commanding officers and probably none of them would care to bother with it. But he consented to Harllee visiting the ships with his sales talk.

"Arms and The Man" had written that the sailors had so

many varied duties to perform with their large and small guns and in the management of ships that their rifle practice must be raised to the highest power of production for the time employed. In other words, the method employed must insure that they be given the maximum of knowledge in the minimum of time. This was Bill Harllee's specialty. He said, "Give me one full day!"

His canvass of the battleships resulted in success with only two ships, the Michigan and South Carolina. Lt. McCandless was Gunnery Officer of the Michigan. Lt. Theodore Gordon (Spuds) Ellyson, the famous first naval aviator, was Gunnery Officer of the South Carolina.

The operation began to look like a notable flop for Bill Harllee. Then he thought about the sixteen destroyers in Guantanamo. The lean, hungry looking greyhounds of the sea, with their speed and informality, and tough, can-do crews had a natural appeal to the soldier in Harllee.

But the renowned Captain William S. Sims was in command of the destroyers. He, with the help of Theodore Roosevelt, had done for naval ship gunnery what Harllee had done for Marine small arms gunnery, and he was to win fame as the Vice Admiral afloat commanding all our naval forces overseas in World War I. However, he was reputed to be hostile to Marines and vituperative on the subject. Harllee had considerable misgivings about approaching Sims, but finally decided that he had to do it to succeed and that if Sims talked rough to him that he was capable of responding in like manner.

When he arrived on Sims' flagship he found him with his officers gathered around him apparently quite interested in their talk. Much to Harllee's surprise, Sims received him with dignified gentility, listened attentively, and responded agreeably, all within a few minutes. Sims said he would be pleased, as Harllee had suggested, to send eight men from each destroyer each forenoon and each afternoon until all hands completed the course. Harllee's earlier conception of Sims was, of course, reversed and he found him a highly efficient, capable officer · and a real gentleman.

When Harllee returned to the range he told his assistant and

175

close friend, Lieutenant George Shuler, to prepare for 16 kinds of trouble the next day with that many squads of "flat feet" from the destroyers coming and to ride herd on them and keep them from running wild.

Shuler told him the next day he was wrong about the "flat feet" from the destroyers and that they were regular fellows and it was a pleasure to be with them.

When the word got around from the Michigan and the South Carolina and Sim's destroyers how interesting the small arms course was and how well the course was run, the range became crowded and the problem became one of how to accommodate all candidates. All ships except one battleship participated.

Later in 1915 Harllee was Assistant Executive Officer (assistant officer in charge, no. 2 man) of the National Matches at Jacksonville, Florida. His boss, Col. R.M. Blatchford of the Infantry, wrote the Commandant of the Marine Corps:

> The indefatigable efforts of Captain Harllee prior to the opening of the matches and his services during the matches have been the mainspring of our success—competitors who have attended this year feel they have been served to a better advantage than in any previous National Matches—and I desire to communicate this information to you and give credit to Captain Harllee for the services he has peformed.

Just to show that he was all-American and could get along in Yankee-land as well as in the South, Bill Harllee got the following commendation from the New England Rifle Association on September 7, 1915 in connection with its annual tournament,

> Every man who had had anything to do with the conduct of the tournament, and I believe every competitor in the tournament, will agree that Capt. Harllee's administration was all that could be desired and was undoubtedly the best that this Association has ever had, although we did think that our past tournaments had been run in a very efficient manner.

And to cap it all off, he was appointed a member of the National Board for the Promotion of Rifle Practice and remained such until 1920.

As a result of his National Press Club membership, Bill

Harllee became acquainted with the writer, Mark Sullivan, in 1914. Beginning in 1915 and for several years off and on, both of them lunched daily in the basement grill room of the Willard Hotel, three blocks from the White House, with a "Kitchen Cabinet". This cabinet included Secretary of War Newton Baker; Harllee's West Point Classmate, Oliver P. Newman, then Chairman of the Board of District of Columbia Commissioners; the other two Commissioners, Louis Brownlow and Judge Siddons; Congressman Robert Page of North Carolina; George Creel, the top national publicist for the Wilson Administration; journalist Gilson Gardner, Herbert Quick and other celebrities. It was from men such as these as well as his own experiences and omnivorous reading that Bill Harllee got the information which was the raw material for his later ideas.

XX
AMERICAN
MARKSMANSHIP—
THE NRA—1916

"Presented to Major William C. Harllee by the Members of the Civilian Rifle Teams Present At The National Matches of Nineteen Sixteen State Camp Florida as a Token of Appreciation For His Continuous and Untiring Efforts In Behalf of American Marksmanship."
—Plaque inscription on a grandfathers clock—a gift of which Bill Harllee was inordinately proud.

1916. World War I, then often called "The Great War," was raging in Europe. Millions of men had lost their lives. Most Americans felt it was not their business, did not want to get into it, and reelected Woodrow Wilson President on the slogan "He kept us out of the war."

But "Preparedness" was the watchword for ever increasing numbers of our citizens. And to Harllee, "Preparedness" meant making America a nation of marksmen again.

179

The Marine Corps and the Navy were on track, headed in the right direction with the speed of an express train, so he began to focus most of his attention on the rest of America. He had been actively interested in civilian rifle clubs ever since his earliest days in the shooting game. He had found in Honolulu in 1904 and at the National Matches of 1908-09-10 that even the Marines of those days could learn something from the rifle club shooters. By September of 1916, these clubs numbered about 1,600 and had about 100,000 members. Typical of those times was a lunch of a hundred men at the Merchants Club in Baltimore, at which Bill Harllee started the rifle shooting ball rolling in Maryland.

The members of the rifle clubs, which were organized all over the country, were red blooded outdoorsmen who shot competitively for sport and loved it. Many were prominent in public life. For example, Assistant Secretary of Agriculture Carl Vrooman said at Winthrop in 1916:

> I have often used a shotgun on birds and small game, and I always regarded shooting a rifle at an inanimate target as somewhat of a bore. But even the little experience I have had so far has shown me that I was entirely wrong. It's great sport, and I want to perfect myself in it.

The rifle clubs, together with thousands of individuals, were organized into the National Rifle Association, the NRA. Bill Harllee and the rifle club members liked each other—they were indeed kindred souls—and he found in the NRA his great ally in pursuing his grand dream of making America again a nation of straight shooters. He became a director of the NRA in 1910 and later a lifetime director. He became a vice president in 1916, and the first vice president (there was then no executive vice president) from 1917 to 1920. He was extremely active in those positions in the Association.

The NRA had a long and honorable record of promoting American marksmanship, dating back to November 17, 1871.

Major General Ambrose Burnside, the Civil War hero, was the first President of the NRA, which started in New York. In 1874, the Association commenced participation in international shooting matches, particularly with Irish, English and Scottish teams. These events attracted thousands of spectators and front page newspaper publicity. The American teams won far more than their share of the matches.

From 1883 to 1884, former President of the United States, General Ulysses S. Grant, was President of the NRA. For the next two years General Philip H. Sheridan held the job.

In 1903, President Theodore Roosevelt wired his congratulations to the NRA for the American victory at the International Matches held at Bisley, England. In 1904, Roosevelt started the custom of writing a congratulatory letter to the winner of the President's Match, the Individual American Military Rifle Championship Match.

Both Congress and President Roosevelt heavily supported the NRA in those days, passing laws in 1903 authorizing the establishment of the National Board for the Promotion of Rifle Practice and in 1904 authorizing the sale of Government surplus ammunition and other military equipment to rifle clubs.

T.R. remained a life-long supporter of the NRA and in 1907 became a lifetime member.

A footnote of interest here was the performance of the NRA shooter Mrs. Elizabeth Servaty (Plinky) Topperwein, not as famous as Annie Oakley, but possibly the best marksman of her sex who ever lived. In 1906, she broke 485 out of 500 clay pigeons in a gusty wind at the Texas Gun Club in San Antonio. She could clip tossed coins consistently with the pistol, using either hand. She and her husband, Adolph, comprised the most spectacular husband and wife shooting team in history.

It is interesting to note that Annie Oakley won a shooting match with Frank E. Butler, a vaudeville star, and then married him. She once shot a cigarette from the mouth of the German Crown Prince (later Wilhelm II) at his invitation. One wonders if the course of history might have been changed if just that one time her marksmanship had not been so good. But according to the World Book, she could hit a playing card with the thin edge toward her at 90 feet.

To illustrate the national interest in shooting, a galley shooting organization called "The National Schuetzen Bund" boasted 130,000 members in 160 clubs located in all parts of America in 1907. In May of that year it attracted nearly 6,000 delegates to its convention in Charleston, South Carolina.

In 1909, the NRA suggested that a match among the six public school rifle teams in the nation's capital would be an inspiration and an example to schools in other parts of the country. President Taft, who was vacationing in Georgia, immediately wired the NRA,

> I approve the teaching under proper regulations of rifle shooting to our boys in advanced grades.

In 1909, Colonel John Jacob Astor presented a magnificent silver cup as a trophy to be held by the winner of the 42 schoolboy teams in a match sponsored by the NRA in 1910. Later that year, the NRA affiliated 73 new school teams.

In 1910, a law was enacted which authorized the War Department to issue free rifles and ammunition to organized rifle clubs. The National Board for the Promotion of Rifle Practice was the agency for distribution of the free material, and affiliation with the NRA was a prerequisite for qualification.

By 1912, the NRA had grown tremendously in stature. Its marksmen had competed against and beaten in direct competition the finest riflemen of five continents, in some cases on their home ranges and in their own specialties. The Scandinavians, for example, had competitive "deer shoots." In a relatively few years the NRA had emerged from an Eastern-oriented organization that was national largely in name into a strong association with a year round program that extended into nearly every state in the Union.

In 1913, the NRA made the decision to reinstate the coveted Hilton Trophy in the Association's annual matches, adding this to their Wimbledon Cup Match, the Individual and Team Palma Matches, and the Herrick Trophy Match. The matches of 1913 exceeded in scope, size, and world-wide interest any that had been held in America. France, Switzerland, Sweden, Argentina, Peru and Canada sent their best marksmen to pit their skills against the Yanks. Canada had a team from each province, and the United States had a team from every state except five. With the District of Columbia and Hawaii and those from the regular services, this meant that 49 American teams were competing.

In 1913, Harllee had the Winthrop Range opened to local civilian rifle teams and members of the NRA. He was beginning to realize his dream.

By 1914, more than 15,000 schoolboy and college riflemen had been or were then enrolled in the NRA tournament programs.

The NRA tournaments were developing some phenomenal marksmen. In 1914, T. K. "Tackhole" Lee ran up an amazing score of 1999 out of a possible 2000 in the National Matches and 500 out of a possible 500 shooting small-bore against the British! In 1915, he made a 2250 out of 2250!

Col. William Libbey, NRA president (1915–1921).

In 1914, the Boys Scouts of America, as a result of NRA efforts, resumed issuing merit badges in marksmanship.

The type of man the NRA had for a President in 1915 is worth noting. He was Lt. Col. William Libbey, a member of the Executive Committee since 1913. Dr. Libbey, sixty and white-bearded, was at once the most scholarly and most versatile of all the NRA presidents up to that time. He held a Doctor of Science degree from Princeton, where he was Professor of Physical Sciences and Director of the Museum of Geology and Archaeology. He was a Fellow of the Royal Geographic Society and Royal Geological Society of Great Britain and of their national counterparts in France. He was an officer or member of a dozen American scientific organizations. He was an author of two books and a vice president of two banks. He was also an expert rifleman and since 1908 had served as assistant inspector of rifle practice for New Jersey. Bill Harllee became a life long friend of this fine man.

In 1915, Thomas Alva Edison became a life member of the NRA, one of 15,000 new members brought in during a 3 months' drive. That year there were also NRA rifle clubs in the plants of General Electric, Goodyear Rubber, Willys-Overland and Jordan Marsh Company. The Association affiliated sixty clubs in the Order of Maccabees alone.

In 1915, Bill Harllee had pushed through his idea of welcoming not only civilians, but women to Winthrop. The principal idea behind this was to attract as many men as possible—more men would come for the day's outing if they could bring their wives, sweethearts (those were the days of "Let Me Call You Sweetheart"), and families. But he also welcomed the ladies as shooters on the firing line. He was familiar with the tradition of Annie Oakley as well as of that of Captain Lee Hall. The Sunday Star of September 28, 1915 wrote in a story headlined "HOME CLUB RIFLEMEN CAPT. HARLLEE'S GUESTS":

Scores made: Miss M. P. Thyson 194; Miss E. A. Lancaster 141.
In one string of ten shots Miss Thyson made 47 out of a possible 50, making six bull's-eyes in succession. Miss Louden, in her first attempt with a machine gun, out of a string of fifty shots made 31 bull's-eyes and 12 fours (next best to a bull's-eye).

The front page of the Sunday April 30, 1916 issue of The Washington Times carried a story headlined "10,000 WASHINGTON MEN AND WOMEN GETTING FIRST PREPAREDNESS LESSON" and again on its first page wrote,

A frail little wisp of a woman manfully blazing away at the targets on the range last Friday, voiced the general sentiment of all her sex who have visited Winthrop.
The nine pound Krag which she was using had recoiled heavily, but because she had held it perfectly, she was unhurt, except for a bit of jolting.
"Hurt, honey?" her husband inquired anxiously.
"Not a bit," she replied, laughing. "This is the best sport I have had in a long time."
And the ladies became acquainted with plenty of such lore as "Never go out without a match" (to use to blacken with smoke the gun sights in a bright sunlight that might cause too much sheen on the sights.)

With Bill Harllee's help, the Virginia Slims baby had already started to come a long way.

In 1916, Harllee and the NRA worked together to write and push through the passage of Section 113 of the National Defense Act of 1916, which earmarked $300,000 to promote civilian marksmanship training. It authorized the War Department to distribute appropriate arms and ammunition to organized civilian rifle clubs, under rules established by the National Board for the Promotion of Rifle Practice. Funds were provided for the operation of Government rifle ranges and the transportation of military instructors to assist civilian rifle clubs. It opened all military rifle ranges to civilian shooters. It provided $60,000 to transport civilian teams to the National Matches. Finally, it created the Office of the Director of Civilian Marksmanship under the National Board.

In 1916, Harllee's "Winthrop Idea" received national attention. It had been kicked off by a parade of notables firing on the range at Winthrop to start the publicity rolling. Included were such personages as Secretary of the Navy Josephus Daniels, Secretary of War Newton Baker, Secretary of the Interior Franklin K. Lane, Assistant Secretary of the Navy Franklin D. Roosevelt, Assistant Secretary of Agriculture Carl Vrooman, Assistant Secretary of War Ingraham, Congressman Oliver of Alabama, District of Columbia Commissioner Oliver Newman and Lincoln Steffens, the great "muckraker". Films were taken for training and publicity purposes which included all of these men and Bill Harllee. This was one of the earliest uses of visual aids for education.

With the interest of the public aroused by the shooting of the "big shots," Harllee opened the range to all who desired to learn to shoot, and civilians, male and female, were welcomed if they were interested in shooting. High school cadets, militiamen, members of shooting clubs and other organizations, as well as individual citizens, went to Winthrop and were instructed in the art of shooting. They were assigned instructors who taught them how to handle the rifle and revolver, and they fired the regular courses. They were supplied with rifles, pistols, and other needs for shooting. They were even loaned

Franklin D. Roosevelt, then Assistant Secretary of the Navy, firing on the Marine Corps Rifle Range at Winthrop, Maryland, 26 July, 1916. FDR knew how to handle the 1903 Springfield rifle and he was active in the National Board for the Promotion of Rifle Practice.

Government notables fired on the range at Winthrop and supported civilian marksmanship training. On this visit in 1916, they witnessed demonstrations of the Benet-Mercie machine rifle and the Lewis light machine gun.
Left to right, Newton D. Baker, Secretary of War; Franklin D. Roosevelt, Ass't Secretary of the Navy; Franklin K. Lane, Secretary of the Interior; and, Henry L. Stimson, Statesman and later Secretary of War.

shooting clothes and given a nominal pay of thirty cents a day, with tent, mattress and blankets free. Winthrop attracted the attention of many of the young men of Washington and many young women, too.

The Winthrop Idea kept its followers busy every minute of the day. The trip to the range was made by a steamer, the Barry, which made a three hour run. The time aboard the ship was used for highly efficient preliminary instruction.

As soon as they left the wharf the instruction began. Sergeant Andrews of the Marine Corps, who was one of the best shots in the United States and who fired on the Corps team in many of the National Matches, took charge of part of the school aboard the steamer with the help of two corporals. These non-commissioned officers taught small groups of students, explaining to them the safety precautions, the proper method of holding a rifle in all the positions of the NRA qualification courses, and the use of the sling to reduce recoil. They then demonstrated how sights should be set; how to squeeze the trigger and snap in; how the rifle was loaded and how the

The "Winthrop Idea" starts aboard the steamer, Barry. Preliminary instruction was given on the 3 hour trip to the Range. Here, Bill Harllee oversees a session with one of his Marine instructors.

breech bolt was worked. Then the pupils were instructed in handling the targets and acting as scorekeepers. In another part of the ship, a Corpsman was giving a lesson in first aid, demonstrating how bandages were applied, how splints could be improvised, and how wounds should be treated with Navy first aid packages.

When this preliminary instruction was completed, the steamer arrived at the Winthrop Range, and each man and woman aboard had a good working idea of what was expected when he or she went on the firing line to qualify with actual service ammunition.

Then the student had plenty of chance to shoot on the range with the help of a coach. If he had brought his wife or sweetheart along, she could shoot also, but at that time most of them prepared picnics and had a social event in the open air. The mess hall was available to those who didn't want to picnic—lunch cost fifteen cents.

Included in Captain Harllee's notice to new shooters at Winthrop was the following:

> Never offer any man in the military service a tip. It is offensive, and he will not take it. He esteems it a pleasure to welcome you to Winthrop and to make the shooting game attractive to you.

Harllee's attitude towards the shooting game was further exemplified by his remarks before a meeting of the Board of the Directors of the NRA at which he strongly objected to a return to the earlier practice of charging entrance fees for the National Matches. He succeeded in fighting this off as a move which smacked of money-making.

All this was done on Saturdays and Sundays. When the student qualified as a marksman, which he did before too long under such auspices, he usually was anxious to continue and qualify as a sharpshooter and eventually as an expert rifleman. His good American sporting and competitive instincts had been aroused. He had the feeling he had added to his value as a citizen, should he be called upon to defend his country.

Bill Harllee's idea was to spread the use of this Winthrop Idea across the whole country by using first the state rifle ranges and then building others in the low cost manner in which he was such an expert. He figured only sixty well trained soldiers would be needed at each range.

He strongly believed that this would be a good measure of preparedness with little expense and interference with civilian vocations. He recommended that certificates be issued to marksmen, with copies kept in Washington. Movies were shown in local theaters in Baltimore and many other cities explaining the rifle range attractions. Thus the shooting game was made attractive to American men and to American women. Such was the Winthrop Idea.

With regard to the training of Marine and Navy coaches and instructors during the week at Winthrop, which was essential, they mastered rifles, pistols, machine guns and three inch field guns. They qualified under Army, Navy and Marine Corps regulations and learned every detail of range work.

They worked hard, very hard, but they had excellent food from the range's own garden, poultry farm and dairy. If they had any time off, the fishing was good and canoes on the Potomac as well as a baseball diamond were available.

They were delighted that there was no pomp and circumstance—there is definitely a place for that in the military but not on a rifle range. Any kind of shooting clothes were allowed. Most wore dungarees, old shirts and Marine campaign (peaked) hats.

So if Ted Lewis had asked his famous question "Is Everybody Happy" at Winthrop, the answer from Marines, sailors, civilians and women would have been—Yes.

But when could the Winthrop Idea be spread across the country?

XXI
ON BEHALF OF
AMERICAN
MARKSMANSHIP
FDR—1916

*I thought you and I enthusiastically
agreed that the way to get the men out
to shoot was to let the ladies accompany
them and also shoot if they so desire.*
—FDR to WCH, May 8, 1916

Monday morning, May 8, 1916. Captain Harllee received
word that Assistant Secretary of the Navy Franklin D. Roosevelt
would like to see him right away.

Harllee duly reported.

"Good morning, Mr. Roosevelt."

This was before Franklin Roosevelt had contracted polio. He
was 34 years old; tall, handsome, athletic, fond of outdoor
sports. He played golf weekly and sailed whenever he could.
Harllee had interested him in shooting at the rifle range at
Winthrop, and he had qualified as a "Sharpshooter." The 38
year old Marine captain was on easy terms with the younger
New York aristocrat. Roosevelt liked what he was doing and
his style of doing it, in spite of the obstructions he had to face.

Mr. Roosevelt led off.

"Good morning, Captain Harllee. No, it's not so good. I thought we had everything rolling along just beautifully at Winthrop. You know how enthusiastic I am about the range and how I've backed you up. And now we've got this article in the Washington Herald this morning that says that considerable feelings exist among the rifle club members because of the order prohibiting women on the range. It says that most of the fifty clubs using the range will pass resolutions of protest. I've also heard that a number of the ladies didn't even know about the order until they got down to the steamer yesterday and then their men had to decide whether to leave them and go on down to the range or cancel out themselves. A fine mess. I thought you and I had enthusiastically agreed that the way to get the men out to shoot was to let the ladies accompany them, and even to shoot if they so desire. In fact, the press had just reported that one-third of the local 10,000 rifle club members are women. What in the world happened?"

Harllee replied, "I'm madder than you are about it; General Barnett (Major General George Barnett, Commandant of the Marine Corps) put out the order over my most violent objections."

Said Mr. Roosevelt, "Ah, well, I didn't think you would be responsible for this. What reason did he give?"

"He gave as the reason that the women would be too hard to control in an emergency. But that's ridiculous. We haven't had and won't have any emergencies in which we and their menfolk can't control them. I don't know what the real reason is."

"So," replied Roosevelt, "We'll fix that up right away. I'm going to write him a note for you to deliver telling him to revoke that order and also to go with you on the steamer to Winthrop tomorrow to find out a bit more about what's going on there. Ha! How do you like that, Bill?"

"I don't like it at all, Mr. Roosevelt. Have him revoke the order, fine. But don't tell him to go to the range with me and don't ask me to deliver the note. He's a kindly sort of a man, and he can do some good work for the Marine Corps, but he's already sore as hell at me for pushing so hard on shooting, and I don't want the Commandant mad at me. I've had plenty of experience with that."

Roosevelt laughed. "Oh, don't worry about General Barnett."

Harllee, "Well, it's still just too rough for me to deliver such a message to him. It isn't right and you know it."

Roosevelt agreed. "All right, but I'll have a note sent over by messenger."

"Frankly, Mr. Roosevelt, I'm delighted you are having the order about the ladies rescinded. That was really a monkey wrench in our business of whipping up enthusiasm for the range."

Unfortunately, the next day when General Barnett went to Winthrop with him, Harllee reported he had never seen an angrier man. Nevertheless, "The Winthrop Idea" flourished, and to Harllee, that was what was important.

In 1916 when Harllee and the National Rifle Association were drafting the legislation (Section 113 of the National Defense Act of 1916) creating the Office of the Director of Civilian Marksmanship to promote marksmanship in America, he arranged with Senator Duncan U. Fletcher of Florida, an old friend who was on the Senate Committee on Military Affairs, to sponsor the legislation. When the bill was before the committee, Senator DuPont of Delaware, at the instigation of the War Department, which was violently opposed to creating that office, made so much obstruction that Senator Fletcher told Harllee that it was difficult to carry on. The Marine officer then informed Mr. Roosevelt, with whom he then kept in close contact. Mr. Roosevelt told him that he would make a special trip during the weekend to see Senator Dupont at his home in Delaware. There he could have a better talk with him than was possible in the Washington atmosphere. The following Monday Roosevelt informed Harllee that he had persuaded Senator DuPont not to oppose their plan any more, and the legislation subsequently passed and the office was created, much to the surprise of the War Department.

Franklin Roosevelt approved an order on September 19, 1916, appointing Captain Harllee Assistant Executive Officer (second in charge) of the National Matches, held at Jacksonville again that year. After these matches, four hundred civilian riflemen signed the following letter to the White House and War Department:

> The undersigned members of civilian rifle teams participating in the National Rifle Matches of 1916, held at State Camp Grounds, Florida, and which said teams were officially selected from the organized 93,000 civilian riflemen of the United States hereby—through our duly authorized representative, M.A. Winter, of Washington, D.C., president of the largest rifle club in the United States and director-elect of the National Rifle Association,—respectfully request that Major (then Captain) William C. Harllee, U.S.M.C., be given the appointment to the office of Director of Civilian Rifle Practice, recently created by Act of Congress.

The press headlined "HARLLEE IS CHOICE OF CIVILIAN TEAMS."

There was no doubt that Harllee was the choice of civilian riflemen for the post of Director of Civilian Marksmanship. Secretary of War Newton Baker decided to appoint him. However, General Albert Mills, who had been Harllee's Superintendent and nemesis at West Point, was on duty in the War Department and had ingratiated himself with Mr. Baker. He persuaded the Secretary of the War not to appoint any Marine, arguing that the Army was much bigger than the Marine Corps and that the Director should be an Army officer, although the law allowed either and the position had been created for the Marine officer, Harllee.

This happened in spite of the fact that nobody even remotely connected with the Army had anything to do with enacting the law and obtaining the appropriation. The responsibility for the work and job were not even claimed by the Army in time for it to request authority and funds from Congress.

Harllee was not really disappointed, as he could still work hard with the Army, Navy, Marine Corps, and the NRA to teach America how to shoot. He was made a vice president of the NRA that year, and he had an excellent spot in the Navy Department, which included the Marine Corps, and on the

National Board for Promotion of Rifle Practice from which to work. He was Recorder of the National Board in 1916.

However, what did bother him was that the hierarchy at the War Department never did really want a Director of Civilian Marksmanship. They probably felt they would be lucky to have some marksmen in the Army and didn't share Harllee's dream of a nation of civilian as well as military marksmen. In any event, they controlled the job and shrouded it ever after in an obscurity that "The Winthrop Idea" had never known.

Major William C. Harllee sketched on the Firing Line at the 1916 National Matches in Jacksonville, Florida, Sketched by C. Duher, 71st New York Regiment and published in the Nov. 2, 1916 Arms and The Man.

195

*Ella Harllee pictured in all her beauty and grace in the High Society days of 1916.
She wears one of the elaborate dance gowns that were fashionable during that time.*

XXII
HIGH SOCIETY—1916

All was not work in the halcyon days of the Wilson administration before we entered the war. Through the good offices of Ella Harllee's Aunt Birdie and her husband, Cone Johnson, Solicitor General of the State Department, the Harllees were included in a group of 25 couples who assembled each Wednesday night at various places— generally the best hotels in Washington, such as the New Willard and Mayflower, for dancing and refreshments. They were the youngest couple and the only one from the armed forces. Also in the club were Miss Margaret Wilson, daughter of the President; Rear Admiral Cary Grayson, the President's physician and than a bachelor; Senator McKellar of Tennessee, the only other bachelor; Secretary of Interior and Mrs. Andreus Jones; Mr. Ord Preston, later President of the Union Trust Bank, and Mrs. Preston, and Joseph W. Davies, later U.S. Ambassdor to Russia and his wife.

When the Wednesday night dance sessions happened to fall on a patriotic holiday, Beau Harllee let himself be persuaded to wear his uniform—the one called "mess jacket" was the one appropriate to such occasions. The jacket itself for a major of the line was dark blue in color with scarlet lining, about a foot of gold braid on each sleeve, and plenty of gold braid in the "shoulder knots" and on the collar. What with the sky blue trousers with scarlet stripes, he made a colorful addition to the party and was about as much out of character as he could get.

Ella's dance frocks were elaborate, but no more so than others of the time. On the night referred to above the gown was made of mauve chiffon with a very full skirt gathered around the waist over satin of the same shade. At the bottom were small ruffles of silver tissue. The top was satin with chiffon draping the decolletage and tiny sleeves. At one side a silver rose with small buds made a shower effect above and below the waist. With this she wore mauve stockings and silver tissue slippers. With her auburn hair and green eyes the effect was most pleasing.

Miss Margaret Wilson wore a pale blue gown of tulle pailleted in silver and crystal beads, with a draped tunic and girdle of satin with a yellow rose at one side.

One night when the dance group (sometimes referred to as "The Administration Dancing Class") met at the New Willard, Beau Harllee was dancing with Margaret Wilson and remarked, tongue in cheek,

"I noticed that the paper said Mrs. Galt (President Wilson's fiancee) is a ninth generation descendant of Pocahontas. I can establish that Ella is an eleventh generation descendant of that Indian Princess. Do you think that makes us kissing cousins?"

Replied Miss Wilson,

"Unless you want to get transferred away from Washington to some place like Guam or out of the Marine Corps entirely, I wouldn't try kissing Mrs. Galt."

Beau Harllee rejoined,

"I think you're right, and I'll remember that when I want to try some other line of endeavor."

More seriously, Will Harllee wrote later in "Kinfolks,"

> Enchantment of Indian descent arose long after the time of ravages by Indians had ceased. In times and places of their ravages they were called savages.
>
> Incidentally, it might be said to the credit of the Indians that they devastated to defend their lands and for revenge, instead of to exploit white people. More proper pride can be taken in descent from their chieftains than from pale faced plutocrats who will not fight but who, by subtle and safer ways, have plundered their own people—which Indians never did.

Margaret Wilson was a lady of great spirit and a talented professional singer, who in 1918 went to France to sing for the troops. She had studied at the Peabody Conservatory and had made her professional debut with the Chicago Symphony Orchestra. She made concert tours on behalf of the American Red Cross and sang at recitals and as a soloist. For a period before President Wilson married Edith Bolling Galt, Margaret was the Presiding Lady at the White House.

Wilson went to sleep election night of 1916 with the New York Times announcing a victory for his opponent, Hughes. It was Margaret who brought him the news the next morning that the Times had an extra out expressing doubts about the election, but stating that there were indications of a Democratic victory. To this he replied with repartee of the day:

"Tell that to the Marines."

On Friday after the Tuesday election word came in of Wilson's 3,773 vote majority in California, giving him a majority in the Electoral College and winning the election for him. He had had a 594,000 popular majority.

Harllee joined the Chevy Chase Club in 1916, a country club just over the District of Columbia line into Maryland and in those days an excellent place to socialize and enjoy fine athletic facilities. He was proposed by his old patron and friend, Major General George F. Elliott, former Commandant of the Marine Corps. He was seconded by Brigadier General George C. Richards, Paymaster General of the Marine Corps.

The New York press stated that:

> The membership of the Chevy Chase Club includes everybody who is anybody in Washington, Cabinet officers, leading Senators and Representatives, public officials, army and navy officers, and nearly all of the Ambassadors and other designations of the Diplomatic Corps are on the list.

Presidents Theodore Roosevelt, Taft, and Wilson were members of the club and active there. President and Mrs. Roosevelt came often for daily horseback rides over an abundance of artificial and natural jumps. On October 20, 1913, Franklin D. Roosevelt joined it, as later did Douglas MacArthur, Warren G. Harding, and Dwight D. Eisenhower, the latter two before they became President of the United States.

Here was a place where the rough Marine could mingle with the great and powerful without waging the private and unauthorized wars upon them to which he was accustomed.

On October 13, 1916 a beloved daughter, Ella Fulmore Harllee, named after her mother, was born to Will and Ella Harllee. She followed a very successful career in education and communications.

XXIII
THE CASE FOR AN ACTIVE AMERICAN ARMY—1917

The American people are not pusillanimous; they have not lost their military virtue . . .

There is an instinct in young men which inspires an ambition to be a soldier, and plenty of young men are willing and anxious to be of service if it can only be done in an honorable and respectable way . . .
—Major William C. Harllee in testimony before the U.S. Senate Military Affairs Committee, January 8, 1917.

The Commandant of the Marine Corps and the Chief of Staff of the Army agreed, "This man Harllee has got to be given a general court martial and thrown out of the Marine Corps."

Here's how it came about:

In 1916, the American press was headlining "PREPARED-

201

NESS" just in case, in spite of eveything, the United States got into the war it didn't want to get into. There were, of course, problems with "Preparedness." One of these was, according to the Boston Record of November 27, 1916:

> The failure of the Hay Army Bill; which made the National Guard our main dependence, and with 1,000 National Guard Officers resigning their jobs, a new plan for a United States Army is needed . . . a modification of the Swiss system or some other idea. One scheme is offered by Major William C. Harllee of the United States Marine Corps.

Although no one could ever possibly doubt that he was a man of action, Bill Harllee, ever since he had become an adult, had done an enormous amount of reading: military history and technical material, the classics (he was known to have a "gift for language"), religion, political history and economics.

His combat experiences in the Philippines, China, Cuba and Mexico combined with his continual discussions with the gentlemen of the press and the political leaders who frequented his rifle ranges and the National Press Club, had together, with his original turn of mind, produced some very clear-cut thoughts on his part as to what kind of an army we should have. These thoughts were not at all pleasing to the leaders of our Army, who naturally favored the status quo. But his ideas captured the imagination of some others, so he began to accept speaking engagements and allowing the press to publish his views. He had always felt that despite the fact he was in the honorable profession of arms and a man under orders that he was still entitled to express fully his beliefs. He had the courage of his convictions and believed that he had made his theories work out in the past, even though they were not those of the top brass.

His old Florida friend, Senator Fletcher of the Senate Military Affairs Committee, heard so much about all this that he talked to Bill Harllee on the subject and decided his proposals should be put on the record in the form of official testimony before the Committee.

It was so done on January 8, 1917. The proposals made by Harllee on that solemn occasion were unique and so well expressed that his statement before the U.S. Senate Military Affairs Committee is reproduced here in full:

THE CHAIRMAN. The committee will hear Maj. William C. Harllee. Please state your name and rank.

MAJ. HARLLEE. My name is William C. Harllee; I am a major in the United States Marine Corps.

THE CHAIRMAN. Major, you were requested to come before the committee, and you have some views on this subject of universal military training. I have talked with you about the matter personally, and we will be glad to have your views, whatever they may be, stated in your own way.

SENATOR THOMAS. How long have you been serving in that branch of the service?

MAJ. HARLLEE. For 17 years.

I belong to the Marine Corps, the soldier corps of the Navy. I have served in the Volunteer Army as private, corporal, sergeant, and first sergeant during the Philippine Insurrection and as a cadet at the Military Academy at West Point for 2 years and for 17 years as an officer of the Marine Corps, appointed from civil life.

Instead of attempting to militarize America and to bring America to the ideals of the present military orthodoxy, why not Americanize our military institution and bring it to the ideals of America?

When you have brought the military system in harmony with things American, you will find a different attitude toward it and no necessity for such drastic measures as compulsory or universal service.

The American people are not pusillanimous; they have not lost their military virtue; they need no system bolstered up by courts, jails, and military constabularies to bring them to a proper preparation for national defense.

Our present military institution violates some of our best American traditions. Purge it on the distasteful things, make it business like, adopt in it accepted American methods, and you will find thousands of willing men—more than you can take care of for military training. They are not willing, however, to enter it as it now stands. I interpret it as a protest against our methods and not as any indication that American manhood is on the decline.

Our military institution is not an American development. It remains substantially unchanged since it was imported at the beginning of our government from England and continental

Europe, from countries where there were two classes of men—gentlemen and common men. The officers came from the gentlemen class, the enlisted men represent the common caste. The system fitted such social structure, but it does not fit America. There is only one class of men here, except in the military establishment.

The law recognizes two separate and distinct classes of men in our military service. They are absolutely separate and distinct. There is a line of cleavage between them. Pride and self-respect are the best elements of military character. Caste crushes them both. Napoleon destroyed caste because it injured the business. The impulse which the French Revolution gave to the French Army has never reached the American Regular Establishment. There was no caste in the Confederate Army nor in the citizen Army of the United States in the sixties. Why breed it in barracks armies to serve as a model for citizen soldiery?

The thing above all others which prevents men from entering the military service is the oath of enlistment. It is an oath of bondage. Any other employer who contracted with men on this basis would be guilty of peonage—a felony under the law of the nation which practices it itself. In my own experience in recruiting I found men unwilling to subscribe to such an oath. It is not fair to men who are unfamiliar with the military service to ask them to enter into any such agreement and it is not necessary. There is an instinct in young men which inspires an ambition to be a soldier, and plenty of men are willing and anxious to be of service if it can only be done in an honorable and respectable way—witness the men who went to Plattsburg—but they are not willing to be branded as men of a lower caste or in time of peace to subscribe to an oath of bondage.

Unhappy or dissatisfied men are of no service to a military or any other body and it is better policy to let them go, and then if everybody should go, to inquire into the cause and seek the remedy. I am opposed to universal service or compulsory service or any other kind of service than that rendered by willing men. I am opposed to it because dumb driven cattle cannot be taught or trained. I am too proud to be comrade with Mouldy, Shadow, Wart, Feeble, and Bull Calf in a Falstaffian host. Like King Henry rather "proclaim it to the host that he who hath no stomach for the fight let him depart for we would not serve in that man's company who fears his fellowship to serve with us." The Persians had universal service. The Greeks did not. It is not the size of your host but it is the quality of it which adds luster to the arms. Unwilling men burden armies, eat its substance, retard its action, and give it panic. Even if there were enough jails and Federal constabularies to enforce universal service without riots among a people it would not be good business to do it. The profession of arms ought to be honorable; spare it from contamination by Mouldys and Bull Calfs.

There is nothing subtle about military training. It does not require years to train a soldier. The individual instruction is simple. It can be done in weeks, and—with the proper machinery developed—in less time than any army can cross any ocean. It was done in the volunteer regiments which went to the Philippines in 1899. Nobody there ever discounted the work of the volunteers. It is done in the Marine Corps all the time. It was done at Plattsburg in a month. To cook, to bivouac, to march, to move from column of march into line of fight, to dig, to shoot, to give first-aid treatment, these are the salient points of a real soldiers' instruction. Yet they are not the features practiced in the life of the barracks.

The art of living afield and the art of handling men afield is not learned in the barracks. Compare your mental picture of life and conditions at barracks with your mental picture of life in the trenches, or anywhere in Europe today, or life in the armies here in the sixties. Can you see any similarity?

The barracks life in idleness impairs the usefulness of a man for the soldier or any other business. It atrophies the talents of its officers. It accustoms all to things not pertinent to the real soldier business and trains men in the wrong habits. It untrains men, or overtrains them. Few officers can withstand many years of this so-called training and preserve their usefulness. Grant, Sherman, and Jackson had but few years of this kind of training. Lee, J.E. Johnston, and Longstreet, were staff officers and had little of the barracks training. Sheridan, Hood, and Stuart were young men who had received but little of it. It is a significant thing how many of the effective officers of both armies of our Civil War fall into these four classes: First, officers who had a few years' service in the Regular Army—and part of that in the War with Mexico—and then went out into civil life; second, those who, while they remained on the payroll, were staff officers and avoided the influences of this so-called training; third, young men who had been in but a few years when the war began; and, fourth, men who had always been civilians when the war began—and it is significant how few of those who had spent their lives in the garrisons arose to the occasion in real war.

My plan for removing the objectionable features and for furnishing a system which will develop habits of organizing real armies and a system of real training is this:

A new army each year. An active army—give it a good name, so it will be proud of its name. Its period of training to be not over six months, perhaps shorter, to accommodate it to the vacation period of colleges; have no oath of enlistment; pay its lowest grade respectable pay, but withhold all except a nominal monthly sum until the end of the period. If anyone wants to quit let him quit, but without compensation. On the other hand, if anyone is not desirable simply discharge him on the same basis, and not resort to jails, etc., to try to reform him or make him obedient. One month at barracks rendezvous for individual instruction, the remainder of the time afield. At the end of the period after marching back to the rendezvous, discharge everybody and tie no strings to them.

Equip it with nothing but working clothes, a gun, some ammunition, a bag for carrying rations, suitable cooking utensils, a water bottle and a blanket.

At the time of discharge reappoint the leaders for the next year. Rearrange the present grades so that the commander of 10 men would be officer in as strict a sense as any other commander and as proud of his job. Appoint him in the same way and give him a respectable salary. The other commanders appointed at the same time, each grade selected by the next higher commander under whom they are to serve, and to be selected from the next lower grade so that an officer must advance a grade each year or go out. This would send into civil life each year officers experienced in all grades, who would have been through the process necessary when we have to form volunteers into armies. It would furnish rapid advancement to young men of demonstrated capacity.

Those who select their own subordinates could be relied upon to select the proper men, because their own changes for future selection would depend upon the work of these men. The only route to the command of this army should be through its ranks. This would dignify service in the ranks.

After the discharge of the army and the selection of the next year's leaders, these leaders could be organized in a school and taught special subjects and advanced military work and be given a normal course in teaching for their next year's work, and a suitable time before the next year's army was to be assembled they could be the force which would recruit this army. And if they fail to recruit their armies under this plan drop them from the payroll.

After one month's individual instruction, the different parts of the army to move out without any tents and with but few wagons and spend the remainder of the time afield at bivuoac and on the march, assembling with other bodies forming larger bodies and moving toward the Government reservations of land where field exercises with actual armies instead of imaginary armies would operate against each other.

An army thus afield would accumulate field habits instead of barracks habits, would furnish the staff an opportunity to cater to actual armies and discover their habits and needs. Federal hospitals could be established all over the country, connected with such a system and also serve as public hospitals.

This army would have no dress uniforms, no garrison life to foster caste. Most of its officers would be without families or dependents and there would be no problem of taking care of their families. It would breed no permanent military class to live on the Government forever, for even its generals would have passed through its processes and into civil life before they became too old to begin civilian careers. Some could go into the permanent staff. There would be no retired list. Such an army would commend itself to business like Americans. It would not be suspected of loafing. It would have no caste—no bondage. It would be thoroughly American. It would furnish a reliable supply of tested leaders and would accustom us to the practice of efficiently using the material which must inevitably be the material for America's wars.

Training nowadays seems to run to getting into a camp with tents. Lee's army had no tents, neither did Napoleon's, and I venture to say that you will find but few tents in Europe today— armies which cannot live afield without tents are not armies— they are camping parties. Caesar tells us that the Gauls did not sleep under a roof for seven years. An army which intends to move cannot encumber itself with tents—and living in tents is not real training for real service.

So little preparation for real service have we had that our field service regulations anticipate connecting with the wagons for rations every day. Men can carry on their persons a week's supply of a simple ration and an army whose habits tie it to a wagon train is not the active army I have been picturing to you.

One of the false ideas which develop among peace-time and barracks soldiery is the fetish for regulation equipment. The soldier needs but little equipment, and as soon as he gets afield he quickly divests himself of everything superfluous. He needs a gun, some ammunition, a blanket, something to tote and cook his rations in, and a water bottle. It doesn't make any difference what is the pattern of his bag or his frying pan, or even his blanket. The only thing that must be of a standard pattern is that his ammunition must fit the gun. When we get down to real business we will be glad to have him bring his blanket, his bag, and his frying pan from home with him—and we won't quibble over the cut of his uniform. This idea is not strange if you will picture to yourself the armies of the sixties, or the men in Europe today.

The true discipline is not the kind which reduces the man to the level of a horse, teaches him to obey and do what he is told and nothing else, and makes within him a fear of his officers and of the law. Such a discipline would not serve you in time of danger.

Real discipline is the discipline which comes from comradeship and community of interest. Active armies are always disciplined. Idle bodies are never so. The joy of labor is the panacea of discipline. Men should be trained to give expression to their thoughts and to depart from instructions in order to accomplish the purpose. An intelligent cooperation is superior to dumb and unreasoning obedience, and the men who are trained to abandon reason are not the kind who possess the true discipline.

Do not put your faith in any system of organizing reserves. When a man separates from the military service let him go without any strings upon him. No man can tell what his condition of life will be in the future, whether he can abandon his civilian pursuits or not. Industrial life in America is restless, men move from place to place. It is a difficult operation to collect men after they have gone different ways and identified themselves in different pursuits. It is easier to start fresh and accept those who offer themselves and want to be accepted. Such a plan automatically accommodates itself to industrial conditions. Only those men who can disengage from industry will then serve. If you attempt to forcibly disengage men from their places in industrial life you will have friction.

America needs not a nation in arms, for we have seen what a nation in arms has brought to humanity, but needs a system and working habits by which willing men, the only kind who are not a burden to an establishment, can be made by American methods into an efficient army—a system which will furnish leaders and teachers who know how to lead and teach and who have practiced the art of organizing, leading, and teaching real armies for real service.

Whatever machinery you build up, whatever monopolies are created for the ground floor people, we will find that in true need new men will spring up into leadership; brave and willing men will gather around them as they did in 1861 and 1898, and unless your machinery is simple and direct it will fail and new and vigorous bodies will spring from the wreckage of your machinery, and you will eventually accept them and call for more, but you will lose time and let enthusiasm dissipate while the so-called trained experts on the ground floor are telling you that they are no good.

If war should come now the most serious problem would not be that people would be lacking to bear arms, or would not bear them with credit to themselves, but it would be in working off the old deadwood which has risen to the top of the military service by the passage of time, men who are entrenched there by law, but who are unaccustomed to the habits of active armies. The development of new leaders and the casting off of the old were the real problems of the war of the sixties. Why not develop leaders now by each year organizing armies for an active life outdoors?

The profession of arms is my profession. What I have said to you is not said in hostility, but in a desire to point out a plan which will bring the profession into closer friendship with the people of our country.

It's easy to understand why the heads of the Marine Corps and Army would want to drum Major Harllee out of the Marine Corps after testimony like that. So they went to Secretary of the Navy Josephus Daniels, for approval, since testimony before a Senatorial Committee and nationwide newspaper publicity were involved.

But Josephus Daniels was a successful newspaper editor in North Carolina long before he was Secretary of the Navy. He was ring-wise in matters of publicity and told them,

"If you court-martial Harllee you're going to make a martyr out of him. After all, he didn't ask to testify, the Senate asked him. The press is using headlines a lot of the public will like. Look at them:

WOULD TRAIN YOUNG MEN IN REAL FIELD WORK

SAYS IT IS A MISTAKE TO THINK IT TAKES YEARS OF PRACTICE

ACTIVE ARMY RATHER THAN REGULAR

TEACH EVERYBODY

KEEP THEM ACTIVE

EVERY AMERICAN SHOULD LEARN TO USE A RIFLE

WOULD SELECT ARMY OFFICERS FROM THE RANKS
PROPOSITION PROVIDES WAY TO OVERCOME PRESENT
BARRIER RAISED BY CASTE

"And those are just the headlines. Whether you like it or not, the public is going to eat that stuff up. Furthermore, you know and I know from personal observation that Harllee has done an excellent job of teaching us all to shoot. The best thing to do is to give him written orders not to speak any more to the Congress or the press on conscription or on the Army. Then if he does so, at least he will have violated orders—which will have to be skillfully written—whereas now he really hasn't violated any orders or committed any other clear cut offense. Of course, you might be able to get him now on the old 'Conduct to the Prejudice of Good Order and Discipline' charge, or 'Conduct Unbecoming an Officer and Gentleman' charge, but that's just what would make it a long drawn out 'cause celebre.'

"Also keep him on the rifle ranges where he can do a lot of good and keep him based in Washington, where we can keep an eye on him. If you order him to Guam or some such place, again he will become a martyr."

Bill Harllee had not only made speeches against conscription, but he had made speeches against the United States entering the war—*before* we declared war on Germany. *After* that he figured the argument was over and he ceased and desisted in any such opposition and bent every effort he could to help the nation win it.

When we entered the war he requested duty with the American Expeditionary Force (A.E.F.) in France. At the beginning of the war there were 86 lieutenant colonels and majors in the Marine Corps; at the end there were 251. Only two regiments and seven battalions of Marines were to see action at the front in France—and of course they won the Corps international and permanent glory. But it is easy to see how difficult it was for majors or lieutenant colonels, his ranks, to get these assignments. Impossible for one in ill favor at headquarters.

In 1917, Harllee's friend, General Henry Hutchings, Adjutant General of Texas, planned the organization of a brigade of Texas National Naval Volunteer Marines under the then existing federal naval militia laws and persuaded Governor Ferguson of Texas to commission Harllee as a brigadier general of Texas N.N.V.'s and place him in command of the brigade. Harllee was delighted. Arrangements were made for the organization of the full brigade and quite a number of the divisions (as the naval companies were called) were organized and some of them were mustered into the federal service—but only as divisions without higher organization. Governor Ferguson made a request to the Secretary of the Navy that Harllee be granted leave of absence to accept this appointment and the request was seconded by both Texas senators and several Texas representatives, but hostility in Washington to this proposal prevailed.

The Reverend Herbert Bigelow, a noted Ohio liberal who presided over the Ohio constitutional convention, like Harllee, was an ardent and active advocate of Henry George's doctrine (the Single Tax) and served in Congress for several years. Bigelow proposed to raise a regiment of volunteers in Ohio or elsewhere with Harllee as colonel and himself as lieutenant colonel, but the draft law broke up all plans to raise volunteer regiments as had been the practice in the past. Like Harllee, Bigelow was a pacifist, but when, in spite of any influence they might have had to prevent war, their country became involved in the war, they both desired to serve at the front under the colors.

E. Paul DuPont of Wilmington, Delaware, was also a supporter of Henry George's philosophy. He arranged for the Wilmington Single Tax Club to invite Harllee to speak to it, which he did one Sunday. Later, after war was declared he sought to go with Harllee in the service and help him organize a regiment of volunteers, but again the draft law put an end to this effort.

Before we entered the war, Bill Harllee was the only officer on active duty in any of the armed services to oppose publicly what he considered propaganda for war. Only one retired officer, General Nelson A. Miles of the Army, opposed it. Harllee was convinced that the munitions makers and financiers controlled the press of the country and therefore its politicans. However he found many senators and congressmen friendly to him as a result of his testimony. Notable among these was the elder Senator Robert M. (Fighting Bob) La Follette of Wisconsin, who in 1924 was the Progressive Party Presidential candidate. The Senator phoned Harllee and requested he come see him. The Marine replied that he would be pleased to go see the Senator, whom he had not previously met. La Follette told him that he approved everything Bill Harllee had said in his testimony before the Senate Committee and that he was glad that someone in the military service had so enlightened the public. He told Harllee that those who were carrying on the propaganda for war would "give him the works" and promised to stand by him to the finish and asked Harllee to come to him direct and promptly when the reprisals began. It was Harllee's conviction that most senators and congressmen were opposed to entering the war, but were intimidated by the press.

His opposition to conscription and to the nation entering the war before it did so, plus Secretary Daniel's orders to keep him based in Washington, continued to frustrate his vigorous efforts to get orders to France until October of 1918 when his good friend, Angus McLean, later Governor of Josephus Daniel's North Carolina, finally persuaded the Navy Secretary to let Harllee go overseas with a Marine regiment. As it turned out, this was too late to get him to France and into combat.

Of course Harllee's proposals for the "Active Army" hardly became the Bible of the U. S. Army. *But*, in later years:

1. His system of infantry weapons instruction was universally accepted.
2. The "caste system" was greatly modified through the years by:
   (a) Commissioning many more men from the ranks (and sending many more to West Point and Annapolis from the ranks),

(b) Raising the age limit for commissioning from the ranks,

(c) Greatly increasing the percentage of officers (in 1917 it was approximately 8%; in 1981 it varied among services but in the Air Force it was almost twice as big a percentage and was much larger in all the others),

(d) Creating higher enlisted ranks such as Master Sergeant and Master Chief Petty Officer, with much improved access to command,

(e) Enhancing in countless ways the dignity and therefore pride of the enlisted men, which is far from incompatible with good discipline (Harllee never advocated or permitted slack discipline). In fact, many senior officers felt that Chief of Naval Operation's Admiral Elmo Zumwalt's famous Z-grams in the Navy in the early 1970's went too far in this direction.

Years later TIME magazine was to write with very considerable inaccuracy: "Colonel Harllee's chief service to the service was to replace enlisted men with civilians as servants," and

(f) Favorably publicizing in press, screen, radio and TV many notable enlisted men and types of enlisted men.

3. The peacetime army before World War II spent more time in the field and less in barracks than before 1917. The following are examples on a scale not hitherto known in peacetime:

(a) In August 1939, the First Army put 45,000 men through field exercises in New York State.

(b) In the winter of 1939–1940, similar maneuvers were carried out by men of the Fourth Army Corps around Fort Benning.

(c) In May of 1940, in a forest area of Louisiana and Texas, a consolidated army of 70,000 men spent a whole month training under war conditions.

(d) In the summer of 1940 a total of more than 325,000 regulars, national guardsmen, and reserves (New York 100,000; Wisconsin 65,000; Louisiana 80,000; the West Coast 80,000) marched, maneuvered, and "fought" in the field.

4. In very recent years, the Navy and Marine Corps have decided they had best let go enlisted men who create too many problems even before they complete their contracted number of years.

5. The highly successful Israeli Army has appointed all its officers from its ranks—and then trained them exceedingly well.

The following excerpt from General S.L.A. Marshall's book "Sinai Victory" (1958) seems to indicate a lot of very strenuous non-garrison training (such as Harllee advocated) for the Israeli Army:

> Accordingly relatively little importance is attached to perfection in the manual of arms, parade-ground drill and other routines familiar in Western armies.
>
> Troops are kept moving about in open country as much as possible. The average recruit is strong in the legs, having hiked around since childhood. . . .
>
> The Army wastes no time in road marching, believing that a thirty mile movement across ridges does more to condition troops than seventy miles on the flat. Most marches are an approach to a combat exercise. Even when the reserves take their periodic training, they are kept in the open and are put over rough ground, traveling by night. Every camp is an armed bivouac on a position suitable for defense; no time is spent at a training base. Say the trainers: That would be a waste. The men would be put on police tasks; we don't call that training. . . .
>
> During training, the reservist subsists on hard field rations. No blankets or overcoats are issued for the bivouacs. The staff feels that the toughening process is furthered by letting the man sleep cold on the ground.
>
> What the Army requires physically of its troops is illustrated in the testing course given the recruit, after it is decided that he is potential NCO material. Such aspirants are divided into packets of three; then each member of the team is put under a twenty-pound load, including his rifle and ammunition. Next, the team is given a march schedule which keeps it moving forty miles per day for three days running, through sharp ridges, such as are found in the Galilee country. Two thirds of the route is covered by day, the other by night, the whole taking approximately thirty hours of the three days.

Harllee's "Active Army" or a modification of it might possibly have been able to work if he had been in charge, but it was, of course, far, far too revolutionary to be accepted then or now. Furthermore the rapid advance of modern technology has changed too many aspects of the army. But it gave a few people a few new ideas—a rare commodity in the military establishment of that day.

Perhaps some other comments on Harllee's amazing statement are in order.

With relation to the pre-1917 field service regulations anticipating connection of the wagons and the troops for rations every day, it is hard to imagine the German blitzkreigers or Patton's Third Army or the Marines conquering the Pacific Islands connecting with "ration wagons daily" in their fighting and lightning-speed days, although perhaps it was occasionally possible. The ratio of the men behind the gun or the combatants to the men of the supply line of communications or the rear echelon forces has so rapidly diminished that it has been reported that in Vietnam less than 8 to 10% of our total soldiers in country were actually shooting at the enemy. We got away with this in Vietnam. Although we met with political disaster, our armed forces were *not militarily* defeated there despite popular belief to the contrary. But if we ever have another war and one against a formidable foe we will need more men manning the weapons. The March 15, 1982 issue of Newsweek quoted General John F. Vessey, Jr., then just selected as Chairman of the Joint Chiefs of Staff by President Reagan, as commenting in the 1970s that "wars are won by riflemen, tank platoons, and howitzer batteries doing their thing and doing it right."

So Bill Harllee was not so far off in advocating riflemen "doing their thing right."

XXIV
MARKSMANSHIP
FOR ALL AMERICANS
1917–1918

"D'you say that you sweat with the field guns? By God, you must lather with us!" say the screw guns, and Kipling's verse expresses exactly the feelings of the Range builders after a week or so of Harllee hurry. But the boys liked it, and they liked the Major and his way of doing business. Also the Major liked them"
—from "A History of the University Divisions, Michigan Naval Militia" by J.R. Hayden and R.M Burley.

On March 16, 1917 Captain William C. Harllee became Major William C. Harllee, "Maje" to his Navy friends.

The United States entered World War I on April 6, 1917. On that day Captain Charles P. Plunkett, U.S. Navy, and Major Harllee left the Navy Department and walked past the White House in Washington. They noticed the sentries with rifles walking their posts, guarding the President of the United States.

"The trouble is, Captain, that those American soldiers who are supposed to be guarding the President probably couldn't hit the side of a barn with those rifles they're carrying."

"Maje, you're crazy," said Captain Plunkett.

"Ask one of them how much he has shot his rifle," said Bill Harllee.

The two officers approached one of the White House sentries.

"Son," said Captain Plunkett, "How good are you with that rifle you're carrying?"

"Don't know, sir," said the sentry. "Never shot one yet."

"What?" Captain Plunkett exclaimed with startled disbelief. Then: "Is that rifle loaded?"

"Yes Sir," said the sentry. "The corporal, he loads 'em for us every morning when we go on duty. But he locks 'em, and he orders us not to fool with the lock."

"Let me see that gun, son," ordered Captain Plunkett. The United States Army sentry gave it to him! Plunkett examined it. It was loaded and locked with the safety on, as the sentry had said. Captain Plunkett returned the weapon, and they walked away.

"Now," said Bill Harllee, "You see what I mean when I fight for rifle ranges. Now you see what's guarding the President of the United States in wartime. A soldier with a gun he's got orders not to shoot! And he doesn't know how to shoot it. No man has any business with a rifle unless he can shoot straight!"

"Maje," said Captain Plunkett, "you go build rifle ranges."

The Captain was in charge of the Office of Gunnery Exercises and Engineering Performances in the Navy Department. Harllee was in his office, in charge of small arms.

Major Harllee had visions of rifle ranges all over the country— at Army, Navy and Marine Corps training stations and near ports of embarkation. He knew that Admiral Benson, Chief of Naval Operations and the rest of the Navy and Marine Corps thought this was the Army's job and that he should stay out of it. So it looked like he was stopped before he started. But he was never more convinced of anything in his life than of his belief that the Army wouldn't do enough and that it needed the Navy's help.

As the Literary Digest of April 5, 1919 reported:

> He found the opposition that usually confronts the enthusiast. The advent of the machine gun, so his critics said, would discount the work of the individual rifleman. He was told that the soldier's musket would have little use in combat except for the bayonet.
>
> Section 113 of the National Defense Act of June 3, 1916, provided funds for the construction and cooperation of rifle-ranges open to any branch of the military or naval service and to all able-bodied citizens capable of bearing arms. The Secretary of War, however, was not inspired by this provision and nothing was done by the Army. Lieutenant Colonel Harllee was awake, however, and prevailed upon his fellow Carolinian, the Secretary of the Navy, to draw upon the appropriation and to go ahead where the War Department hesitated. Mr. Daniels empowered Lieutenant Colonel Harllee to carry out his scheme.

Major General Johnson Hagood, one of General Pershing's right hand men in France, wrote later in his book, "We Can Defend America":

> During the summer of 1918 we sent 200,000 infantry soldiers to France who had never fired a rifle . . . they arrived, and some of them went to their death without having been instructed in the use of their rifles.

So Harllee fought a continuous battle during the rest of the war to build ranges and train men to shoot, the professional risk to himself be damned. He was definitely not what would later be known as a "careerist" or "ticket puncher."

His views were borne out later by General Pershing, the "Black Jack" Pershing of Harllee's West Point days. He gave staunch support to National Rifle Association programs. He became exasperated at the poor marksmanship of the recruits who were swelling his command in France. He sent a communique to the Secretary of War, made public in October of 1917, which stated,

> You must not forget that the rifle is distinctively an American weapon. I want to see it employed. . . . Longer experience with conditions in France confirms my opinion that it is highly important that infantry soldiers should be excellent shots. . . .
>
> Thorough instruction in range practice, prescribed by our Small Arms Firing Manual, is very necessary. Our Allies now

fully realize their deficiency in rifle training. It is difficult to secure areas for target ranges in France, even now when crops are off the ground. Much greater difficulty soon, when plowing begins. After ground is secured in France, considerable time will be required for troops to construct ranges and improvise target material. In theater of active operations this time should be available for intensive training with new weapons and formations.

I therefore strongly renew my previous recommendations that all troops be given complete course in rifle practice prescribed in our firing manual before leaving the United States. Specialty of trench warfare instruction at home should not be allowed to interfere with rifle practice, nor with intensive preliminary training in our School of the Soldier, School of the Company and School of the Battalion.

I cannot too strongly impress upon the War Department the absolute necessity of rigid insistence that all men shall be thoroughly grounded in the School of the Soldier.

"Arms and the Man" reported that although the British had won some brilliant victories with the rifle, the French believed in bayonetting and bombing. But Pershing was a man of great conviction and determination.

General Barnett, the Marine Commandant, required Marines to qualify as marksmen or better before he would send them to France. He claimed he made a trip on a transport with 11,000 Army troops and found that very few of them had ever fired an Army rifle! The White House sentry was not unique!

General Johnson Hagood in his book also stated that:

On March 21, 1918 when the Germans were starting the great drive that destroyed the Fifth British Army and separated the British from the French on the Western Front, the Allies cried to America for help.

and sent this desperate appeal to Washington:

We must have riflemen. We must have machine gunners . . . or we are lost.

Hagood recalled that on the very same date the War Department in Washington demonstrated its notions of how to win the war by issuing the following instructions to the generals commanding troops in the United States:

The two greatest weaknesses in the American soldiers' training are (1) the slovenly salute, and (2) lack of uniformity in dress.

But back to April of 1917 and the new Major's job. When America entered the war, there had already assembled at the Naval training stations tens of thousands of eager young recruits, and more were coming by train. No range facilities existed that were adequate to handle a hundredth part of the vast force. These youngsters had to be kept busy, pending the completion of additional accommodations for housing and training, and it was realized that an excellent way of holding their interest was to give them a chance to learn rifle shooting.

At last the Winthrop Idea, or a form of it, could be spread across the country.

Major Harllee looked over the experts among the high school cadets of Washington, D. C. with whom he had been working closely and selected four young men, all from McKinley Manual Training School. These men were enrolled in the Naval Reserve Force and promoted to the rating of chief yeoman. He took the youngsters to Great Lakes, near Chicago, because his first break popped up there, and they served as the nucleus of his force of instructors.

In his talk to each new group of men, Bill Harllee began with the statement that if they found life rough and hard not to blame him for such was war. He said he was not in favor of war and had done his best to oppose the starting of it but, now since other people had got us into it, he and they were going to do their very best to bring it to a close as soon as possible, and to a close victorious to the United States.

The State of Illinois, at his request, turned over to the Navy their fine rifle range at Camp Logan near Zion City. He had difficulty with the Executive Officer of the Great Lakes Training Station concerning men for duty on the range at Camp Logan. He then took from the Training Station range, which he had previously built and put in operation, 24 men of a company of National Naval Volunteers. He sent 18 of them to Grand Rapids, Michigan, their home city, to round up some good recruits for the ranges. They stirred up Grand Rapids and caused over 500 splendid young men to come at their own

221

expense to Camp Logan, where he enlisted them in the Navy, without any authority but with good results in the end.

Two divisions of the National Naval Volunteers from the University of Michigan were already at the Great Lakes Training Station when Harllee arrived. There were also some officers, very recently commissioned from the University of Michigan.

When Major Harllee stooped to enter that officers' mess tent at Great Lakes Naval Training Station, none there knew that their wartime future had entered with him. Little did they know that they were to be the commanding officers of his nation-wide-to-be spread of rifle ranges.

Silent and ill-at-ease, the brand new Navy officers from the university militia looked askance at his light blue, red-striped trousers, his dark blue coat and Marine Corps insignia. What strange bird was this, which had come to further embarrass their ill-assorted group? His formidable aspect did not reassure them.

Yet it was not a day till one of these embryo officers was hard at work with him creating a new Navy Rifle Range on the lake shore north of far-spreading Camp Paul Jones. And, in less than a month, two others were in Massachusetts and Virginia on similar projects.

For things moved fast after Major Harllee arrived. In two weeks the new lake shore range had been built by selected blue jackets, and was in strenuous operation, training thousands of the newly enlisted sailors from the Great Lakes camps.

Then over a hundred of the Michigan militiamen entrained for Wakefield, Massachusetts, to act as a nucleus of the force which repaired and developed the Wakefield range and camp. Another detachment took over the Virginia Beach range. Then, always expanding—always developing new human material, at first from Wakefield, then from other ranges, for range officers, construction chiefs, commanding officers, petty officers, range forces, cooks and construction gangs—this great enterprise grew and spread out till fourteen Navy Rifle Ranges and camps were established and in operation in all parts of the country.

The rifle range game was a hard one. Opening up a range

usually meant working fourteen hours a day, on canned-willie rations, and living in the wet for several weeks, while no slight hardship was involved in keeping the firing lines and butts in operation through bitter winter days.

For the first time the ranges were kept open all winter instead of closing in mid-December. And the winter of 1917–1918 was unusually severe. This meant lying down on icy ground, working stubborn bolts, squeezing triggers with frosty fingers and facing snow glare. At Great Lakes, it meant cold winds from Lake Michigan, and there were snow drifts at Wakefield, Cape May, Glen Burnie and other ranges. But neither Bill Harllee nor the other men at the ranges ever forgot how much they wanted to get to France, therefore, they wanted to do as much as they could to prepare themselves and others for that day. The Major built more rifle ranges than anyone in history.

Great Lakes, Wakefield, Virginia Beach, Philadelphia, Cape May, N.J., Charleston, S.C.; Rumford, R.I., Annapolis, Glen Burnie, Md., Peekskill, N.Y., Camp Logan, Ill., San Pedro, Calif., Mt. Pleasant, S.C., Caldwell, N.J. and an airplane machine gun range at Pensacola, Florida completed the roll of the ranges. Machine gunnery was taught as well as the use of the rifle and pistol. Caldwell had 250 targets and was then the largest small arms training range in the world. It was built without appropriations, and in defiance of direct orders not to build it from a brass bound senior officer.

Harllee was even warned of being court-martialed for ignoring red tape. "Court-martial and be damned," he said. They didn't court martial.

The following excerpts from Bill Harllee's letters illustrate his attitude towards military punctilio and obstructive regulations at the height of the war:

> The National Naval Volunteer, a Lieutenant Commander, in command of the Sewell's Point Station, has a good line of talk, and he probably is pretty efficient as far as Navy Regulations, saluting, and that sort of thing is concerned, but I cannot conceive of any live man with a range in his front yard not using it to its utmost capacity.
> AND . . .

The Commandant committed the business to my charge. If there have been any irregularities in the proceedings, the fault is mine; and if any suspensions or checkages are involved, the omission is mine, and I hereby assume it.

These bills are correct and just, and should be paid with the same promptness with which the material and service were delivered and performed by business parties who responded to urgent requests with the spirit and manner befitting the times, and in good faith that I was a responsible representative of the Government authorized to transact the business.

If verbal proposals and agreements are irregular proceedings, this procedure was in this case nevertheless necessaryu in order not to suspend the construction—and the construction limits of three weeks—a record time—and in order to do it at a minimum cost for the layout.

No obstacle was allowed to stop construction or operation of the ranges. Red tape was used so long as it brought results— and a skillful sea-lawyer can do wonders with it—but was violently thrown aside when it threatened to check operations. "Damn it, man, sign anything! Get the job done" rang for years in the ears of many a prudent commanding officer, who feared to take some action that might "hang him" later.

It is amusing to note for example, that one member of the New York State Commission controlling the rifle range at Peekskill, New York, complained on March 4, 1918, that he "understood from the Adjutant General of this State (New York) that Peekskill was turned over to the Marine Corps or to the Navy under some kind of agreement entered into with Major Harllee" and that "I am very much surprised that . . . I have no knowledge in the matter."

This letter went to a Marine Corps General at headquarters who was an old adversary of Bill Harllee from the days when he was General Elliott's Aide-de-Camp and was battling the staff corps people then permanently stationed in Washington on behalf of the General. But the Major didn't let little things like this get in the way of the rapid progress needed in "The Great War."

None other than Franklin D. Roosevelt, as Assistant Secretary of the Navy, had written on January 8, 1918, that "The State of New York has authorized the use by the Navy of the State

Camp and Rifle Range near Peekskill, New York. The Navy will occupy this range with a permanent operating and instructing force of one hundred and fifty men."

Furthermore, Bill Harllee was not above giving a few thousand rounds of Government ammunition to rifle clubs to use where they could to promote American marksmanship. Especially if he knew they couldn't get to his rifle ranges and if he was sure the ammo would be used to train new men who would be going in the armed forces. To hell with regulations if they got in the way!

Another example of his highly unorthodox procedures was his solution to the problem of getting his men to the excellent two weeks course the Lewis Machine Gun School operated at the Savage Arms Corporation at Utica, New York. Under the regular arrangements there, the board and lodging cost $2.00 a day for each man. In spite of Harllee's efforts, so successful in many directions, he could not get the Navy to pay the men more than its regular commutation rate of $1.25 per day. The Marine Corps was paying its men more for their board and lodging than was paid by the Navy. The machine gun course was so good that Harllee told the men that if they would volunteer to pay the difference and graduated with high honors they would be advanced in rating, giving them much more money than the $10.50 involved. Furthermore, he later found them good board and lodging at the homes of local patriots at bargain rates! There were plenty of volunteers!

Technical problems had to be met, too. For example, the Colt Machine Guns had to be reamed out another $1/100$ inch, by cooperation with the Colt factory at Hartford, to make the certain types of ammunition work without stoppages.

There were, of course, some rough bumps on the road to American marksmanship. One day early on, the Chief of Police of Zion City, the nearest town to Camp Logan, phoned the Major and told him that his then principal assistant, the very able Ensign Albert Jenkins, was under arrest and could not pay his fine. Bill Harllee rushed right into town to find out what in the world could have happened. He discovered that Jenkins had been arrested for smoking a cigarette! Zion City was the home of the Dowie religious sect, which was very strict in observing its beliefs, one of which prohibited smoking, and others of which prohibited all other vices common to most of mankind. They actually had passed an ordinance against smoking cigarettes in the city and had been active in enforcing it against motorists passing through. Harllee knew that if it were enforced against the sailors there would be constant friction and trouble. So he decided to put on a parade and banquet for the city fathers of Zion City and persuaded them to suspend the law against smoking for men in uniform for the duration as a contribution to the war effort. In fact, after the people of that city found out what fine officers and men were at Camp Logan, they showed them much cordial hospitality, taking them into their homes.

Occasionally there were humorous moments. It wasn't always possible to find the best of every trade and profession at every range, so sometimes men had to be "volunteered" by the Major for certain jobs. A cook had to be thus found for the Mt. Pleasant, South Carolina range. The cook kept muttering, "I ain't rightly never cooked that many grits to once." Incidentally, Mayor Hyde of Charleston led the civilian shooting effort there.

Harllee built the Caldwell rifle range squarely across the path of France-bound American troops, 40 minutes from Hoboken. He went out and sent out his officers, like salesmen, to colonels commanding regiments waiting to board their transports for France.

"Bring your regiment to Caldwell," he invited. "Let 'em learn to shoot straight before they reach France. We'll house 'em, feed 'em, provide ammunition; rifles too, if you need 'em. We can get you back to shipside in 40 minutes."

Grateful regimental commanders thronged with their men to Caldwell, cutting red tape as Bill Harllee cut it, to the cry: "There's a war on."

So in spite of it all, Bill Harllee told the world that he could take any man and in less than a week bring him up to 90 per cent of his possible shooting efficiency, and he did it.

At the time of the Armistice, 1,200 targets were in operation and the permanent range forces consisted of 30 officers and 6,000 men. The ranges accommodated about 10,000 transients in training, fired 500,000 rounds daily, and each day turned out over a thousand men trained in the rifle, pistol and machine gun.

Civilians and state troops were always urged to come and made welcome. The theory on which the ranges were run was that America should be a nation of riflemen; that every citizen has a right to keep and bear arms, as guaranteed by the Constitution; and to know how to use them. The thinking behind this was that a nation of riflemen is likely to be a nation able to maintain its liberties.

More than 500,000 American soldiers, sailors, marines and civilians learned to shoot straight on his rifle ranges, under his command. No other American officer ever equalled that record.

The cold record of these accomplishments can never give a true picture of the facts. These far-flung camps and ranges first existed only in the mind of Bill Harllee. Even the vision of them existed nowhere else, and there were many in high positions who would have stopped the program instantly if they could have dreamed of its existence.

Yet, taking young and unproved men, gathered from all parts of the country and all sections of life, he brought this vision to reality. Callow college boys and raw-boned men from Texas, miscellaneous young males who ranged all the way from aristocrats to the sweepings of the gutter—blended under his driving inspiration into a force which could do anything and do it well.

Promotion was rapid for those who made good. It was a great democracy of work—with money no object to the worker. They made their own officers, their own petty officers, their own specialists in the various fields of construction and operation. Men of every trade and profession were found or enrolled, and it is doubtful if so much training was ever done with so little in this or in any other war.

They wrought with their own hands the barracks they lived in, the halls in which they ate and the telephone lines over which they communicated. And of course the rifle ranges—from the massive target butts to the farthest firing line.

Sometimes they were criticized for their lack of polish—by those who had more time than they did for polish and criticism. But, even there, Harllee did his best to keep them up to the mark, and on occasion they could turn out a creditable inspection and parade.

He successfully indoctrinated all with their mission—to teach the nation to shoot! And especially to teach those who were going to the battlefields—how to shoot before they went there! A doctrine too often ignored by those who should have known better.

He effectively delegated authority to these inexperienced young men—scattered from coast to coast—yet never lost control over anyone or any situation!

Boys in years became men in character and capacity under such a regime. Until the end of their days they thanked him for awakening and developing them. Fortunate were they—to find their military years a stimulant to their initiative—instead of a sedative.

According to "A History of the Michigan Naval Militia University Divisions, by J. R. Hayden and R. M. Burley:

> From the standpoint of personal development no more fortunate thing could have happened to University of Michigan men than to have served under such a leader. Every individual who came into real contact with Colonel Harllee and made good, became a better worker, a straighter thinker, a harder fighter and the devoted admirer and friend of his chief. Further, identification with the Navy Rifle Ranges enabled a large number of Michigan men to render war services of the greatest value, besides opening the way for many of them to further useful duty afloat or in France.

As far as Bill Harllee himself was concerned, he had always worked hard—even into the smallest hours of the night—but he surpassed even himself now in an effort to get the job done and get himself to France.

He always looked upon his physical strength and his strong constitution as assets to be used in the service of his country in the profession of arms, and not as something to be carefully nurtured and built up. By 1917, the former 6 foot 197 pound football player was described in the press as slender. He weighed 153 pounds.

He believed in the principles so well expressed by Major C. A. Bach, United States Army, in an address on leadership delivered to the graduating officers at Fort Sheridan and reprinted by the U.S.M.C. Recruiting Publicity Bureau in New York on March 25, 1918:

> Self-sacrifice is essential to leadership. You will give, give all the time. You will give of yourself physically, for the longest hours, the hardest work and the greatest responsibility is the lot of the captain. He is the first man up in the morning and the last man in at night. He works while others sleep.
>
> You will give of yourself mentally, in sympathy and appreciation for the troubles of men in your charge. This one's mother has died, and that one has lost all his savings in a bank failure. They may desire help, but more than anything else they desire sympathy.
>
> Don't make the mistake of turning such men down with the statement that you have troubles of your own, for every time that you do YOU KNOCK A STONE OUT OF THE FOUNDATION OF YOUR HOUSE.
>
> Your men are your foundation, and your house leadership will tumble about your ears unless it rests securely upon them.
>
> Finally, you will give of your own slender financial resources. You will frequently spend your money to conserve the health and well-being of your men or to assist them when in trouble. Generally you get your money back. Very infrequently you must charge it to profit and loss.

Harllee urged economy for its own sake—urging the cause of the taxpayer in a day when millions were being squandered, recklessly by others! For example, at Cape May, New Jersey, the site for the range was rented for a dollar a year!

The story of the Navy Rifle Ranges would not be complete without a description of an outgrowth from them—their teams at the National Rifle Matches.

In the summer of 1918, Harllee gathered up his best marksmen from the Navy Rifle Ranges then in operation. He took them to Camp Perry, where the Army was conducting the National Rifle Matches of that year. He was Assistant Executive

Officer of the Matches. His men were divided into teams—to compete against the veteran riflemen of the Marine Corps, Infantry, Cavalry, Artillery, National Guard and civilians from New York to the Philippines.

These young Navy men had been shooting for months, whereas their competitors had been shooting for years. And long range competitive rifle shooting is usually an art that takes years to learn. Yet the Navy Rifle Range teams landed six out of the first ten places, including second, third, and fourth—losing first place by a narrow margin to a wonderful team of Marines. And the oldest cup in existence, for prowess in rifle shooting, the Leech Cup, was won by a man from the Rumford, R.I. Navy rifle range. This cup was awarded twenty years earlier by Captain Leech of the Irish team which then visited the United States. The 200 yard rapid-fire match was won by R. S. Tubbs of the Virginia Beach Navy rifle range. These were two of the several National Rifle Association matches. The successes of the Navy Rifle Range Team and individual members were impressive testimony to Harllee's unique skill in developing riflemen.

For the National Matches, including the NRA competitions, still the seminal institution for fine marksmanship, Harllee argued for such liberalizing and progressive measures as allowance of the squatting position, among other positions; latitude in selection of sights; and a provision designating for use the service rifle as issued, star gauged, targetted, and equipped with special drift slides to take care of abnormal zeroes, or if desired, equipped with any sight not containing glass.

When Admiral Plunkett sought to interest the Navy Department in mounting fourteen inch naval guns on railway mounts and sending them to France, one of the weightiest objections to his scheme was the absolute impossibility of taking enough trained officers, petty officers, and men from the fleet to furnish the personnel of the expedition. "Where'll you get your men?" he was asked, with sort of a triumphant finality.

"Never mind about the men," replied the Admiral, "I'll get the men, and they'll be damned good ones, too."

"Where?"

"From Harllee's rifle ranges."

And the men from the ranges went to France with Admiral Plunkett and the five great 14 inch naval gun railway batteries, the biggest land guns the Allies had, that wreaked such long range havoc with German troops, railway junctions, and ammunition dumps.

Finally, the following are some of the descriptions of the results of marksmanship training in World War I:

> From "The Literary Digest" of April 5, 1919:
> Under the fiercest fire, they (the U.S. Marines) calmly adjusted their sights, aimed at a particular man, and got him. While the soldiers of our Allies used their small arms only when the foe was within two hundred yards, the Marines began bagging Germans at 1,000!

> From the "Engineman's Magazine," August, 1940:
> With all due respect for machine guns, tanks, airplanes, and the other necessary implements of modern war, there is nothing so terrible to face as accurately aimed rifle fire. It reaches out to two thirds of a mile and says to each individual foe—this means you.

Of course, Harllee's rifle ranges trained infantrymen and aviators in the use of machine guns as well as rifles and pistols.

It should be noted that Colonel Robert D. Heinl, Jr., in his superb book, "Soldiers of the Sea," uses the more conservative figure of 400 yards for "dropping men" with the '03 rifles at Belleau Wood. German intelligence reported the remarkable marksmanship of the Marines. Since Premier Clemenceau of France said that battle "saved Paris," Heinl wrote that the repulse of the German "great attack was in some sense responsible for today's Marine Corps."

Even in the matter of defeating machine gun nests, two U. S. Army General Staff officers who had been in the thick of the fighting reported the value of accurate rifle fire. They said that in some cases American riflemen had been able to get on one or more of the flanks or to the rear of machine guns nests at some distance and had been able to fire their Springfields with such accuracy that the machine gunners were often shot through the head or vital parts of the body. When this was possible, it was certainly to be preferred to frontal attacks with grenades and bayonets.

On August 28, 1918, Bill Harllee was promoted to Lieutenant Colonel and was called "The Colonel." In those days, unlike later days of inflation in ranks as well as in everything else, this was considered a high rank. He became technically a "brass hat," although in the stuffy sense of the expression, he never was one. As was noted in "The Trigger," the magazine of the Rumford, Rhode Island rifle range, he was not a "sycophantic pursuer of empty titles," and this promotion meant little to him at a time when his mind was concentrated on American marksmanship and getting to France. In view of the way he stuck his neck out, the promotion mildly surprised him.

He could take pride in the fact that despite the firing of forty million rounds of ammunition—more than the Navy had ever fired in peace or war in all its previous history—not a single accident, death or injury to personnel was due to carelessness or fault on the part of anyone.

After a long and sometimes bitter struggle to get to France, Harllee found himself in October of 1918 assigned to the 15th Regiment of the U. S. Marine Corps at the huge base at Quantico, Virginia, preparing to go overseas into combat. Armistice Day of 1918 found the regiment embarking for France. It was a big disappointment to him that he had not been "over there" earlier. But later on, he did have the satisfaction of reading in the December 26, 1919 issue of "The Leatherneck," the Marine Corps Magazine:

> It is generally admitted that to Colonel Harllee more than any other individual is due the wonderful marksmanship which made the Marines famous on the battlefields of France.

. . . and in an official letter from Rear Admiral Charles P. Plunkett, his Navy boss during the war:

> In fact, out of practically nothing, Colonel Harllee built up a force which, with an almost neglible expenditure of money, produced greater results than any other effort by any branch of the Navy or the Army during World War I.

232

XXV
THE NATIONAL
MATCHES—1919

*Caldwell, N. J., will become the
Mecca tomorrow of the man with the
rifle. The biggest national marksmen's
contest ever held in the United States is
to be staged there. Americans will fore-
gather in force to vindicate the reputation of their sharpshooting forebears.*
    *It is due chiefly to Lieut. Col.
William C. Harllee of the Marine
Corps that the match is to be held.
Colonel Harllee for many years has
been a strong advocate of the theory
that every person should be familiar
with the handling of a gun.*
—**The New York Times, August 3, 1919**

The National Rifle Matches of 1919 were held at the last and
greatest of the Navy Rifle Ranges—with Lieutenant Colonel
Harllee as Executive Officer—which meant he was in charge.
He was the first Navy Department officer to run the National

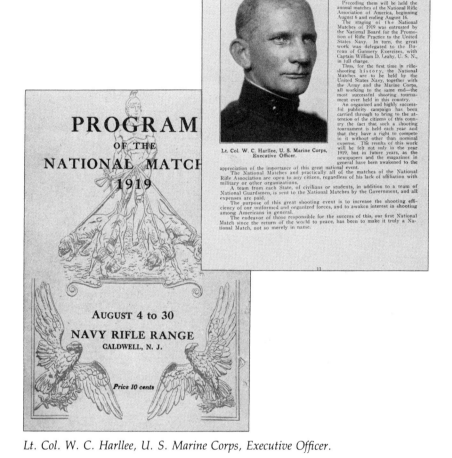

Lt. Col. W. C. Harllee, U. S. Marine Corps, Executive Officer.

Rifle Matches and the first one to be a vice president of the National Rifle Association.

Two thousand bluejackets and Marines labored all summer to complete this range at Caldwell, hewing it out of the wilderness of great trees which covered its site. Just before the matches everything was in the pink of condition. Then came the flood.

The great flood of the Bible could not have caused more consternation among Noah's neighbors than did this later deluge among the multitude assembling for the Matches. Torrential rains descended. A great dam up the Passaic River burst. The waters rose swiftly—till the flood raced waist high through the streets—sweeping everything loose before it. It was a black night never to be forgotten—with telephone warnings of further floods—and urgings that the camp be abandoned.

The next day revealed unimaginable devastation. Whole firing lines were gone. Tent floors had been swept a thousand yards away and piled up in the butts. Boats navigated the streets of the camp. The flimsy army exhibition barracks, recently set up, stood awry in water six feet deep in places. The steam shovel, completing the last target butts, lay on its side in muddy water.

Thousands had arrived and thousands were arriving—with the Matches at hand. Some of the men who had labored so loyally turned sulky at the sight of the destruction of their work. It was a time for a strong man and a leader. This man was Harllee.

The Colonel was everywhere, driving and encouraging. He was waist-deep among the stumps on the new range—setting an example for his Sailors and Marines. He was arranging for the feeding of the arriving multitude, appointing range officers, organizing the publicity department, pacifying horrified admirals, generals and distinguished visitors.

Not satisfied with the havoc already wrought, the rains continued to descend every one of the thirty days and thirty nights of the matches. The mosquitoes rose by millions from the quagmire—and had to be quelled with oil. Fastidious riflemen lay down in the water and mud to fire their "string." It might have been a nightmare.

But it was not. As so aptly put in *Americans and Their Guns*, "Harllee, however, was a stubborn Marine with a reputation as a drop-of-the-hat fighter." A legion of the veteran riflemen, who had known Harllee at Jacksonville and other former matches, remained steadfastly loyal to him. His confidence and persistence, which no one else could ever understand, considering the strain, kept all going forward. Good cheer abounded in the great mess hall for officers and distinguished guests and in the rain-soaked tents of the riflemen.

The National Rifle Association matches held that year were the largest held up to that time. There were seventy-two separate teams on the field, with hundreds of entries in the individual events. Harllee arranged to have at the range the biggest exhibit of war material ever seen in this country, according to "The Leatherneck" magazine.

Even though the rain, mud and mosquitoes were something to try to forget, there were moments to remember. There was entertainment every night, and on one special night there were three bands and two orchestras with which to make merry. On that night Miss Selma Sellinger, the shooters' regular songbird, was giving a concert when the Colonel stepped out and said, "Come on, Miss Selma, let's dispense with dignity and cut up a little."

He helped her get on the top of a table in the middle of the crowd and asked the crowd to sing "Salvation Lassie" with her. The Salvation Army Chief, who had done much for the shooters, said he had never heard it sung so enthusiastically. The first thing you know they were singing "Pack Up Your Troubles in Your Old Kit Bag," never sung more appropriately this side of the ocean; "There's a Long, Long Trail A'Winding"; "Tipperary"; "Over There"; "When I Leave the World Behind Me"; "Oh, How I Hate to Get Up in the Morning"; and the other popular songs of that era.

The Colonel wrapped up the night with the wish of Scotland's poet in his "Cotter's Saturday Night," "That your lives be blest with health, peace, and sweet content."

Even Major General Commandant George Barnett, who disapproved of some of Bill Harllee's machinations, was moved to write him on October 1, 1919:

> the undersigned desires to commend you upon the successful completion of the National Matches which were recently held at the Navy Rifle Range, Caldwell, N.J.
> The difficult conditions which you had to overcome in order

to get the range ready for the matches are fully appreciated by the undersigned. It was only through your indefatigable efforts that it was possible to hold the matches at Caldwell at the appointed time, and you are deserving of great credit for having successfully carried out the program as originally planned. Your work, under the handicap of a shortage of men and adverse conditions, showed a spirit of tenacity which is highly commendable.

General Barnett had said in a speech at the National Matches on August 28, 1919:

> The marksmanship of our Marines at Belleau Wood surprised and astonished our allies. I was told by a French officer that the most surprising thing that he had ever seen during a battle was when the men of the Marine Corps actually stopped to set their sights during the struggle at Belleau Wood.

He also sharply rebuked those critics of Colonel Harllee's policy who had intimated that the Caldwell range was unfit for habitation.

It is amusing to note that Harllee's official record states:

> Fitness reports covering that period are excellent, but he was admonished, by letter from the Major General Commandant, dated July 23, 1919, for irregular methods of procuring a detail of men from Quantico for duty at the Navy Rifle Range, Caldwell, N.J. He was commended by the Major General Commandant October 1, 1919, for his services which resulted in the successful completion of the National Matches in 1919.

Assistant Secretary of the Navy Franklin D. Roosevelt visited the National Matches at Caldwell in August 26, 1919 and in the speech he delivered said,

> The primary object of the National Matches is to develop interest in rifle shooting among civilians. The ranks of the Army, Navy and Marine Corps must be built up from our civilian population, and the finest military training in the world is embodied in the firing of the service rifle.

The National Match News of three days later reported that Mr. Roosevelt was chiefly interested in bringing the civilian population to the rifle range. It added that at every opportunity he had encouraged both by precept and example the doctrines which Colonel Harllee and his staff had endeavored to impress upon the men who had taken part in the National Matches.

Harllee's final beau geste to the riflemen of America has been reported in two quite different ways. Colonel Robert E. Barde's "History of Competitive Marksmanship in the U. S. Marine Corps" states that his career was almost ended by the theft of three million rounds of Government ammunition from the range at Caldwell. And as can be imagined he did have to answer quite a few letters about this. But his career never came first with Beau Harllee, and nothing bad really came of it anyway.

On the other hand, the National Rifle Association's magazine, "The American Rifleman" of January 1945, wrote much more accurately in his obituary:

> All the unpleasantness (of the flood at Caldwell) was, how-ever, forgotten at the end of the matches when the small arms ammunition dump was conveniently left "unguarded" so that the civilian riflemen might return home with ample supplies of the 1917–1918 ammunition! Some of that ammunition was still helping to promote civilian small arms practice when World War II started . . .

Then Harllee tendered to the Army, Marine Corps, Navy, whatever part of the Government that would take it, the world's greatest rifle range, which collier's Weekly then called "one of the lowest-priced insurance policies that Uncle Sam can ever have," with the flooding and mosquitoes controlled, as a permanent world capital of the rifle, pistol and machine gun. No dice. Nobody in high enough authority was interested any more. Weeds, bushes, undergrowth and trees slowly replaced this range where thousands of men could have been trained to shoot in a week!

XXVI
FOUNDING THE
MARINE CORPS
INSTITUTE—
"The Damned Education"—
1920–1921

June 2, 1920

Dear Colonel Harllee,

Many thanks for sending me the textbooks. My daughter and I are going to get busy on them this summer and I am proud to be a student in your university.

Always sincerely yours,
Franklin D. Roosevelt
—from "Soldiers of the Sea"
by Colonel Robert D. Heinl, Jr.

The Great War was won. The postwar blues had "set in," in earnest. The excitement of preparing to go "over there" was over, and drills in the armed forces seemed pretty boring and dull to the boys in khaki. The big morale problem that occurs in armies after every war was cresting.

Secretary of the Navy Josephus Daniels had hopes of making

the Navy an organization which would help men get an education while serving their country, but he had to give this up as impractical.

In 1919, Congress was obviously bent on radical retrenchment in the War and Navy Departments. The days of free spending were over and the day of reckoning at hand. Military minds, ever as alert as any others to any threat against the source of their funds—congressional appropriations—began a counter-offensive.

The Army must be popularized among the parents of the nation. What better way than to broadcast it as a great educational institution—and thus bridge the post-war reaction against things military? So the Army set up an elaborate system of schools—on paper—and the Marine Corps must needs follow suit, but in the end, as we shall see, became first.

The Marine Corps, in the person of Major General John Archer Lejeune, decided to grab Lt. Col. William C. Harllee for the job of starting this education. After all, as it was later written in the Marine Corps Gazette, he "was notorious throughout the Corps as a schoolmaster." But it was also written there that "Bo Harllee was anything but the traditional schoolmaster type."

His early and hard-realized dream of getting a commission in a soldier service, and his dreams on behalf of American marksmanship have been mentioned. He was very proud of his role in the events in this chapter, which were written up in the lead article in the February 1950 issue of "The Marine Corps Gazette" under the title, "The Story of a Dream."

Bo, to use his nickname during this period, reported to the Marine Base at Quantico, Virginia, on December 20, 1919, later to be recorded as one of the most important dates in Marine Corps education history. The educational activities which had been going on at Quantico were renamed "The Marine Corps Institute" on that date. Harllee's title was "Assistant Chief of Staff in charge of Vocational Training," and he was to serve under Generals Lejeune and Smedley Butler.

On January 2, 1920, Post Special Order No. 299 at the Marine Corps' Quantico, Virginia base, by far its biggest, announced

240

that 13 new schools would open on January 5. These schools were those of: Typewriting, Stenography and Clerical Work; Equitation; Forestry; Concrete; Carpentry; Electrical Mechanics; Band Music and Playing; Blacksmithing; Painting; Plumbing; Cooking and Baking; Motor Transport; and Drafting. A simple reading of the list is enough to make one realize that these courses were set up to train men for a more useful service career and for an opportunity to enter a gainful occupation upon discharge.

A great many Quantico Marines—actually most of them— took quite a different view of what they called "the damned education" than Congress, Secretary Daniels, and Generals Lejeune and Butler. They looked upon the schools as "sissified nonsense." The "schoolboys" had to pass through lines of jeering Marines on their way to classes. The Marines, particularly the old-timers, figured that the Marines' job was to fight, not to go to school. In the beginning, only 5% of the 5,000 Marines at Quantico chose to attend the schools. In spite of this, Bo Harllee held fast to his rigid policy that the education must be voluntary on the part of each individual Marine.

He wrote later:

> The decision and effort to learn must come from the men. The Marine Corps Institute does not propose to instruct those who do not want education, and who are not willing to put forth the effort to get it, even if at times there are difficulties in the way.

Harllee knew that most grownups have an aversion for classroom work, especially the Marines of that day. To them it felt like a reversion to childhood days, with unnecessary restraint and discipline and even homework.

"The Leatherneck," of April 1939, wrote that "he knew the sentiment of the service in regard to education, a hostile sentiment which he did not feel himself capable of overcoming." But this was only true with regard to *compulsory* education of a general nature or of a kind designed to be useful to the individual after he left the Marine Corps, benefitting the Corps only indirectly. This was, of course, just the type of education the Secretary of the Navy and the Marine Corps Generals desired be conducted.

So Bo Harllee faced the same kind of opposition he had faced in making the Corps learn to shoot, only much, much more so. To make things worse, the infamous flu epidemic of 1919–1920 forced the schools to shut down a short time after they opened. But they were able to reopen on February 2, 1920, with several new courses, and that date is now considered the founding date of the Marine Corps Institute (MCI).

Harllee, with the encouragement of General Lejeune, decided to travel all over the country checking colleges and schools at all levels to see how best to tackle his problem. He chanced upon the answer right in the Quantico Y.M.C.A. when he noticed the famous "Looking Ahead" bulletin of the International Correspondence Schools of Scranton, Pennsylvania.

He shouted with joy! He had found the answer! It was utterly impractical to have trained teachers and classroom schools in all the courses in which men might be interested, even at Quantico, much less in small and large detachments scattered all over the world, where most Marines were. He was looking ahead from his Quantico schools to schools for all the Corps.

Also Marines constantly came and went from stations individually and in groups on an irregular as well as a regular basis. That was one of the glories—maybe even the chief glory—of the Corps—first to fight—always ready. But it ruined any hopes of regular schedules and school years and graduations.

Furthermore, all commanding officers and other supervising Marines could not be expected to be enthusiastic about such schools. In fact, most of them could be expected *not* to be enthusiastic about them.

But correspondence courses! That was different! They had a flexibility that compensated for all these problems. And the courses could be sent out from a central Marine Corps office and sent back there to be graded. Harllee figured it was like the shooting game when he had insisted on all the coaches and instructors being trained at a central point (Winthrop) instead of leaving their training up to hundreds or thousands of officers or non-coms who might or might not be well qualified.

As his thoughts raced ahead in this manner, he decided to present General Lejeune with his discovery. The General was so happy with it that he sent Harllee up to the International Correspondence Schools (ICS) office in Scranton, Pennsylvania, where President Ralph E. Weeks and his staff treated him with every courtesy. After spending two weeks there, the rough Marine ordered $4,000 worth of textbooks for Quantico. He had no authority to expend such funds, but he persuaded Mr. Weeks that the good old Marine Corps would not let its man down and would pay the bill, which it did—eventually.

The arrangement was made that a fixed percentage of the lessons (10% at first) were to be sent to Scranton to be graded and that all final examinations would be processed there. When a student completed a course he would receive a certificate from the I.C.S. as well as from the M.C.I. Arrangements were also made for some Quantico Marines to be trained as instructors in the I.C.S. courses.

To insure the totally voluntary nature of the program, Harllee proposed that no entries be made in a man's record about quitting a course; only completions would be noted.

In reply to criticism of correspondence courses he replied that a man must learn by his own effort. He wrote that when a man receives a college education, he merely stands upon the threshold of an education for his life's work. He quoted:

The heights by great men reached and held
Were not attained by sudden flight
But they, while their companions slept,
Were toiling upward in the night.

He pointed out that Franklin, Lincoln and Edison never attended a college. He said that no man need despair of educating himself as long as he can read, and even blind men have ways to learn from books.

However, he did promise that the Marine Corps Institute would offer its services in trying to place men where they could be of most service to the Marine Corps, and after that was done the Corps would try to enable them to have better opportunities to come into contact with the practical phases of their courses.

He also stated that commanding officers should provide encouragement, advice and help and should arrange places for the men to study in their off-duty hours. He noted that in many cases instructors would be available and voluntary classes could be formed.

Military drills and instructions were conducted for the Quantico Marines in the morning. They were given the afternoons off from work if they wished to attend the schools. The "school boys" were excused from guard duty. In spite of this, the June 1939 issue of "The Leatherneck" reported:

> It seems apocryphal that healthy men could take pride in ignorance—many of them could scarcely write their own names—but the hostility exemplified by the Quantico Marines during the first days of the Marine Corps Institute was similar to that which had previously wrecked the educational projects of Secretary Daniels in the Navy.

Harllee persisted. Nothing could stop him. No detail was too small for his attention, no hours too long. Every part of this new and difficult work was carefully organized and charted. As the Marine Corps Gazette wrote:

> Without Harllee's power to defy tradition, without his tremendous drive and vitality, the success of General Lejeune's school might not have been so successful.—The success of the program was largely due to the intelligent, fiery and even rebellious nature of Col. Harllee.

But on March 5, 1920 the Colonel had to dust off his "Chaw Brannon" (Chicago publicity and recruiting) side. That was the day the House Naval Affairs Committee and the Secretary of the Navy decided after a hearing by the Committee on the subject to inspect the Marine Corps Institute at Quantico. A transcript of that hearing is as interesting to read as the best fiction. The apparent attitude of the Committee was: Is it possible to turn these schoolboys into an effective fighting force? Is the reverse possible? Gen. Lejeune was firm in his convictions:

"You know there used to be an old theory that the soldier ought to be illiterate and like dumb, driven cattle. I think our experience in this war shows the more intelligence, the more education, and the more initiative a man has, the better soldier he is."

He went on to describe the original morale-lifting goal of the Institute.

These were the sentiments voiced earlier by Harllee in his testimony before the Senate Military Affairs Committee on "The Active Army."

Harllee, when he was told about the Congressional inspection, determined not to have his program endangered by the temporary aberrations of the Quantico Marines.

He ordered every man at Quantico to have a book in his hands and to be reading it whenever possible while Congressional Committees inspected the base. Some of them may have been looking at the books upside down, and there was a certain incongruity about tough old Marines looking at books like "Little Lord Fauntleroy," while smoking and chewing tobacco, but the visitors expressed themselves as being very happy with the educational efforts being made.

Editorial pages of the nation's leading newspapers began to praise the "Quantico Idea" (shades of the Winthrop Idea) and Marines began to request duty at Quantico so they could go to the school. In April of 1920, any man who wished to do so could enlist in the Marine Corps for duty at Quantico where he could take the M.C.I. courses. But what about the men of the Corps who were not stationed at Quantico?

On May 11, 1920, the threat of trouble in Mexico gave Bo Harllee the break he needed. The 16th Marines were sent there aboard the transport USS HENDERSON. Many of the M.C.I. students requested permission to continue their studies aboard ship. This could be the first time for the "damned education" in the Marine Corps to spread beyond Quantico. Harllee moved fast and had the materials packed up in locker boxes for the following courses:

| Automobiles | 80 textbooks |
| Drafting | 6   " |

Bookkeeping   20   "
Spanish   180   "
plus, an Amberolo Phonograph with a complete set of Spanish instrumental records.

In less than three weeks, lessons began pouring into Quantico. Dozens of new enrollments also came in. The Marines were the first with correspondence school education! The dreams of Secretary Daniels, Generals Lejeune and Butler, and Bo Harllee began to be realized.

Such distinguished personages connected with the Marine Corps as Assistant Secretary of the Navy Franklin D. Roosevelt began taking M.C.I. courses.

The tide had turned. It ran so rapidly that when General Lejeune was appointed Commandant of the Marine Corps on July 1, 1920, one of his first orders was to direct Bo Harllee to extend the scope of the Marine Corps Institute to the entire Marine Corps.

He also ordered Harllee to duty at Marine Corps Headquarters in Washington as Chief of the Educational Section.

When Harllee left Quantico, the staff of the M.C.I. gave him a surprise send off on the 5:41 P.M. train, complete with guard of honor which deeply affected him.

But after he left Quantico, the Institute floundered, according to "The Leatherneck", despite its operation by persons well fitted for the work. Insufficient students were enrolled at stations all over the Marine Corps. It looked like the Marine Corps Institute was a failure after all.

The Commandant and General Smedley Butler, then in command of Quantico, returned from a trip to Haiti and Santo Domingo about this time. They asked Harllee how the Institute was making out. He replied that they had better transfer him back to Quantico or transfer the Institute to Washington where he could take personal charge. The difficulties of forcing "the damned education" down the throats of the Quantico Marines were such that even Harllee's friend that great Marine fighter, General Smedley Butler, said, according to "The Leatherneck", "I will be glad to get rid of the thing."

General Lejeune decided to transfer the M.C.I. to Washington and gave Harllee the triple job of Officer-in-Charge of the Marine Corps Institute, Commanding Officer of the Marine Barracks in Washington, and Chief of the Educational Section at Marine Corps Headquarters. This decision was made on November 20 and that very night Bo Harllee transferred the men, desks, texts and all the rest of the school to Navy barges. By sunrise of the next day the Marine Corps Institute was cruising up the Potomac River to Washington. It was transferred from the Washington Navy Yard to the famous old Marine Barracks at Eighth and Eye Streets, S.E., in pushcarts furnished by the local police sergeant.

From then on the Marine Corps Institute flourished and, in a figure of speech, lived happily ever after, even unto today.

The Commandant, General Lejeune, generously gave Harllee the following credit in an official letter to him:

> In other words, during the entire period in which you were connected with the Marine Corps Institute, from January, 1920, to July, 1921, you conceived its plan, obtained the cooperation of the International Correspondence Schools, organized the staff of the Institute, drew up complete instructions for its management, and enlisted the cooperation of the officers and enlisted men of the Marine Corps in making it a Marine Corps school in the broadest sense. So successful were you in your efforts in creating this institution, that even after your detachment from duty in connection therewith, the Institute has continued to develop and grow along sound lines.

The Institute was suspended only for nineteen months from its inception until the present day—those months were from July of 1940 until January 19, 1942. During the first 30 years, the Institute processed well over two million lessons. In 1924 the Commandant ordered all officers to enroll in a foreign language study. Officers, as well as enlisted men, took other courses. In 1950, the Marine Corps Gazette estimated that every Marine officer then on active duty had studied at least one course.

The list of graduates for the month of December 1925, discloses diplomas given in almost every course on the lists of the International Correspondence Schools. A major with a diploma in Poultry Farming (this was a very popular course) leads the list. Accounting, Traffic Management, Commercial Law, Civil Engineering, Electric Lighting, Auditing, Automobile, Aeroplane Engines, Blacksmithing, Shop Practice, High School Courses, Stenographic, Good English, Pharmacy, Railway Postal Clerk, Fruit Growing, Soil Improvement, Machine Shop Practice, Handicraft Designing, Mathematics and Physics, Radio and many other courses all showed their graduates.

Through the years until Harllee's retirement in 1935, about one quarter of all Marines took M.C.I. courses.

And what was the cost of this plan? The Commandant reported in 1934 that the cost of graduating a student was $23.86; the cost per student enrolled was $1.29 and the cost per lesson was 34 cents! These costs were paid by the Government, and as had been the case with the rifle ranges, Bo Harllee had a crazy phobia against sticking the taxpayers.

"The Leatherneck" wrote in December of 1934 that "the original plan of organization was well conceived and has remained unchanged." The I.C.S. was still being used.

An example of what could be done by the M.C.I. for a Marine—if the Marine wanted it enough—was the case of John Smith. After the eighth grade he had to leave school to support his family. After many jobs for four years, winding up as an overcoat salesman, he joined the Marines. He started M.C.I. courses. In five years, he turned in almost 500 lessons; he completed ten courses, one a standard high school course. He became a regular Marine Captain and received a high school diploma and the equivalent of two years of college. Only the name is fictitious. An extreme case to be sure, but it showed what could be done.

As all armed forces, including the Marine Corps, began to acquire more complicated equipment and more technical military knowledge became necessary, the M.C.I. in 1953 changed the list of courses it offered to MOS related, or U.S.M.C. occupational courses, except for mathematics, spelling and punctuation. The organization of the M.C.I. remained the same, however. It reported 178,000 Marines enrolled in 1981, with 113,000 completions that year.

The M.C.I. was the prototype for the Coast Guard Institute,

the Army Air Forces Institute, and United States Armed Forces Institute (which closed in the 1970's), all designed to extend educational and vocational training to the armed services.

"Our Army" magazine in August of 1935 stated, "It is significant that the present plan of Mr. Robert Fechner, Director of the Civilian Conservation Corps, is providing educational facilities for the expanded CCC with 600,000 members coincides along general lines almost exactly with what Colonel Harllee has advocated all his life."

General Lejeune said,

> Here in the Marine Corps Institute, we offer a man the opportunity to learn. We do not urge it on him. And the man who can apply himself and study in the face of the difficulties of a military life is the man who is worthwhile. Whether a man is on shipboard or whether he's stationed in some post in China we are able to offer him an opportunity to improve himself— to make himself a better Marine while he is in the service, and a better citizen when he is out of the service.

Lieutenant Colonel Harllee said,

> A man must be able to read understandingly and to write, and if he can do these, even if only tediously, and will exert himself he can hope and expect to lift himself above the common level and to become the kind of man industry needs and pays for liberally. He can then go forth into the world creating for the Marine Corps the reputation not only as a corps d'elite of soldiers but as a training school for economic usefulness for the advancement of human prosperity and happiness.

Finally, Will Harllee said in a speech to a graduating high school class in Midway, South Carolina in 1935:

> It has been my lot to direct the education in the art of using firearms of many men, several hundred thousand of them. That stern duty is a necessary feature of military training. But the arts which give real values and should be the glory of life are not those which destroy but those which create. As I approach the time for crossing over the river to rest under the shade of the trees my most abiding satisfaction derives from the part I have played in many years of military service to carry on the work of an educator to enrich life and create some spiritual as well as material values.

On July 27, 1921, Lt. Col. Harllee was detached from Marine Corps Headquarters and ordered to Santo Domingo.

By following General Harllee's original plans, the Marine Corps Institute has, during the years, given education and training to thousands of Marines, thus strengthening their character and their ability to meet the problems of both military and civilian life.—Ralph E. Weeks, President, International Correspondence Schools

XXVII
SANTO DOMINGO
Sorting Out Guerrillas With The Cordon System 1921–1922

"Sorry, impossible to review your fine regiment. I praise their accomplishments which could only be possible through their discipline, endurance, and superior determination. These qualities are only possessed by efficient troops. They have my earnest admiration. Lee"
—Radio message from Commanding General, Second Brigade, Santo Domingo to Lt. Col. Harllee, Commanding 15th Regiment and Eastern District Santo Domingo, November, 1921.

In 1916 after numerous coups d'etat in Santo Domingo and the incurring by Dominican Governments of debts to European nations which they would not or could not pay, President Wilson sent in the U. S. Marines. Their mission was (1) to stabilize the political situation, (2) to enable the collection of customs revenues with which the European borrowers could be repaid enough to prevent their intervention, and last but not least, (3) to protect American investments there.

The Marines had done their usual excellent job of landing and getting the situation well in hand. After the initial battles in 1916 and for a short while thereafter, they sent out patrols of usually less than 30 men under a lieutenant or sergeant to cope with an assortment of political and other opponents to the American regime. In addition to local patriots, this melange included highwaymen and other criminals; desperate unemployed sugar cane cutters imported from Haiti, Jamaica and other West Indian Islands; and peasants forced into collaboration with these groups. Such men were all called "bandits" by the Americans. In later wars, they would be termed "guerrillas." The Marines lost 20 men killed and 67 wounded from 1916 to 1922 in this manner and underwent the type of frustration later familiar in Vietnam. They couldn't tell who was a "bandit" and who was not. As a result they were alleged by some Dominicans to have been guilty of serious misconduct, and this was one of the reasons for an active interest on the part of the U. S. Senate Committee on Foreign Relations.

On August 5, 1921, Bill Harllee reported to the Commanding General of the Second Brigade of Marines in the capital, Santo Domingo City, for duty. He spent a month and a half there with Brigadier General Harry Lee, much of it in Lee's home. He had travelled down to Santo Domingo with General Lee. He also made trips around the country and found out what was going on. He decided what he would do when he got a chance.

The bandit activity had always been primarily in the Eastern District, the provinces of Macoris and Seibo. That was where the big sugar estates were concentrated. The jungle-like terrain of large sections of the Eastern District afforded the bandits excellent protection.

General Lee decided to assign Harllee to command the hot spot—the Fifteenth Regiment and Eastern District, with a strict injunction to bring the bandit activity to a halt as soon as possible. Lee knew him and his reputation and figured he was the man for the job.

Marines in the Eastern District of Santo Domingo conduct a search operation of native huts to ferret out bandits and arms.

12:35 A.M. September 28, 1921. San Pedro de Macoris, Eastern District, Santo Domingo. Lt. Col. W. C. Harllee, who had taken command 35 minutes earlier, was awakened by a messenger galloping up to his quarters on horseback with the message:

"Mr. Thomas Steele, the British subject in charge of the Angelina sugar estate five miles away, has been abducted by bandits."

Harllee had already made up his mind what to do the moment anything happened, and he had decided to do it fast, right away. He called his second in command, Major Gerard M. Kincade and told him, "Get the entire regiment ready to move out with me, immediately. Steele has been kidnapped."

They both knew that Illinois Senator Medill McCormick's Special Investigating Committee of the U. S. Senate was en route to Santo Domingo to look into just such occurrences as the snatching of Steele, and to see how the Marines were handling the situation.

Harllee took the entire regiment of 36 officers and 814 enlisted

Marines ready for combat in Santo Domingo as they set up a cordon in a section of Jagual Wood.

men into the field and surrounded a section of Jagual Wood with what the history books would call a "cordon." He selected the part which was known to include the hiding place of the dreaded Ramon Nateras, who had abducted Steele. Before the abduction, Nateras had demanded $5,000 from him.

The bandit camp was on high ground between two deep arroyos and was so well concealed that it was invisible from trails passing through the arroyos. There were about sixty men in the camp and another party of thirty men arrived later. The bandits were well supplied with good rations, including chicken.

The "General" demanded that his hostage kiss the Dominican flag and threatened to put him in a cave with rats, snakes and spiders. The bandits saluted the "General" profusely and gravely by bending the knee and raising the right hand.

In the words of a report of the day:

> All the men wore shoes and the trousers were generally blue jeans. The "General" was well dressed with jean trousers, which had been bleached by having them frequently washed. . . . Woman in camp about 22 years old, good looking; also girl fourteen years old.

Harllee drew a cordon formed by his regiment around the area bounded by a line between Chicarrones, Las Yayas, Mata de la Palm, El Salto, La Paja, Monte Coca and Chicarrones and gathered *all* the people in this area. In the meantime, he had located two local women of good reputation, Maria and Rosa Belen, who had been badly mistreated by Ramon Nateras' bandits. These women were not prostitutes or locally notorious, as legend later had it, but had been forced to live with the bandits and understandably had no love for them.

That night Harllee put a bright light on each of the 600 or so inhabitants he had rounded up in the area and had the two women, for their own protection unseen by the other Dominicans, identify the bandits. One hundred and five bandits were identified in this particular roundup. Thus was solved the problem of all guerrilla wars—how to find out who is a guerrilla and who is a peaceful peasant.

During the operation, on September 29, 1921, Marine Gunner Robert W. Reid had led a detachment of eight men up a precipice under close range fire from eighty armed bandits and drove them from their stronghold. This was a good example of the type of action involved.

Bill Harllee addressed the following remarks to the people, who had been rounded up, translated, of course, into Spanish, and even into Haitian Creole for the few Haitians there:

LET ALL THE PEOPLE LISTEN:
During the past month, bandit leaders have robbed many stores and many people. They have taken away Mr. Steele, an English citizen and Manager of the Angelina estate. They held him until he paid money to get away. The Marines have caught the man who caused that mischief and almost all the men in that bandit camp, and they have been punished.

The bandit leaders have written to managers of all the Sugar Estates and have demanded money.

The bandits have told the sugar estates managers that they are forming an army to make them pay money to the bandits and that they will rob the sugar estates if they do not pay.

You people here have been afraid of these bandit men, because you believed that they would hurt you, and you were afraid to give any information about them.

255

They have told you that the Marines could not catch the bandits.

The bandits have robbed bateys (stores) in the cane fields and also the settlements in the woods, and then have scattered and hid in the woods. You must not let them live in your country any more.

The Marines are obliged to find the bandits. The bandits put away their arms when the Marines come, and it has been hard for the Marines to recognize bandits from the other people, so we have been obliged to collect all the people in these woods.

We now have with us people whom these bandits robbed and injured. These people are helping us to pick out the bandits. There are many more people who wish to help us find these bandits. Heretofore, they have been afraid to help us, but you now see that we will not let the bandits know who tells us about them. You now see how well and how easily the Marines can find out who are bandits and how well we keep secret those who give us information. If any of you at any time, wish to give us information, the bandits will not know about it.

You also see that the Marines will not let any bandits go free in this country. We intend to find all of them and to make it impossible for bandits to live among you. You will then be happier and free to go about your work and not be afraid to inform on bandits or help us find them. You now see that the bandit leaders are no longer big men. We will make them afraid to come among you.

You may now go to your homes, and you may feel that we are here to protect you and that you can come to our officers and our soldiers and give them information and that we will not permit bandits to hurt you. I hope that we will not have to assemble you again, but we will have to do this again if we learn of any more bandit groups in your country. We are friends of the good people of this country, but we will not stop hunting for bandits until we have put them all in jail.

We are going to use these bandits to work on your roads and do other things for your benefit. This is the only kind of bandit armies that you will see in this country.

You may now go home. You will be safe, but if you wish to stay here tonight, you may do so and you will be fed tomorrow before you go.

We wish you a pleasant trip to your homes.
ADIOS!

The people were mollified, and many stayed for breakfast. Between then and December 23, 1921 and from January 2,

1922 until March of 1922, Harlee conducted eight more of these cordon operations. A Marine officer who could speak Spanish, together with a Dominican officer, were put in charge of the interrogation unit on later cordon roundups, although Harllee always participated.

Radios, which had not hitherto been available for such tactics, were used, as well as air dropped messages.

Harllee flew in the U. S. Marine DH-4B aircraft, an improved version of British designed World War planes known as "Flying Coffins," over the terrain as an observer himself time and again until he had learned the district perfectly from the air. After each operation he carefully made the same talk to the non-bandits.

With the cordon system, Harllee and his 15th Regiment captured over 600 bandits in less than six months. There were two other regiments in 2 other districts in Santo Domingo almost from the beginning in 1916 until it was all over in 1922. In mid-1922, the Marines only claimed 1,137 bandits killed or wounded in all Santo Domingo since 1916 as compared to Harllee's 600 in six months. And not one single Marine under Harllee's command was killed!

And what did he do with the captured bandits? Did he put them in prison? No. He set them to work building a gridiron of roads through the jungles. These roads ran both east and west and were ony 500 yards apart—less than the range of a rifle—and automobiles could traverse them, as they were ten feet wide. Major General Commandant Lejeune commended him by official letter for destroying the bandits' rendezvous and hiding place in such a new and resourceful way. After the cordon operations were over, bandits started surrendering voluntarily, as they had no place to hide. Harllee also had the caves in which they had hidden blown up.

The prisoners, most of whom were unemployed and hard-up, were treated humanely and fed so well that there were even reports of men trying to break *into* the prison camps.

The Dominicans were happy—only those very few sympathetic to the bandits and those employed by one of the big and powerful American owned sugar estates complained. British

Vice Consul Reverend A. H. Beer of the St. Stephens Episcopal Church of San Pedro de Macoris, the dean of the diplomatic corps there, was very happy with the operation.

Frank Garnett, Administrator of the big "Ingenio Porvenir" sugar estate wrote to Harllee on March 16, 1922:

> The district at the present time is freer of bandits than we have ever known it to be. I wish to emphasize the fact that during the entire time of the military occupation of this Island, it is only during your regime that any real common sense activity had taken place in order to put a stop to banditry.

Lieutenant General Edward A. Craig served under Harllee in Santo Domingo as a young officer. He was the hero of World War II and the Korean War who told his brigade upon embarking for Korea, "No unit in this brigade will retreat except on orders from higher authority—you will never receive orders to retreat from me."

General Craig, in his oral history at Marine Corps headquarters forty-seven years later, reported about Harllee's Santo Domingo operation.

"I think this drive did more to defeat the bandits down there than at any other time, any other operations that we had. It was the first real coordinated drive that I saw."

In a letter in 1981 he added,

> Colonel Harllee's plan was a success as many of the bandits were convicted in court and others surrendered soon after the drive ended. From this time on organized groups of bandits ceased to exist.

Also,

> I am thankful and proud that I had the opportunity of serving under Colonel Harllee during the period described.

Dr. Allan R. Millett's authoritative history of the Marine Corps, "Semper Fidelis" states,

> In a five-month period the regiment (the 15th) conducted nine well-planned, skillfully run cordon operations to seal off and screen entire village populations for guerrillas.

and, reporting no casualties for the 15th regiment, also declared:

> The cordon operations and more patrolling finally brought the campaign to an end as the remaining bandits surrendered or were tracked down.

XXVIII
SUCCEEDING TOO
WELL—SANTO
DOMINGO

In fact, it would appear that during long and faithful service, he had added glory to the annals of the U. S. Marine Corps.
—Judge Advocate of General Court Martial on Lt. Col. William C. Harllee

Parodoxically, Bill Harllee had succeeded too well. It's a strange tale.

In March of 1922 a gathering storm of faults found with the administration of the 15th Regiment burst loose. He had been told to be with his troops and to leave the administrative details of the regiment up to his staff. He had done both. He had been with his Marines on all nine cordon operations but had worked day and night (on one occasion for 3 days and 2 nights with no sleep or rest) on the paperwork, because he knew there was national, and especially Senatorial, interest in the United States in what was happening in Santo Domingo and much of the paperwork was designed to provide a record to take care of this interest. President Warren G. Harding had made a campaign pledge to get the Marines out of Santo Domingo, which was the desire of many Americans concerned about what we were doing with armed force in Latin America. They called it "Dollar Diplomacy" because we were intervening at least in large part to protect American dollars invested there.

March 23, 1922 was the date. Harllee was relieved of command then, in spite of the fact that the British Vice Counsul, who visited the estates and mingled with the people, wrote to him on March 21, "I do not know of one person who has spoken in favor of your removal. In fact, the expressions have been quite to the contrary." Colonel Charles H. Lyman relieved him and proceeded to find fault with the spit and polish aspects of a regiment which had been active in the field for months. Their leggings were not blancoed! And so forth.

Harllee was ordered to appear as an interested party, and later as a defendant, before a Court of Inquiry looking into the morale and discipline of the 15th Regiment and compliance with orders and performance of duty by Harllee and his regiment. This was done by General Lee, who had commended him after he started his cordon operations; who had had many drinks with him while being informed in detail by Harllee of what he was doing; and who had so often entertained him in his home!

What had happened? Some felt that jealousy on the part of others had played a part in poisoning the General's mind. But that was not all. Harllee knew that the price of raw sugar had gone from 3 cents a pound to 30 cents a pound in 1916 because of World War I. A great American financial institution had invested in sugar estates and had, in effect, encouraged the banditry by importing the 20,000 laborers, mostly black men from Haiti and the British West Indies, for the sugar fields and mills, and then throwing them out of work half the year—after paying them 30 to 40 cents a day when they worked. It was to the interest of that bank, Harllee believed, that the banditry continue so that the American occupation would continue and their sugar estates would not have to contend with taxes and other problems from the pestiferous Dominican government, which was why he was sure that they encouraged the banditry.

In those days, he was convinced that the bank had great power at the seat of our government. Many people asked him later on how he happened to wind up before a court of inquiry and a general court martial after doing such a good job. He told them that the bank had the word passed down from its powerful friends in Washington to have him removed because he was causing too much trouble for them, e.g. conducting an investigation into the alleged complicity of the Consuelo Sugar Estate with the bandits. And in his view it was always possible for jealous people to find something wrong with a military operation such as his and to thus get him out of the way.

Mr. Kilbourne and Mr. Bass of the American-owned and operated Consuelo Sugar Estate had complained about Harllee, who claimed that they were friends of Ramon Nateras, the notorious bandit. He thought this because he had sworn testimony from not one, but five witnesses to the effect that the Conseulo Sugar Estate was paying the bandits! This sworn testimony was taken by a Board of Investigation of four Marine officers and established that this Estate had paid Nateras so well that he shot and killed in premeditated fashion—murdered, or executed, if you will—four of his Dominican countrymen for robbing the bodega (store in Dominican Spanish) of the Consuelo Estate and that he warned other bandits not to rob it or other American-owned estates! Marines might be fair game for Nateras, but not the property of the American bank!

Harllee's successor and obviously no friend, Colonel Lyman, claimed that the officials of the Consuelo Sugar Estate cooperated with the Marines. Would they be likely not to, said Harllee, after they had been exposed?

But in spite of all this and all the good work, the 15th Regiment as well as Harllee himself, was put on the spot—its morale, discipline and performance was on trial! Nothing was done to Consuelo or the bank. Is it any wonder Harllee saw sinister influences at play? And that he saw them as coming from the powerful New York bank! Colonel Lyman and Rear Admiral S. S. Robison, the Military Governor of Santo Domingo, called the evidence used by the Board investigating the Consuelo Sugar Estate doubtful, but the Marine officers hearing it had believed it—and their findings and opinions were reached after Harllee had left the District and no longer had any authority over them.

The Court of Inquiry on Harllee and the 15th was a monster—it lasted from March 23, 1922 until June 19, 1922 with 50 days of meetings and 1,388 pages of testimony, not counting hundreds of pages of exhibits. Bill unsuccessfully challenged 2 of the 3 members of the Court on the grounds of personal bias and prejudice—one of them with such gusto that when they recommended the general court martial for him, they included contempt of court as one of the specifications. This in spite of the fact that the member concerned had used the words "ridiculous," "puerile," and disingenous" with regard to Harllee before he was ever challenged.

As an example of the attempts to convict him, the Brigade Surgeon testified as to the horrible condition of the hospital at San Pedro de Macoris. Harllee's medical officers told him that the Brigade Surgeon's testimony was false; that he was drunk the day of the alleged inspection and had not gone further into the hospital than the porch. The next day, Harllee's counsel, Major Kincade, introduced witnesses to establish this non-inspection, reported as an inspection, on the record. Harllee then moved to impeach the Surgeon's testimony. The court refused to strike it from the record, but nothing further was heard from the court about this witness and his testimony.

The phony quality of the charges against him are illustrated by the following samples of testimony by Bill Harllee in his defense:

7.Q. State what you know of your alleged failure to make any report of the alleged rape of one Altagracia de la Rosa.
I had Captain Garcia, a native Dominican officer, and Lieutenant Whitmire question the women, and I questioned them myself and made inquiries of other Dominicans present who lived in that section. There was no division of opinion on the part of Captain Garcia, Lieutenant Whitmire, myself or anyone else present that the complaint was a crude fake. It was so palpably so that it was annoying to follow it up. Notwithstanding, I gave Lieutenant Whitmire orders to take them to the place

where they claimed to live and to carry them throughout our lines in that sector and have them view the men. As a matter of fact, they said their house was on the Saco River, and our lines were not within several miles of the river. Every statement that they made concerning their assumed knowledge of where our troops were located was wrong. In fact, they could give no account to support their claims. These women were loathsome and repulsive beyond description, filthy, and one of them with open sores upon her person which made one keep well away from her.

I had been ordered to the capital to be present during the hearings of the Senate Committee, and I left camp that evening and went by plane to the capital the following morning. There I was for four days with the Commanding General as a guest at his house. During this time I related this case to him. I did not refer to them by their names. I told them that these women were in camp ready for the Senate Committee and that we could convince the Committee of the fake nature of the reports they were receiving by introducing these two women. The General said we'd better let the Committee run its own investigation. I gained a clear impression that my report in this case was satisfactory and sufficient, and when I returned to my troops in the woods and found that Lieutenant Whitmire had taken the women to all the troops along the sector, that the women would not take him to the place where they claimed to live.

8.Q. Do you wish to make any statement about la Cruz and Private Cadow?

Now, about Domingo la Cruz and Private Cadow. Private Cadow adorns the uniform he wears and whether that uniform be faded or whether his hat be blocked or belt be blancoed, does not adorn him any more. Private Cadow is my comrade. He is not a murderer, if he goes to jail, I go with him. I hereby take upon my own shoulders the responsibility which you might think belongs to Private Cadow. That kind of thing makes morale. Lay it on me.

9.Q. What about the break-in at 88 Bazan Street?

The man at 88 Bazan Street, for instance, is a newspaper man. His story was so outrageous that I never for a moment even believed that Marines had even been to his house. When ever a man states that after a bunch of men had tried and failed to push open a door, they then placed a horse in position and had the horse kick the door open, I do not believe it. Especially if there are no horse-hoof marks upon the door and I considered that the investigation conducted was sufficient.

Some idea of the attempt to railroad Bill Harllee can be gained from the following excerpt from his testimony.

The defendant waives nothing. I have been before this court of inquiry during a period of well nigh three months. I have listened with utter disgust to testimony offered here covering a period of over two months, introduced by the court, the judge advocate and his array of his assistant and counsel. I have observed the spectacle of witnesses who have given some of the most pusillanimous testimony that had ever been offered before a military body.

This court, after consuming over sixty days in introducing testimony against me and in the case of one witness, Major Miller, whose testimony was hostile and antagonistic to me, consumed all of the court days for two weeks in the testimony of that one witness. For the testimony of the approximately thirty witnesses which I have introduced in my behalf, I have been allowed exactly the same time as was consumed by this one witness, who appeared to be the chief witness against me in this court. Now, I have hastened the proceedings of this court to the very extreme of human endurance during these two weeks in which I have been presenting my case.

Now I submit that this proposition of stopping my direct examination within a limited number of hours after its beginning is outrageous and iniquitous, and if this be contempt make the most of it.

The following question put to a lieutenant of Harllee's 15th Regiment during the Court of Inquiry and his reply speaks for itself with regard to Colonel Lyman, who made many of the reports against Bill Harllee:

6.Q. Some reference has been made to alleged relations of yourself with some of the personnel of the Bernstein Carnival, do you wish to make any statements in that respect?

6.A. Colonel Lyman told me in Macoris that it was rumored in the Capitol that I was engaged to one of the Bernstein Carnival girls. I told him at that time that it was not so. I was not in any position to even think of such a thing. Colonel Lyman told me at that time that he was going to investigate it and if he found it to be true, that he would give me a general court-martial. I have been told since that General Lee and Mr. Bernstein did investigate it and that I wish to state here under oath, that the rumors are absolutely false.

All of this so damaged the efforts being made to defame the 15th Regiment and its Commander that the Court of Inquiry was moved from San Pedro de Macoris to San Domingo City and the files of the Regiment were closed to Harllee.

He and his friends were suspicious of a phony record being kept so that the wife of one of his officers took the entire proceedings down in shorthand.

The Military Governor of Santo Domingo, Admiral Robison, sent for Harllee and his counsel and told him that if any more attempts were made to humiliate officers before the Court as was done to the Brigade Surgeon, he would have them tried for "Conspiracy." Harllee replied that he had not started the iniquitous proceedings of that Court but that he had nothing to fear from them and that the Admiral could be assured that nothing he said would deter Harllee from defending himself to the best of his ability and from impeaching any other witnesses who gave false testimony. He also told the Admiral that when he talked about "Conspiracy" between him and his counsel he evidenced the same lack of knowledge of law and propriety that he did when he sought to suborn testimony on the proceedings of a court of any kind and as he did when he attempted to threaten and intimidate him when he was a defendant before a court. That stopped the argument. The Admiral had nothing further to say.

Such was the Court of Inquiry.

So on September 7, 1922, Admiral Robison "ordered him tried by general court martial on 10 specifications of "Disobeying the Lawful Order of His Superior Officer" and 2 specifications of "Conduct to the Prejudice of Good Order and Discipline," but not for "Conspiracy."

The maximum sentence for these charges and specifications was death!

It was really a case of throwing the book at him: the specs started out with such ridiculous items as expending without authority three hundred dollars of fines (which he had properly collected) on feeding the prisoners he had captured and was working. They ran through not carrying out exactly a detailed training schedule while his regiment was in combat and of not marking his maps exactly as ordered. In fact, his maps were better than ordered. They had contours, which were prohibited but necessary. They wound up with accusations of murders and rapes by Marines of the 15th Regiment, accusing Harllee of not investigating them fast enough. What it amounted to was that he and his officers in the field had been far, far too busy to comply immediately and fully with all the paperwork thrown at him when he had been told in the first place to leave such matters to his staff! Furthermore the regiment was twelve officers short of its complement of 45.

But he was a gone goose; in a military organization, theoretically, one carries out orders, period!

There were not enough officers senior to him in Santo Domingo to comprise a general court martial, so they had to order several down from the United States.

Harllee was now in a battle for his life, with the cards stacked against him. So at every stage of the game he vigorously and successfully fought with the facts, and the officers and men of the 15th stood by him, at great risk to their careers, because he had been relieved and was apparently going to be junked.

They testified that Harllee had been on the front lines with them, on horseback and afoot; had visited the forward outposts at such times as 2 and 3 A.M., and had worked so hard that they feared for his health.

In respect to these matters, the following testimony before the Court of Inquiry of Major Gerard M. Kincade (he had been Harllee's second in command, but Harllee had been relieved) is pertinent:

> At no time did I hear any murmurs or complaints, besides that the individuals or squads had to cook and prepare their own meals. . . . They seemed to be cheerful and spirited under these hardships. I recall an incident which was reported to me by Mr. Garnett at a gathering of officers and civilians after the Jagual Woods operation had been on for three weeks. He said "I was to Jagual today and I saw some of the men. They looked dirty but cheerful, and I asked them how they liked the work. They said "The old man (Harllee) is working as hard as we are, if not harder, and if he can stand it, we can."
> These and other observations lead me to believe that even

the highest duty the Regimental Commander could ask of his men would be performed in such a way as to omit of any complaint and I believe the morale and discipline of the 15th Regiment was excellent.

With respect to this morale and discipline the court found as follows:

"The court has been impressed with the exhibition of loyalty to their late commanding officer shown by the officers of the 15th Regiment and with the general spirit of contentment and harmony among the commissions of personnel of that regiment. The uncontradicted evidence also shows that there was a spirit of cheerful and uncomplaining obedience to orders among the enlisted men; such a spirit among officers and men is not compatible with a low state of morale."

The General Court Martial lasted from September 11, 1922 to October 10, 1922. The testimony ran for 250 pages. Harllee's enemies had awfully bad luck with the general court—the President, Colonel Ben H. Fuller, later Commandant of the Marine Corps, and the members were all fair men. Even the Judge Advocate of the Court, the prosecuting attorney in a military court, Lt. Col. E. B. Manwaring, stated in the next to the last paragraph of his final argument,

The character, reputation, and ability of the accused (Harllee) have not been attacked, it being cheerfully conceded that the integrity of purpose of the accused in the service has heretofore always been unquestioned. In fact, it would appear that during long and faithful service, he had added glory to the annals of the United States Marine Corps.

So on October 9, 1922, the President of the Court called Harllee before the court and announced to him the verdict, "Acquitted on all charges and specifications."

A letter from the Office of the Judge Advocate General of the Navy dated Feb. 17, 1982 states:

A search of the files of the Office of the Judge Advocate General for the years 1921–1925 reveals that notice of the results of the case of Lt. Col. Wm. C. Harllee were not published to the naval service, although the results of certain other courts martial during this same period, including acquittals, were so published.

This is typical bureaucratese. The facts were that the powers that be knew very well that the best procedure to follow in this case was to cover up all notice that it had ever occurred. This was one war with the great and powerful that Bill Harllee did not ask for but won hands down.

And here again, as at Vera Cruz, he learned first hand what was wrong with our relations with Latin America.

Sumner Welles, Under Secretary of State for President Franklin Roosevelt, was to say in 1927 that the benefits which Washington derived from eight years control of the Dominican Republic "have been of infinitesimal importance when compared to the suspicions, fears and hatred to which the Occupation gave rise throughout the American continent, and when compared to the lasting hostility towards the American people which the Occupation created in the hearts of a very great number of the Dominican people."

XXIX
HAITI AND BACK TO WASHINGTON 1922–1926

HAITI

In November of 1922, Bill Harllee was ordered to the First Marine Brigade in Port-au-Prince, Haiti.

Haiti retained its independence from 1804 until 1915, when the Marines landed and took control of the country for reasons similar to those which had occasioned their landing in the eastern half of the island of Hispaniola, Santo Domingo. The changes in regime in Haiti had been much more frequent and much bloodier than in Santo Domingo.

But by 1920 the "Cacos", as the bandits or guerrillas were called in Haiti, had been subdued by the Marines. The name "Caco" came from a bird of prey. The country had been pacified and politically stabilized. The natives were illiterate, poor and lived in primitive conditions. It only took the presence of a thousand or so Marines in the First Brigade to successfully, even tranquilly, occupy Haiti. So Bill Harllee's duties were routine, but he travelled all over Haiti by auto, horseback and aircraft. He learned enough about the country to stand him in good stead then and on a later, much more interesting tour of duty there.

WASHINGTON, D.C.

He was to be ordered back to Haiti in 1926, but in July of 1923, Bill Harllee reported for duty as Executive Officer, Division of

Operations and Training at Marine Corps Headquarters in Washington.

He learned that after the dust had settled on his Santo Domingo court—a failed attempt at a frame-up as he saw it—that he was going to get choice assignments from then on. Nobody wanted a Congressional investigation of what had gone on down there.

He then described this job as follows:

> I am a regular bureaucrat. I have a high sounding title, and when I go away on leave it makes no difference. The office is just as well off when I am away as when I am there. In this respect I am no different from any other bureaucrat. Still, I am glad to have a job with nothing to do for a change.

In the midst of these strenuous duties he found time to attend the Progressive Party convention at Cleveland as a delegate at large. He also attended the Democratic convention in New York, where he met again Franklin D. Roosevelt.

The Colonel loved the war-like spirit and the humanitarianism of the elder Senator Robert LaFollette of Wisconsin, the Progressive Party Presidential nominee, because he found in these qualities a parallel to his own two-sided nature. He followed LaFollette with the same loyalty and enthusiasm with which he had followed Henry George, the Single Tax leader, whose doctrines he had espoused since 1912. He could be a follower as well as a leader, when his heart and mind were enlisted in a good cause. But he could not follow authority for its own sake.

Senators Brookhart and Shipstead, Congressmen Keating and Crosser, former Assistant Secretary of Labor Louis Post—these were some of his friends in those days. So were a host of others in rebellion against injustice and oppression. He was the loyal friend of anyone whose spirit was devoted to the cause of human progress—even though their methods may have differed from his.

THE CRUISE—THE MOVIES

During this tour of duty, he was ordered to make a training cruise with the U. S. Fleet to Panama, Los Angeles and Hawaii. It was a dream cruise. In Panama, where bargains then abounded, he bought lifetime supplies of china, linen, perfume for Ella, and a goodly quantity of cigars, all duty free.

In Los Angeles, or rather Hollywood, he was invited by William C. de Mille to visit him for several days.

Bill de Mille was not as famous as his younger brother Cecil B. (whom he called C.B.) C. B. had gone from New York to Hollywood many years earlier than Bill, but the older brother had been a highly successful writer and producer of plays on Broadway from 1900 to 1914. For eighteen years thereafter in the movie capital, he directed fifty-six motion pictures and produced many more. After 1914, the two brothers worked closely together. C. B. in those days was exceeded at the box office only by Mary Pickford and Charlie Chaplin.

Bill Harllee had met Bill de Mille through mutual friends in the family of Henry George, whose daughter, Anna, Bill de Mille had married. He wrote a play, "Classmates", in 1907 about some of Harllee's West Point classmates going adventuring in South America after leaving the Point.

Shortly before the de Milles went to California in 1914, they visited the George family in Washington—Henry George's son was a Congressman from New York. Automobiles were rare then—the Marine Corps did not even own a motor vehicle until 1909, but Bill Harllee had a Ford, and he and his car were requisitioned to show the New York de Milles around the nation's capital for a couple of weeks.

So when Harllee finally got to Southern California, he found that bread cast upon the water had come back as very fancy cake indeed. De Mille took him to his office with him day after day and gave him the run of the Paramount Studios. What a candy store in those days! The producer also gave a party in honor of the big Marine, who particularly liked Adolphe Menjou and Greta Neilson. He described Menjou "as a very modest and pleasant gentleman." Neilson was being featured in one of Bill de Mille's pictures.

There was national interest in the Hollywood parties of those days. The public imagined them as latter day Roman orgies. Plenty of space was made available for dancing, some of it by stars and starlets on table tops. Caterers supplied gourmet food even if there was no vomitoriums, which Bill Harllee had seen in Pompeii.

Despite Prohibition, there was plenty of strong liquid refreshment as well as gaming, so that either "wine, women, and song" or "drinking, singing, and gambling" were available. Finally, the grounds of the estates of the movie moguls had plenty of very attractive secluded nooks.

A party given by a producer such as de Mille did not lack for aspiring actresses seeking roles. Hollywood then ground out five to seven hundred films a year.

Wandering through a party for Harllee late at night, de Mille asked,

"Having a good time, Bill?"

He replied,

"There are some Marines I've known who would give up their chances at the Pearly Gates to be here."

Late the next night the two Bill's relaxed over some Bourbon and started talking:

de Mille,

"Bill, what do you think of the picture business? C. B. and I are happy that you have had a chance to meet some of America's idols and goddesses. You know I've directed Mary Pickford, Clara Bow, Victor Moore, Thomas Meighan and plenty of others you've met."

Harllee,

"Yes, I appreciate tremendously your hospitality. It would do justice to the good old South. And I admire your having the guts to stick to the principles of Henry George. I know they are not popular here. You've even been quoted as saying that the people of a state have certain inalienable rights to its natural resources. That certainly won't endear you to the people who have bought up all those natural resources."

de Mille,

"Sure, Bill, and I know we are in agreement on the laborer being worthy of his hire. Believe me, we've had one hell of a battle out here with the early Trust and financiers in order to see that producers, actors, actresses, directors, writers and all the rest of us who actually make pictures, realize some of the rewards. But, that's not what I asked you. What do you think of the picture business and the picture people?"

Harllee,

"Bill, movies were very useful to me in Haiti and Santo Domingo. I took some reels with me when I inspected the small posts out in the country and at night set up a screen and showed them. When the trains in the film seemed to come at the natives in the audience they jumped up and ran until I stopped the train. Same with horses coming and the guns firing at them. They thought I was a magic man—had Voodoo. More seriously, Bill, to be perfectly frank with you, naturally I like the people here, but I prefer to find my heroes in the people who have actually done the things—like Captain Lee Hall—fought the battles, beat the crime, won the games and races, made the inventions, led the people well, and so forth, instead of the people who are acting out their roles. I think its more than a little absurd that so many thousands of people will wait so many hours to see movie stars enter or leave a Hollywood premiere when they wouldn't do anything like that for, for example, the President of the United States or Sergeant York."

de Mille,

"I see you've got a lot to learn about our business, Bill. Let me give you lesson one, old boy. Our stars are symbols of romance, courage, adventure, nobility, unselfishness, virtue and high standards which everyone would like to represent, but which most of us can only closely identify with through those symbols on the screen. Furthermore those stars are in the long run selected not in any artificial manner but by seventy million moviegoers in this nation, supplemented by many millions in Europe and South America. They cannot become stars unless the public pays their nickels, dimes and quarters to see them.

"And its been a long uphill fight for the movie pioneers. When Mary Pickford had her first starring role she was paid only five dollars a day. Many is the month that I and others have worked 16 hour days. It was a battle back at the beginning of the century to get stage and other people to think of movies as respectable; another battle to shift from one reelers to feature length movies. The one reelers used to be called "chasers" because they were used to chase the audience out of a vaudeville house before the next vaudeville show. Writers had quite a battle to get paid anything for use of their material. And the picture business is dangerous. We've had a man, Bob Fleming, accidentally killed by a rifle bullet, whereas you like to claim that you had nobody killed on your rifle ranges where half a million men learned to shoot. Back in the early days, C. B. was shot at twice while carrying film home to prevent its sabotage, which had ruined our first film for us and almost put us out of business before we started.

"And you should go on some of our locations with us. Snakes, tarantulas, wild beasts, desert heat—not nearly as comfortable as your Marine barracks.

"And marksmanship, my friend? You should have seen a scene we shot with a young actor on top of a wall raising a water jar over his head to throw on his attackers below. Old Frank Hopkins had to break the jar with a 30-30 bullet passing eight inches above the actors head, and he did it.

"Also, the movies have provided more entertainment for more people than any other art form. Movies are seen by millions—stage plays by thousands. So don't you sit there and tell me that the public shouldn't have a little enthusiasm for the people who give them all this entertainment."

Harllee (smiling): "O.K. Bill, tonight you win. Tomorrow night I'll tell you about the Philippine Insurrection and the Boxer Rebellion. But you have certainly aroused my interest in America's most popular entertainment. And after all, you were the First Sergeant in the Paramount Company in World War I. As you may recall, I was a First Sergeant in the Volunteer Army in the Philippine Insurrection. So, as one first sergeant to another I won't let you down."

In Hawaii he saw his old friend Merle Johnson and others from the rifle days. His old Japanese cook and friend, Nasako, and his wife came down to the fleet flagship to see him with a huge basket filled with edible delicacies. Only after he left did Bill Harllee find a gallon of fine okolehau, a delicious Hawaiian alcoholic beverage, buried in the middle of the basket. He had only two friends aboard ship with whom on very rare occasions he dared imbibe such liquid refreshment—the Admiral was very strict in enforcing Josephus Daniels' prohibition, court-martialling any offender automatically. The three of them had a rough time taking care of such a glut.

On July 25, 1925, Bill Harllee was promoted to the rank of Colonel.

THE ARMY WAR COLLEGE

In August of 1925, he was ordered to the Army War College, then in Washington, D.C.

In June of 1926, he motored up to the twenty-fifth reunion of his West Point class of 1901. A book was published to commemorate the occasion. It contained pictures and biographies of the classmates and a fairly serious, if at times light-hearted, account of the reunion. But the editors considered one incident, and one incident only, worthy of a special page. In those days "shot" and "half shot" were the popular slang for being under the influence of alcoholic beverages. This page follows:

SHOT AT SUNRISE

It becomes our painful duty to record an appalling tragedy which occurred in connection with the Reunion. Two beloved classmates met with a shocking disaster. They were none others than Harllee and Jimmie West. On Thursday night—the big night, when hearts swelled with feeling from renewal of friendships and fond remininiscence—Harllee and West struggled manfully through the long hours. None suspected the bitter fate that awaited them at daylight. In song and story they strove to outdo all others and—thanks to the cheering spirits present— they well nigh succeeded. As the night wore on, no hint of the impending tragedy revealed itself in their demeanor. With a loyalty and faithfulness for which they have ever been noted, they looked smilingly towards the dawn. In fact, the nearer the dawn approached the broader became their smiles. Others gave up the vigil and silently stole away to their cadet cots, in mute testimonial to the endurance and cheerful determination of Harllee and West. Finally, none remained but them. Gazing into each others eyes, they realized that their hour, at last, had struck. They stood a moment, their arms about each others shoulders, almost overcome by emotion. Then they lifted their heads proudly, turned and marched out of the barracks arm in arm. West in a slightly used dinner coat suit and Harllee in pajamas.

Dawn was just peeping up over the eastern hills across the river. A soldier sentinel, solemnly and shiveringly walking his post in front of barracks, halted and looked upon the two brave men of Nineteen-One with approving envy. Harllee and West stood proudly and erectly upon the grass plain. They snapped to attention and brought their hands to a salute as the great orb of day flashed over the horizon. The last of the class to survive the night, they were shot at sunrise.

Although Harllee graduated from the Army War College in June of 1926 with a recommendation for high command, contingent upon successful command of a brigade, the highest recommendation the War College gave, he was undoubtedly more touched by the page his West Point classmates gave him and Jimmie West in their 25 year book.

During these years, he joined the New York Yacht Club, citing tongue-in-cheek that his service as an oiler on the steamer Mascotte and as a Marine captain aboard the USS FLORIDA had given him a considerable interest in yachting.

More seriously in 1894 he had made a trip from Tampa Bay in the 5 ton yacht "Mischief" down around the Florida coast to the empty land where Miami now stands and back to Tampa. "Mischief" was the fastest sailing craft in those waters then. Captain Frank Cooper and young Will Harllee, the entire crew, visited all the inhabited keys and some of the uninhabited ones. They saw not only the "Conchs" who were Will's relatives, but quite a few fugitives from the law. Captain Cooper was a gentlemen, an accomplished seaman and excellent cook and taught young Will enough of these arts so that he thought he could lay claim on membership in the Yacht Club.

He was always interested in ships and boats and would later become Fleet Marine Officer of the U. S. Fleet. He had friends at the Club from rifle range days and political interests. He felt that the headquarters of the New York Yacht Club, on 44th Street near 5th Avenue, where he could and did occasionally rub elbows with the Vanderbilts and their like, was one of the most interesting places in New York and the place which served the best steaks.

FLYING IN FLORIDA—1925 and 1928

In Harllee's early days, fear of flying—with such nicknames for aircraft as "flying coffins"—was much more prevalent than today. One man, after riding on a photographic mission with a few aerobatics thrown in by the famous Marine aviator, Lieutenant Hayne D. Boyden, told him,

"Thanks a lot, Lieutenant, for those two airplane rides."

Boyden replied, "What two rides?"

The answer, "My first ride and my last ride."

In 1925 an opportunity opened up for Bill Harllee to help out aviation in his birthplace, south Florida. The Mayor of Tampa, Perry G. Wall, a treasured friend and former employer of his brother John, knew that Bill had spent a great deal of time flying over Santo Domingo and Haiti to learn the terrain and to have rapid transportation. Harllee was not an aviator, although he requested aviation training and duty. However, he had studied all aspects of it as well as any non-aviator could, and had planned and built several airfields in his district in Santo Domingo. Perry Wall had great faith in him. The Mayor wanted an airport for Tampa, and he wanted Bill Harllee's advice in selecting the location.

The Tampa Tribune of July 23, 1925, referred to Col. W. C. Harllee as a native son who had had a distinguished and colorful career.

The Tribune went on to report that he pointed out the necessity for progressive cities to recognize that aviation was no longer a novelty. He said that in order to attract air mail service good landing fields were essential.

He pointed out that Pensacola and Jacksonville had good airports, but that there were only emergency fields in Florida south of those. Tampa, as a fine water port, would be an excellent strategic location for a good air field, as all naval maneuvers in the future would have to include aviation.

He mentioned that aircraft had replaced horses for reconnoitering and that the country from the air is a perfect map for both the observer's eye and the photographic facilities of the aircraft. He also noted the value of communications by air.

277

He went on to report that the field must be at least two thousand feet in length, in the shape of a right triangle with the longest leg in the direction of the prevailing wind, and that it would be an advantage to have it near the water because of seaplanes.

Typical of the era was his remark that there should be attendants to clear the field when airplanes were landing and taking off. He gave them much further information such as the desirability of a hangar, the need for a wind vane and tanks for the special grade of gasoline used by aircraft.

He picked 160 acres of a 320 acre tract which he found free of ditches, knolls, and other obstructions and sketched the details of a proposed airfield for his hosts.

After the Tampa airport was opened, Mr. R. Wallace Davis, General Chairman of the enterprise, wrote the Commandant of the Marine Corps, as follows:

> The formal opening and dedication of Tampa's Municipal Airport on February 22nd was no doubt the most stupendous ceremony of like character ever held and was witnessed by at least one hundred thousand people. Perhaps no other opening had received the publicity as did ours. In addition to the ceremonies at the field a number of social affairs were held.
>
> Without a doubt the splendid celebration was due largely to Colonel William C. Harllee, whose reputation and respect, amounting to a great deal, caused him to be called upon a number of times to make addresses and his responses to the wishes of the people upheld the reputation, not only of the Marine Corps as a whole, but its officers.

Mayor Perry G. Wall of Tampa wrote the Commandant,

> "Little enthusiasm had been shown and no action taken toward establishment of a landing field here until Colonel Harllee's arrival."

Bill Harllee visited Jacksonville en route back north in a Curtiss-Falcon plane with a Marine pilot with whom he had flown in Santo Domingo. A Jacksonville newspaper reported that he mentioned that the winds in Florida were generally mild and yet strong enough to help the fliers. It also reported that he prophesized that Florida, because of its geographical location, layout, climate, and the aggressiveness of its people, would become a mecca for aviation.

XXX
THE SOUTHERNER AND THE BLACK PATRIOTS HAITI 1926–1927

Haiti is a stick, in habitual use throughout Central and South America, with which to belabor the United States.
—from The Times of London, December 1929

Haiti.

The only country in the world in which a slave rebellion ever succeeded.

Haiti.

The only completely black nation in the Western Hemisphere—the land of Voodoo, pride and poverty.

Port-au-Prince, the capital of Haiti, is where Colonel William C. Harllee, U.S.M.C. the man from the deep South whose role models were the heroes of the Confederate Army, arrived on July 30, 1926.

As the Royal Dutch Mail Steamer, Poseidon, pulled in to the wharf at Fort Ilet, Bill Harllee saw his old friend, Julius Turrill,

THE MARINE FROM MANATEE

through the tropical sun on the pier, complete with brass band. He had marvelled at the lush green beauty of the port city as the ship approached, but he knew that as he saw it close up, the city itself would not be so beautiful but would reflect the real poverty in which most Haitians lived. But he knew that the Haitians, in spite of their bloody history, were happy, kindly and generous when they could be, dignified and proud in spite of their poverty. They had not been led by television, radio, movies and other such influences, or even by politicians, to expect a lot. As long as white people did not try to enslave or exploit them, they were as friendly as could be.

Colonel Julius Turrill, U.S.M.C., was Major General Julius Turrill, Commandant of the Gendarmerie d'Haiti (later known as the Garde d'Haiti) which was both the Army and Police Force of that country. As the ship drew nearer, Harllee could make out his friend's mustache and his football player's physique. He remembered ragging him about Vermont. Turrill was typical of the most rock-ribbed and taciturn Vermont Yankee. He had been a battalion commander and a real Marine hero at Belleau Wood, in World War I, where the Marines took frightful casualties but became internationally famous.

Turrill had requested Harllee as his Assistant Chief of the Gendarmerie d'Haiti, with the rank of Brigadier General. The Gendarmerie's ranks of captain and above were then filled by the U. S. Marine Corps.

Finally the ship moored, the gangway went down, and Bill Harllee met his new boss.

He told him, "Greetings from the Commandant and all hands in Washington, Julius, and thanks for having some confidence in me and most particularly for inviting me to stay with you and your wife and mother—that is, if they will let us do a little drinking and maybe even some singing and gambling."

Turrill replied, "Welcome, Bill, and I think we've got a good opportunity to do some good here with these Haitians. As you know, they can be fine people."

Haiti had had a most colorful history. A thumbnail sketch of it is necessary to an understanding of Harllee's tour of duty there. In the eighteenth century, it had been a jewel among

280

France's colonies with plantations of sugar, cocoa, coffee and indigo, making many Frenchmen, of whom there then were up to 30,000 in the country, rich at the expense of brutal exploitation of well over half a million African slaves. The Spanish had earlier committed genocide on the indigenous Indians with their type of slavery.

Colonel Robert D. Heinl, Jr. and Nancy Heinl in their "Written in Blood," unquestionably the best over-all history of Haiti ever published, give a vivid idea of that brutality (partly from a passage written by Vastey, Henri Christophe's secretary and privy counselor, who had lived half his life as a slave):

> Have they not hung up men with heads downward, drowned them in sacks, crucified them on planks, buried them alive, crushed them in mortars? Have they not forced them to eat human excrement? And, after having flayed them with the lash, have they not cast them alive to be devoured by worms, or onto ant hills, or lashed them to stakes in the swamp to be devoured by mosquitoes? Have they not thrown them into boiling caldrons of cane syrup? Have they not put men and women inside barrels studded with spikes and rolled them down mountainsides into the abyss? Have they not consigned these miserable blacks to man-eating dogs until the latter, sated by human flesh, left the mangled victims to be finished off with bayonet and poniard?
>
> Besides the atrocities cited in Vastey's outcry, colonial archives tell of tin masks hung on slaves to keep them from gnawing cane; of cinders, aloes, salt, pepper, and citron rubbed into flesh raw from the lash; of red-hot irons laid across buttocks; of boiling wax poured into ears; of gunpowder exploded inside a slave's rectum.

In 1804 after some fourteen years of fighting, the slaves and other "men of color", as they were called, threw out the French as well as some Spanish and British who had shown an armed interest in Haiti.

Needless to say, the blacks repaid the French in kind for the terrible cruelty of which some of the French were guilty. Again, the Heinls' "Written in Blood" has a vivid description written by a Frenchman who escaped such repayment (if it can be called that):

> . . . but on 17 and 18 March, 1804, they (the whites) were finished off en masse. All, without exception, have been mas-

sacred, down to the women and children. A young mulatresse, named Fifi Pariset, ranged the town like a madwoman, searching the houses to slay the little children. Many men and women were chopped down by sappers, who hacked off their limbs and smashed in their chests. Some were stabbed, others mutilated, others "passes par la baionette," others disemboweled, still others stuck like pigs . . .

. . . Riding down a white woman, he (Clervaux) snatched her nursing baby by the leg and smashed its skull against a boulder. As the sticky blancmange of blood and brains trickled to the ground, the soldiers roused themselves and fell to with saber and bayonet . . .

The passing masters of the French Revolution back in Paris adopted various policies towards the rich whites, poor whites, men of color and slaves of Haiti, but to no ultimate avail as far as preventing Haitian independence was concerned.

Among those sent to Haiti by Napoleon were his sister, Pauline, and her husband, General Leclerc, who died there of malaria and yellow fever.

Although malaria, "yellow jack" and other tropical diseases killed tremendous numbers, in some cases majorities of the French regiments sent to Haiti, Harllee always felt very strongly that the Haitians had won their independence by force of arms. They fought mightily with inferior weapons, in many cases machetes, hoes, pickaxes and the like, and sustained tens of thousands of deaths.

Haitian history clearly indicates a fact unpalatable to Americans of today—an operative racial division between those having both black and white blood, known as men of color "jaunes", or "mulatres" (in English, yellows or mulattoes), constituting 10 to 15 percent of the population, generally educated and with some means; and the "noirs", or pure blacks, almost all uneducated and poverty stricken.

The ignorance of the illiterate blacks, forming 85 percent of the population of the country, mostly peasants scratching out a living at a subsistence level, created a condition which was not compatible with American type democracy and which led to political instability. Haitian history is replete with violent changes of government. The U. S. Navy sent warships into

Haitian waters fifteen times in the last century to "protect American lives and property" and in this century sent them there during twelve different years before 1915.

The Haitian government became involved through those years with debts to foreign nations, particularly France. Germany was concerned about the welfare of her merchants in Haiti. These matters caused the U. S. Government to be apprehensive about potential violations of the Monroe Doctrine.

On July 27, 1915, General Oscar, a close friend of President Sam of Haiti, ordered every political prisoner in the prison at Port-au-Prince, Haiti, to be put to death. There were 200 of them, some belonging to the most prominent families. Ex-President Zamor was among the prisoners. They were butchered in what has been described as "an incredibly brutal manner." President Sam took asylum in the French legation, but when the people learned of the slaughter in the prison, they broke into the French legation on July 28, 1915, and tore his body into bits. This was the first time a foreign legation had been violated in Haiti.

So the U. S. Marines landed, starting an occupation and control of Haiti which lasted until August 21, 1934, the day set by President Stenio Vincent as the Day of Second Independence. Of course the Marines did not make the final decision as to how long they would stay there. The purposes of the occupation were declared to be humanitarian, economic and strategic.

The humanitarian purpose was expresssed by Secretary of State Lansing as follows:

> To terminate the appalling conditions of anarchy, savagery, and oppression which had been prevalent in Haiti for decades, and to undertake the establishment of domestic peace in the Republic in order that the great bulk of the population, who had been downtrodden by dictators and the innocent victims of repeated revolutions, should enjoy a prosperity and an economic and industrial development to which every people of an American nation are entitled.

The economic purpose was to establish order and stability in Haiti in order to encourage American investments in Haiti rather than to favor special concessions to American business interests, according to "The Foreign Policy Association Information Service" issue of November 27–December 12, 1929.

The strategic purpose related to the Panama Canal and the denial of the coaling stations desired by Germany for her ships, which the U. S. Government feared could be easily converted into submarine bases during World War I.

Having carefully collected all possible information concerning what led up to the American Occupation of Haiti and made judgements concerning the best course of action, Harllee believed that he and his friend and boss, General Turrill, who entirely agreed with him, should act accordingly. They pulled the Haitian gendarmes, then about 2,500 in number, in from the small stations at which they were posted all over the country and concentrated them and their American officers in the larger cities, the district headquarters, with six mobile companies. They did this because:

1. The country had been peaceful and crime-free since 1920. As Bill Harllee wrote,

> No country in the world is safer for its sojourners and citizens than Haiti.

2. Many of the small detachments of Gendarmes, under low ranking, non-commissioned officers had fallen victim to the temptation of bullying and preying upon the populace.

3. These detachments could not be given any real training in the posts at which they were stationed. In their larger concentrations at the district headquarters they were not only given military training by higher ranking officers, but also were started in courses which would give them a basic education; i.e. would teach them to read and write. The majority of them were illiterate. Harllee's plan was to fit them to be teachers, as he had been, for literacy could be the key to Haiti's emergence from its age-old political instability and poverty. This, he felt, was the real answer to Haiti's problems—elevating the educational level of her people, so that they would be capable of properly utilizing aid and assistance. And this would put the

United States in the best light. The Haitians loved education and military training and were enthusiastic about this program.

Turrill and Harllee started efforts to promote Haitian officers much more rapidly above the rank of captain so they could take over their own army and police force as soon as possible.

Harllee found hundreds of poor, harmless Haitians in prisons for such petty offenses as being vagabonds, idling their time away under disgusting conditions. With Turrill's hearty approval, he put them out at work on the roads and trails, issued them tobacco, fed them well, and they became useful and happier.

Harllee, although a white Southerner out of the last century and proud of it to the last drop of his blood, engaged in social intercourse with Haitian officers, the lack of which had seriously offended the proud Haitians.

For example, he wrote in later years:

> One of my best friends in the Gendarmerie is Col. Kebreau Devisin. He was lately the Department Commander at Cap Haitien but I have an impression that he is not there now.
>
> Devisin's home is at Croix de Bouquets, not far from Port-au-Prince. When I was in the Gendarmerie, he was the local Gendarme commander at Croix de Bouquets and was a first lieutenant, one of the senior lieutenants. The policy then was not to advance the Haitian officers. When Russell was relieved and the Marines had soon thereafter to evacuate Haiti, the Haitian officers had to be advanced rapidly and Devisin became a Colonel.
>
> Devisin is a big handsome black, a striking looking man, impressive in his appearance and bearing. He would make a magnificent motion picture character to dramatically represent Christophe (King Henri), Toussaint Louverture, or any other famous Haitian strong man. He is a real soldier who has been tried by fire. He is magnificent under fire and in any danger. He is a soldier and a gentlemen unafraid. His fidelity had been tested, too. We in the Gendarmerie knew that we could trust Devisin.
>
> Gen. Russell disliked Devisin and Devisin disliked him, but it would not have been proper or ethical for me to discuss Russell disparagingly with Devisin, and I never did so. The Puppet President Borno disliked and also feared Devisin. Devisin had the merit of real patriotism, real love of his country, and

had contempt for a traitor to it like Borno and Borno knew it. He had a pretty good idea that Devisin would 'bump him off' if he got a chance.

I have ridden the woods day and night with Devisin. I enjoy his company, for I know him to be a man and a soldier. I have had him in my home in Port-au-Prince and at my table and drunk rum with him there and have enjoyed his fine hospitality in his home and drunk rum and champagne with him there.

Senator Shipstead, U. S. Senator from Minnesota, is a great friend and admirer of Devisin. I took the Senator and Mrs. Shipstead to Croix de Bouquet, and Devisin threw a party for them which startled the natives and also Borno and Russell. Devisin gathered the "Real McCoys" of the Cul de Sac (the great plain around Port-au-Prince) at a large dinner of banquet at Croix de Bouquet and speeches were made, some not at all pleasing to Borno. Some of the politicos there were not buddies of Borno.

Borno and Russell wanted to do something to Devisin and also to me, but they thought it best to desist. After all, Shipstead was a U. S. Senator.

On October 15, 1926, after a four and half month absence on leave in Europe, General Russell, to whose rescue Harllee and so many others had gone at El Tejar near Vera Cruz in Mexico in 1914, returned to Haiti and cancelled everything Turrill and Harllee had done. As High Commissioner, he had authority to do so.

When Harllee heard that Russell said their actions in his absence were illegal, he said to Turrill,

"Julius, Russell is apparently claiming we acted illegally. They say he did a good job here in the beginning but you know what I think of him. I think you ought to see him and ask him to his face what was illegal about our actions. You and I know damned well that what we did wasn't against any orders and was in the best interests of both Haiti and the U.S."

Replied Turrill,

"I've already asked him what was illegal about what we did. He said we made too many changes without his authority or that of President Borno when he was absent. But as far as the illegality is concerned he was evasive."

Harllee then said,

"Do you have any objection to me seeing him? I've been

told he thinks I'm plotting against him. And I don't like the smell of these rumors about illegality. You remember what happened to me in Santo Domingo."

Turrill told him,

"I don't think it will do any good but go ahead and see him if you want to."

So Harllee saw General Russell. He looked the General in the eye and said,

"General, I understand you have said General Turrill and I are guilty of extensive illegal actions. Will you please inform me as to what was illegal about what we did?"

Replied Russell,

"I'm not going to discuss the matter with you, Harllee. I have asked for a legal opinion on the matter and will send it to Turrill. You are answerable to Turrill, not me. And that is all."

Said Harllee,

"Yes, and I stand behind everything Turrill has done. But I believe I am entitled to face my accuser."

Replied Russell,

"I've told you once that you are working for Turrill, not me. And that's all, Harllee."

Harllee persisted,

"Yes, and in Santo Domingo I thought I was working for General Lee and then the people over him made a mighty attempt to clobber me. They failed but it was a very rough experience all the way around. You'd best not try it again."

Concluded Russell,

"I've told you once that that's all. Leave at once, Harllee."

And that was that.

Russell dredged up a legal opinion to the effect that the Turrill-Harllee orders were illegal. He wrote the Commandant of the Marine Corps that the orders in question hadn't been issued by Turrill until Harllee arrived, but Turrill issued them and had planned to do so before Harllee's arrival. The illegalities were technicalities which could have easily been changed by the High Commissioner and his puppet President Borno.

Turrill and Harllee had to comply with Russell's orders, but they attempted without success to persuade him to change his course and, within the framework of his orders, tried to act in accordance with the 1915 Convention with Haiti, to prepare for evacuation, and to leave the Haitians as friends of the United States instead of enemies.

Then in March of 1927, matters came to a head. Senator William H. King of Utah, a member of the Senate Naval Affairs Committee, which had jurisdiction over the Marine Corps, decided to come to Haiti to survey the situation for himself.

Harllee was convinced that General Russell did not want Senator King in Haiti. President Borno of Haiti issued orders to Turrill to keep the Senator out of Haiti and to arrest and deport him if he entered. Turrill, of course, told Borno that he could not comply with such orders unless they were in writing and from the American High Commissioner, General Russell, from whom his orders came. Borno then issued written orders, but Turrill remained adamant. Russell then tried out oral orders, but again Turrill insisted on written orders, which Russell finally issued in the form of orders to comply with Borno's orders. Turrill and Harllee were then obliged to comply.

Russell, of course, was very unhappy at having to show his hand. So on April 20, 1927, he left Port-au-Prince for Washington, and Turrill and Harllee were shortly thereafter both ordered away from Haiti. Harllee was ordered to leave on the next ship and Turrill a little later.

Harllee reported to the Office of the Major General Commandant on May 24, 1927. After a month there, he was ordered to the Naval War College at Newport, Rhode Island, as a student.

The interest of the United States and its political leaders in Haiti is illustrated by the fact that before Harllee left there, he was visited for twenty-four days by U. S. Senator Henrik Shipstead, Farmer-Labor Party, of Minnesota, and Congressman Robert Crosser, Democrat, of Cleveland, Ohio. They shared Harllee's view, as expressed by the London Times, that Haiti was a stick with which all Latin America could beat the United States, and they wanted to do away with that stick, which President Franklin Rossevelt finally did, evacuating the

Marines on August 19, 1934. It is well known among the experts that FDR's Good Neighbor Policy was the most successful one the United States ever had in winning friends in Latin America. General Russell was replaced as American Minister, highest in-country official in Haiti, in May of 1930 by Dr. Dana G. Munroe, a civilian.

This replacement was the result of recommendations of President Hoover's "Forbes Commission." The commission treated Russell kindly but recommended what Turrill and Harllee had advocated at such risk to themselves: turning Haiti over to the Haitians as rapidly as possible and ending the occupation. They recommended that the military ruler be replaced by a civilian. All this is what Senator King and Shipstead and Congressman Crosser had strenuously urged.

"Labor," a weekly magazine published in Washington, D.C., included in "Lonergan's Comment" in its November 30, 1929 issue:

> Someone with authority and a robust regard for Uncle Sam's good name should look into what is going on in Haiti.
>
> Theoretically, the little black republic is a sovereign nation; actually it is governed by General John H. Russell of our Marine Corps. He is called high commissioner, and what he says goes and nothing goes without his "O.K."
>
> Back in Wilson's administration, our Navy Department wrote a constitution for Haiti, after we had intervened at the suggestion of New York bankers.
>
> It contains a neat "joker." The President of Haiti may "postpone" an election. In that event the Council of State runs the country and the council is named by the President.
>
> Louis Borno, the present President, has taken full advantage of that provision. He has kept himself in power for years and has just "postponed" the election of the national legislature.
>
> He has given the New York bankers everything they wanted and has changed the constitution so American "development" companies may grab the natives' land. There is evidence that the "graft" runs into the millions.
>
> The Haitian people can do nothing. Their constabulary is officered by Marines and a detachment of the "leathernecks" is always on hand, ready to move into action at a sign from the high commissioner.

A fitting last word on when we should have left Haiti came

from the man who was Secretary of the Navy when the Navy and Marines took over Haiti in 1915, Josephus Daniels. He wrote in the July 12, 1930 issue of the Saturday Evening Post that "long ago we should have come out".

It is interesting to note the reaction of the Haitian press to the departure of Turrill and Harllee, despite the fact that the press was controlled. President Borno imprisoned editors without trial, including one M. Jolibois, who had inveighed against Russell. Borno had even been high-handed enough to close Haiti's top social club, the Cercle Bellevue, because he thought the members sympathized with editors imprisoned without trials. Some excerpts from the Haitian press of the day follow (they are translations from French made by the Military Intelligence Department of the Gendarmerie d'Haiti):

LE NOUVELLISTE, 6 May 1927

General Harllee, we have never met him. But we have learned that he is an officer who does not hide his ideas. He calls a cat, a cat, and the COOPERATION (between the American Occupation and Haiti) "BLUFF." That's his character. His desire was to elevate the Haitian element in the Gendarmerie and to give the Haitians the occasion to play a preponderating role in the affairs of this country. The Gendarmerie, in his opinion, was sufficient to maintain order in Haiti.

It is for these reasons that we sincerely congratulate him.

LE TEMPS, May 10, 1927

HAITIANS GREET GENERAL TURRILL AND GENERAL HARLLEE!
THEY ARE HONEST PEOPLE WHO GIVE HONOR TO THEIR FLAG.

They had both the reputation of being not only well considered among the Haitian Society, but also very respected and very liked by their officers, non-commissioned officers, and enlisted men at the same time.

Everywhere it was said of General Turrill that he is simple, good-natured, severe, and just. One knew that he is not a "fetard" (a man who likes enjoyments); that, just like the Chief of the Occupation, Colonel Myers, he confined himself to the unique execution of the duties of his functions, and attended only when duty required the receptions and political affairs, enjoying above all the family pleasures.

As far as General Harllee is concerned, he was of a nature as correct, but more ardent, of a very high intelligence, of a remarkable education and experience, and he stood with still less patience the activities of the American military occupation which, directly or by means of "cooperation" uselessly offend the rights of the Haitian People, do damage to the influence of the United States here, and only lead to create a universal and deep hatred against everything which is American, business, persons, and the good and the evil.

And all that had made these two Americans respectable and respected, more beneficial to their country, more useful to the policy of Washington than the unbearable conceit and the unscrupulous doings of other American representatives.

The measures taken by Generals Turrill and Harllee, solely responsible toward Haiti and in the name of the United States, for the peace of our Republic, positively meant the discontinuance of the military rule which grasps all the civil services of the Treaty; crushing our country for eleven years.

The High Commissioner (General Russell) coming back to the country undoubtedly had his attention called to these actions by someone who adores his chain and who is neither conscious enough, nor conscientious enough to understand that this chain strangles and humiliates, not his insignificant personality, but this country.

The reform of Turrill and Harllee was immediately abolished.

Then Senator King had the idea to come and see what is going on here to justify the maintenance of the occupation, *so prolonged that it by no means gives honour to the ability of the officials of the foreign policy of the United States.*

King was barred. The responsibility for the measure was beyond all Haitian authority and went back to the supreme direction of the American forces here (General Russell).

But Shipstead came. Crosser came. And, due to introductions by Turrill, of Harllee, they saw with their own eyes the conditions which had led to the changes made in the course of the autumn of 1926 to the improvement of the public force in Haiti; they understood by themselves and with the facts, how these conditions would have resulted on the part of the United States in the immediate adoption of a policy more suitable to their own interest and more suitable to the rights of the Haitians.

An excerpt from an editorial from LE NOUVELLISTE of May 11, 1927 follows:

Parade through the streets of Cape Haitiem, Haiti, August 6, 1934, after the American flag was lowered and the Haitian flag was raised.

What has General Russell ever made to allow the Haitian citizens to also express their vote? Nothing, absolutely nothing; to the contrary!

The final chapter in Harllee's Haitian episode was written on August 24, 1935, a year after the American Occupation ended and over eight years after Harllee left Haiti, when his old friend, Colonel Demosthenes P. Calixte, then Commandant of the Garde d'Haiti (formerly called the Gendarmerie d'Haiti) notified him that President Stenio Vincent of Haiti, on behalf of his nation, had awarded Harllee the Haitian National Order of Honor and Merit in the Grade of Commander. After the American Occupation, medals were not awarded by the Haitians to those whom they felt had unnecessarily prolonged what they considered their national humiliation. Bill Harllee felt happy about this, because he felt it was in the interest of the United States to have the good will of Haiti, and for that matter, every other country in the world.

Finally, it must be said about Haiti that it needed and still needs help, especially educational help, from the United States, but military control . . . NO.

XXXI
FINISHING UP THE TWENTIES

To seek and to find military objectives and to engage the enemy with little regard to its size and to question where is the objective, rather than how big or dangerous it may be.

Each private at some time drills the company.

NAVAL WAR COLLEGE

In June of 1927, Bill Harllee reported to the Naval War College at Newport, Rhode Island, for duty as a student in the U. S. Navy's top professional school. He studied hard in that most pleasant place, very hard. He even mastered such deadly dull texts as the Navy's "Communications Instructions," which Naval officers had tediously learned through years of experience as communications officers, but which senior Marine officers were not really expected either to know or to learn. In writing his thesis and other papers, he displayed his original turn of mind.

As a result of these efforts, Admiral William V. Pratt, who

was President of the Naval War College then, was pleased to accept him as Fleet Marine Officer a year later when he became Commander-in-Chief, U. S. Fleet.

Bill Harllee enjoyed very much the atmosphere of the War College and Newport. When his only grandson was born in Newport in 1941, he took some kidding from his friends about having a New England Yankee to carry on his very Southern name. He retorted that Newport had first been made famous as a resort by Southern planters and was thus really a Southern town in heritage. This seemed a bit far fetched even to his family, but the July 1983 issue of the magazine "Travel— Holiday" carried a cover article on the subject which included the following:

> "Newport was a magnet for the wealthy long before the era of the Four Hundred. As a successful shipping port in the 1700's, the city became a summering place for Southern planters and their families who rented homes near the harbor each year. Today, Newport boasts what is perhaps the country's most extensive collection of authentic Colonial-era buildings, with more than 400 pre-Revolutionary houses, many of which have been carefully and authentically restored."

Bill Harllee was quite expressive concerning leadership in a paper required by the Naval War College on that subject. Excerpts follow:

> Leadership springs from courage—a noble quality of character which inspires devotion and respect in it subject forces.
>
> It is amplified by knowledge and is stimulated by opportunities for application to a definite purpose.
>
> A real military leader should have ingrained into his code of action the determination to seek and find military objectives and to engage the enemy with little regard to its size. The question in consideration should be where is the objective rather than how big or dangerous it may be.
>
> Indeed, safety lies in quick and courageous engagement in war—not in over caution or safety-first measures. My own experience, and also history, teach me the truth of that doctrine- which I feel is not properly emphasized in our war colleges.
>
> What made Nelson a great admiral and General Robert E. Lee a great captain and what has characterized other great commanders was that they had the quality of mind and soul

which lifted them above the little, mean, and low-down arts of imposing upon their subordinates, and the contemptible trick of seeking to burden them with blame when responsibility for misfortunes rested higher up.

General Lee rode through his lines after the disaster of the third day at Gettysburg and accepted the blame which many historians have ascribed to others (Author's note: the big Marine would have highly approved of the leadership aspects of his son's friend, President John F. Kennedy, taking the blame for the disaster at the Bay of Pigs and President Ronald Reagan's taking the blame for the catastrophe suffered in the October 1983 suicide bombing of the U. S. Marines in Beirut, Lebanon).

In my earnest study of history and biography, trying to learn what qualities characterize greatness and high military character, no lesson stands out more clearly than that. The great commanders are those who through these high attributes of character have won the confidence and respect of their subordinates and have thus been able to mould their forces into a force pulling together in the same direction instead of being torn asunder by suspicions, distrusts, hatreds, and other such sentiments.

Let me cite from my own observation an example of the kind of loyalty which is characteristic of real leadership:

Once in Washington a young Lieutenant of Marines under Captain Charles P. Plunkett of the Navy (later Rear Admiral) was suspended unjustly from promotion. Secretary Daniels had signed the notification. Captain Plunkett took the paper and laid it before the Secretary of the Navy and said, "This is a sorry sample of Navy justice." He said lots more. It took courage to say the things he said because the case concerned something towards which Mr. Daniels was known to be unrelenting (liquor) and Captain Plunkett's vigor and boldness jeopardized his own prospects for advancement. This paper was cancelled, the record of it expunged from the files, and the suspension removed. Captain Plunkett would not leave the Secretary's office until he had settled that difficult matter upon which he had staked his own chance for promotion. That was loyalty.

And finally, no army which was devoid of a spiritual force called morale ever prevailed over an army which possessed it. Morale is not a product of moving pictures and "welfare workers" to amuse and wet nurse "the boys". It comes from a desire for accomplishment, and is most often nurtured amidst severe conditions—never by softening processes. Caesar suppressed the agencies which effeminated his soldiers. There were no Jazz-bo artists in the wake of his legions.

NORFOLK

During the year after the Naval War College, Bill Harllee was given command of the Marine Barracks at the Navy Yard, Norfolk, Virginia. The barracks and yard were actually in Portsmouth, Virginia.

At Norfolk he decided to make a school out of the barracks.

Lieutenant (later Rear Admiral) Alexander S. Wetherspoon inspected the school, called "The Sea School," for the Navy Department and was so impressed that he took a set of all their questions and answers for use in Navy Training Courses. He also reported that each private was required at some time to drill his company in order to develop his self-confidence and interest. He found the concentration perfect in the Spanish language classes, conducted because of Latin American campaigns then going on. These classes were conducted by enlisted men. He noted that there were no brig prisoners, and that there was a very high state of morale.

In December of 1928, Bill Harllee received his last commendation for work on the rifle range. It was from the Commandant of the Coast Guard for his work on the Virginia Beach range and spoke of his "careful planning, earnest cooperation and skillful supervision."

FLEET MARINE OFFICER

In May of 1929, Bill Harllee reported to his old friend, Admiral Pratt, for duty aboard the flagship USS TEXAS as Fleet Marine Officer of the U. S. Fleet. He was delighted to get this assignment, because ever since his happy days aboard the USS FLORIDA, and even before, he had considered duty aboard ship the feature which distinguished Marines from Army soldiers. In those days, Marine detachments from ships had formed important parts of the Marine units which had performed so well all over the world.

His tour of duty as Fleet Marine Officer was altogether pleasant with another trip to Panama, Los Angeles and Hawaii. In the small Flag Mess aboard the USS TEXAS, he was fortunate to find his close friend from USS FLORIDA days, Captain Royal E. Ingersoll, who later became Commander-in-Chief of the Atlantic Fleet during the critical years of World War II, and who was one of the finest officers the U. S. Navy ever had.

Then, too, there was a sentimental touch for him in the name of the fleet flagship. His beloved wife was born and raised in Texas, and he had started his soldier's life as a private in the 33rd U. S. (Texas) Volunteer Infantry.

THE TWENTY-ONE YEAR CLAIM

It is really rather amusing from the perspective of many years to consider the minor victory over red tape and the big brass that Bill Harllee won on February 28, 1927. That was the date Private Law 414 of the 69th Congress was enacted. It reimbursed him for the loss of all his household effects, which were burned up in a fire on the U. S. Army's Arlington Docks at Seattle, Washington on May 7, 1906.

This was long before "Catch 22" had entered the language, but it was a perfect early example of that expression.

The Army paid all Army personnel for their losses, but said it could not pay Harllee, because he was "in the Naval service (the Marine Corps being in the Navy Department)."

The Navy said it could not pay him, because the destruction took place on Army property.

And they both kept repeating variations of this for twenty-one years.

Harllee had tried to avoid his belongings even going to Seattle. He had arranged to remove them by tug from the Army Transport Sherman at smoking San Francisco, in April of 1906, to the USS CHICAGO. He was stopped because no cargo was manifested to San Francisco. The Sherman left for Seattle and the Chicago remained in San Francisco Bay, where Harllee was assigned to duty. But since the Sherman would not permit this transfer, his goods were taken to the Army dock at Seattle.

The Secretary of the Navy in 1907 made the following ridiculous statement (written, of course, by some underling):

"Further, an officer is not obliged to accept free transportation of his household goods offered by the Government."

Imagine an officer being transferred on permanent change of station duty orders from Honolulu to Mare Island, California, as Harllee was, and not accepting the Government transportation offered free for his household effects!

And then in 1914, the Secretary of the Navy quibbled about what was included in the claim, recommending total disallowance of the silver set and drawing instruments as well as 24 other items. Apparently a first lieutenant's total earthly possessions, including wedding presents, and all household goods, were supposed to add up to only $1,125.90 in value, rather than the $2,392.60 Harllee requested! The Secretary had to concede that Harllee had only used a very small fraction of the 5,100 pounds allowed, but as late as 1926 the Secretary was still recommending disapproval! Furthermore, the Secretary had been backed up in 1916 by a Court of Claims decision with a lot of gobbledegook as to how none of the existing laws quite fit the case and therefore the claim had to be disapproved!

No wonder it became popular in later years to attack the Government bureaucracy in Washington.

But again, Bill Harllee was never one to take a raw deal lying down, so after twenty-one years of trying to go through the proper channels—after all this was only money, this wasn't teaching the nation to shoot or defeating its enemies—he decided to work towards getting a private law passed. His good friends, Senator Duncan U. Fletcher and Representative Herbert J. Drane, both of Florida, promptly got a private law passed without opposition reimbursing him for the full $2,392.60, not even quibbling about the Chinese kimono or vase or the white fur rug.

But even here, he gave the taxpayers a break—he didn't request the twenty-one years interest on the money!

XXXII
NEW ORLEANS—
REVOLUTIONIZING
RECRUITING
1930–1935

Only high school graduates will be accepted.
—**Colonel William C. Harllee—1930**

In November of 1930, Bill Harllee was assigned to command the Southern Recruiting and Reserve Division of the U. S. Marine Corps with Headquarters in New Orleans. He was offered the Middle West with Chicago as headquarters, but he wanted to realize a long-held dream of writing his family history, which he would call colloquially, "Kinfolks." The "kinfolks" were in the South.

But before writing his book, he turned recruiting upside down, and to good effect. He had nine of the finest sergeants in the Corps with him in New Orleans.

When he gathered them around him he said:

"I want all the recruiting posters and ads taken down as soon as possible. We will put out the word that the Marine Corps is well supplied with men; that it takes influence to get in the Corps; that nobody will be accepted who is not a high

Bill Harllee's recruiting staff in New Orleans
Top: Sergeant Benjamin Franklin Hearn, Jr. (left First Sergeant Joseph William
Peden (center) Sergeant Albert LeRoy Jenson (right)
Center: Sergeant William Elwood Farmer (left) Sergeant Major Harvey Steffens
Newgarde (center) Sergeant William Thomas Faulk (right)
Bottom: Sergeant Joseph Newton Swearinger (left) Sergeant Arthur Sherwood Hotte
(center) Sergeant Joseph Balla (right)

school graduate; that for starters each applicant must submit three letters of recommendation from well-known local people and must have a preliminary physical exam in their home town at their own expense; and that they cannot appear for final examination by the Corps until they meet these requirements and receive written authority from us. Any questions so far?"

Sergeant Major Harvey Newgarde,

"Colonel, how are we going to 'put out the word' if we take down posters and ads?"

Replied Harllee,

"The newspapers and magazines will tell the story of the United States Marine Corps for us. When they do, high quality recruits, not the sweepings of the bars and pool halls, will batter at our gates to get in the Corps. And the Corps deserves and needs high quality men."

Sergeant Benjamin F. Hearn,

"Colonel, this has never happened before. How can it happen now?"

Harllee,

"It happened when I had charge of recruiting at Chicago, our biggest headquarters. It's a question of making friends with the newspaper people—the editors and reporters—and being honest with them and giving them something they can use; hard news, if possible, and feature news if not. We've got something about as rich in public interest as you can get to give them. If we do it right they'll print it and the public will know that a U. S. Marine has a chance to render really unique service and to educate himself at the same time. You know about the Marine Corps Institute. And most young American men want adventure while they are young, and we can offer it to them. . ."

The sergeants were skeptical of the whole approach. It flew in the face of all the great recruiting traditions, from the British press gangs down to the modern U. S. Marine Corps recruiting posters, some of the finest military art available.

It took the U. S. Army 52 years to catch up with Bill Harllee with regard to high school graduates. "The Washington Post" of April 3, 1982, reported on the front page,

> The Army . . . for the first time is accepting only high school graduates. The Army "has never been closed completely off before" to men without a high school education. . . .

The consensus of the sergeants was that it wasn't going to work. True, there was a depression, but at that time a Marine private was paid $21 a month and most men remained privates for several years. There was absolutely no attempt then to achieve parity of pay between the armed forces (especially enlisted men) and civilians. That came along decades later. Advertising had already been proven—"reach for a Lucky instead of a sweet." Harllee's Chicago success was a quarter of a century past and the sergeants did not have personal knowledge of it.

But Hearn said,

"The old man is all right. Harvey and I know him from the "Texas." He was Fleet Marine Officer then, believe us, he will do what he says he will do."

Said Newgarde, "Hearn is right. Colonel Harllee is not like some folks I've seen that would go and lie to a poor Marine."

Harllee had learned well the publicity game in Chicago in 1907 and 1908 and ever since nurtured his association with its practitioners at the bar of the National Press Club during his years in Washington.

Of invaluable assistance in this work was a colorful newspaper genius named Meigs O. Frost. He had won a Pulitzer prize for his reporting in Mexico during the Mexican-American troubles there. He called himself a Connecticut Creole, since he started out in life as a New England Yankee, but spent the rest of his life in New Orleans. He could make an interesting story out of an every day boiled beef dinner in a blue collar worker's house. He was such a superb raconteur that officers on Navy ships would rather hear him talk than see movies in their wardrooms.

Meigs Frost had co-written "A Marine Tells It To You" with Colonel Frederic M. (Fritz) Wise. He knew and loved the U. S. Marine Corps, and he and Bill Harllee became close friends for the rest of their lives.

One fascinating story after another began to appear in

Southern newspapers about individual Marines from the Southern Recruiting District. As a result of his reversal of recruiting approach, i.e. making it a privilege to join the Marines instead of begging young men to do it, Harllee was able to close all 30 of his substations, keeping only 3 district stations; reduce his total staff from 75 to 25 men; and save the Marine Corps a quarter of a million dollars a year.

But even more important was the fact that he was able to maintain a waiting list of highly desirable applicants for the Marine Corps in the Southern District three times as big as could be accepted to fill all the vacancies in the Marine Corps.

In a letter dated Nov. 10, 1932, the Major General Commandant of the Marine Corps wrote that he,

> . . . notes with great satisfaction the excellent results obtained by the Southern Recruiting District in the procurement of a high type of applicant for first enlistment. The filling of the ranks of the Marine Corps with men of advanced educational qualifications is beneficial to, and highly desired by, the Corps. . . .

And long before that, the sergeants had grown to like and admire the old man. The New Orleans press referred to him as "a grizzled, What Price Glory type of Marine." He had been a sergeant himself. He was not only capable, but decisive, an indispensable quality in a military leader, and he had the welfare of the sergeants at heart. Most of them even switched to smoking the same brand of cigarettes he smoked—Lucky Strikes (he had smoked Piedmonts in his earlier years). And on special occasions, they used Bourbon whiskey with him to celebrate. They voluntarily rendered so much assistance to him in his authorship of the "Kinfolks" volumes that he published their individual pictures and names in the Preface, although he did not include his own picture.

After a most pleasant, though hard working, five years living at the St. Charles Hotel in New Orleans, Colonel William C. Harllee was retired from active service in the U. S. Marine Corps on June 30, 1935, after 38 years service in the armed forces of his country.

The New Orleans Tribune of June 17, 1935 carried an editorial which praised his conviction and force and which said that he had the indefinable qualities of a man who might have performed the deeds of Stonewall Jackson or Nathan Bedford Forrest if he had had the opportunity. It recorded what he had done in the field of marksmanship instead of the field of combat action which he had so coveted in The Great War.

Brief excerpts from the Major General Commandant's lengthy comments on Harllee's retirement follow:

> Col. Harllee has served almost in every place where marines have been assigned to duty in the last quarter of a century. It was his shooting formula that gave the Marines the enviable reputation of being crack shots. . . . He served with distinction in Cuba, the Philippines, China and the Dominican Republic. . . . The privilege of every officer and man in the Marine Corps of being able to take a correspondence course in over 100 different subjects is credited to his ingenuity.
>
> As Col. Harllee retires on July 1, he leaves behind him a host of admiring friends, and the Marine Corps loses one of its most colorful officers. . . .

XXXIII
KINFOLKS—BACK TO THE ROOTS: 1930–1935

MAKE ME A MAN
BY O. LAWRENCE HAWTHORNE

Lord, give me the strength of the pioneer
And the faith of his hardy soul!
Provide me with courage to persevere;
Make me fight till I reach my goal.
Let weaklings indulge in a sheltered life
Where they curse when their luck goes bad,
But fit me for battle with storm and strife;
Give me brawn like my fathers had!
—from "Kinfolks" by William C. Harllee

Will Harllee had always had an unusually strong family feeling, arising perhaps from the fact that he was orphaned at an early age and brought up among so many loving relatives. This feeling was much more common in his day than in later years, particularly in the South. People looked to their families for sustenance, spiritual as well as material. Will believed inspiration was to be drawn from the lives of his relatives and ancestors.

305

He wrote in his final work:

A people that take no pride in the noble achievements of remote ancestors will never achieve anything worthy to be remembered with pride by remote descendants. (Macauley)
The same would be true with the word remote omitted.
The only Biblical commandment with a promise is: "Honor thy father and thy mother, that thy days may be long upon the land which the Lord thy God giveth thee." (Exodus 20:12)
By honoring them and by like reverence for our forefathers, which we can have only when we have some knowledge of them, we honor and exalt ourselves.

During his earlier years on active duty in the Marine Corps, he had automatically accumulated material on the history of his family and that of his wife and had the intention of some day compiling it into the usual modest volume on the subject.

In New Orleans, he was so successful in his Marine Corps assignment with the expenditure of so little time that he spent more and more of his spare time as he travelled through the South expanding the scope of his family history. Finally it grew into a monumental three volume 2,964 page genealogical classic listing 27,841 persons, who were ancestors of his two children, John and Ella Fulmore, and descendants of those ancestors. He utilized a unique system of designations devised by himself.

He wrote:

The purpose of this work is to provide for our children a record to inform them concerning their kinspeople, to translate from tradition to record as much as could be learned of their progenitors, and then to trace to the present time the descendants of the progenitors.
The collection and publication of the information herein was undertaken in the hope that it may be of interest and perhaps of some value to the many descendants of the ancestors of our children and to the multiplying numbers of their future descendants, and that its interest and value will increase with the passing of years.
Incidental to this work, glimpses are reflected here and there of our Southland and its people in colonial times, Revolutionary War times, ante-bellum times—"before the war" for Southern Independence, and mis-called "Reconstruction" times when all semblance of decent government was destroyed and government, as well as social and economic life, had to be reconstructed after the ruins of that spoliation era, worse than the destruction of war, were cleared away.
In estimating the character of our Southern people, if sacrifice in

defense of homeland be a measure of nobility of character, let none be persuaded that the poverty and ruin which befell the Southland after the war of its invasion were sacrifices in an unholy cause, nor feel humiliated by the poverty which followed. Their sacrifices are a heritage of character, richer and more enduring than possessions which can be gotten without honor and likewise dissipated, a heritage that is a title to real nobility as long as its character is preserved.

If this work, by informing our kinspeople and future generations of them of the noble character and achievements of our forebears, the men and women who have struggled and sacrificed to make a goodly land for us to live in, inspires an abiding faith in the principles and aspirations of our forefathers, and strengthens and broadens the span of the ties of kinship, the hope proceeding from the purpose of this work will be fulfilled.

This writer had been reminded, and already knew, that KINFOLKS is not a dictionary word. But KIN and FOLKS are both good dictionary words and by combining them to form the title of this work, the writer hopes he does not offend the literary taste of ultraliterate kinsfolks by a homely term he loves and to which his ears are attuned by its long-sanctioned usage among his unpretentious, but none the less respected kin and homefolks.

He noted with regard to the ladies:

It may not be improper to state, in spirit of levity and of tolerance of the wish of many good ladies not to have their dates of birth revealed, that some of the dates are not reliable. There are instances where reliable records have been found showing the date of birth to be earlier than the reported. In no case has the date shown in reliable records been later than the date reported.

His true blue Americanism showed up in his comments on coats of arms:

Claims to coats of arms and other heraldic pretensions among American families have been omitted from this work.

Coats of arms and like heraldic devices pertain to only the one person with which each is invested, and not to their families. In olden times, heralds made visitations to smash up the equipment of those who displayed heraldic devices to which they were not entitled.

What must the foreign possessors of those privileges think of the pretended claims to their devices by those in our country? Our Constitution states, "No title of nobility shall be granted by the United States."

Claims to descent from William the Conqueror, the kings and the dukes, and other foreign titled personages, claims which are generally fanciful or spurious, and sometimes made by those who are not reliably informed who were their immigrant or less remote American ancestors, have been critically examined or rejected.

The book also had its humorous sections, such as the story about old man John R. Bethea, who during the Civil War subscribed to Parson Brownlow's, "The Knoxville Whig," a violently anti-Southern newspaper, although he himself was a strong Southern partisan. His friends and neighbors, all red-hot Confederates, were so irritated about this that they got Harris Covington, an excellent writer, to send in an article to the "The Knoxville Whig." The article was an obituary of John R. Bethea. It set forth in strong language the difficulties under which he lived, surrounded by such a horde of Secessionists and fire-eaters that at times his life was in danger and he did not dare to show his face for fear of assassination; that he could not worship God in peace; that he was scorned and spurned; that he was hissed at and insulted; and on one occasion was pelted with rotten eggs; but, notwithstanding these severe trials he had remained faithful to the glorious cause of Republicanism and that when he came to die his last words were. "Union, Union, UNION!" Old John R. was astounded when he read his obituary and then raved and fumed as much as his friends laughed. He stopped his subscription to the "The Knoxville Whig."

With the expansion of the book came the inevitable expansion of the cost to the final point at which it added up to $30,000 in 1935 dollars.

Even after he had made every conceivable sacrifice, how could he possibly finance this?

At that stage of his life, he could not hope to pay for this himself without good sales. Long gone were his Boxer Rebellion loot, his poker winnings from the Philippines, and the money he had earned from his rifle instruction books. He still had some of the Florida land he had inherited—one eighty acre parcel, one forty acre, and one ten acre—but this constituted a birth-right he had hung onto through half a century, which had included a twenty year lawsuit he had fought and won against a lawyer team, including a future governor of Florida. Furthermore, unimproved land in the location of his was not moving then, and if he had sold it, it would have been for a song.

So, what to do? Failure stared him in the face.

As it had so often before when despair threatened, fortune smiled upon him. His cousin, William Donald Carmichael, with whom he had been raised and with whom he had attended the University of North Carolina, came to the rescue. Will Carmichael was President of his class at the University of North Carolina and was Vice-President of the Liggett and Myers Tobacco Company. His unsolicited generosity was acknowledged in the book as making its publication possible.

Even so, there were problems. The book was printed on fine paper, bound well and was full of photographs. It was published during the depression, and it was hard to sell a $15 set of books that was more of a reference work than a story, although there were many sections which included short stories and information for longer stories. Yet the books had to be sold.

Will Harllee was determined to leave a record of what pioneer Americans had done to inspire their descendants and he continued to effect every economy he could, including seven cent breakfasts, in order to save money and enable himself to leave this literary monument to posterity. And fortune smiled again.

Mr. Ralph Weeks, the President of the International Correspondence Schools, with whom he had worked so successfully in starting the Marine Corps Institute, arranged to have the I.C.S. purchase 500 sets of "Kinfolks" for presentation to libraries throughout the country.

Henry Morton Robinson, a Senior Editor of the Readers Digest, the best selling author of "The Cardinal," "The Great Snow," and other works, was an enlisted man in the World War I Navy. He had then served as Editor of the Rumford, Rhode Island rifle range magazine, "The Trigger." Such was his affection for his old chief that he, too, came to the rescue with a major purchase of "Kinfolks" for distribution. So ultimately several thousand sets were put in circulation.

The book was widely acclaimed by newspapers and genealogical publications and organizations throughout the South, and in Pennsylvania and Utah.

A typical appreciation was the one written by Sue Ruffin Tyle in the July 1935 issue of "Tyler's Quarterly Historical and Genealogical Magazine":

> There were so many delightful bits of intimate and vital history and biography tucked here and there, and it was read with increasing absorption. It compasses the whole sweep of our United States history with passages back and forth from England, Scotland, and Ireland to New York, Pennsylvania, Delaware, Virginia and the Carolinas . . . a veritable "Arabian Nights," containing many invaluable, first-hand stories such as "The Story of James Adair"—"Robin Adair"—"Memoirs of a Southern Gentlemen"—"Bombardment of Fort Fisher"—"Escape of Judah P. Benjamin"—"Robert Watson's Diary" . . . Again and again we see of what sturdy stuff these "kinfolks" were made; how they grappled with the barbarous Indians; . . . how they displayed ingenuity that wrought the sword from the plow-share in the 1770's and—in the 1860's—and best of all we see that "the home that puts its indelible impress upon its citizenship" is the one whose elders, "like Enoch, walk with God" and "create gallantry and inspire chivalry," whose children go forth "intolerant only of falsehood and dishonesty."

XXXIV
THE POLITICAL CAMPAIGN IN SOUTH CAROLINA 1935–1936

I shall do my utmost to disband the host of federal bureaucrats which now infest our people and to make the federal government a frugal government, the only kind of government which will ever be an honest government.
—**William C. Harllee, June 2, 1936**

Will Harllee had been closely associated with and a friend of President Roosevelt, and he had strongly supported him and the Democratic platform in 1932. He felt that the emergency measures of the first 100 days were necessary. But he believed that the emergency was over in 1935 and that Roosevelt was betraying the platform of 1932. His feelings against the New Deal in 1935, when he retired from the Marine Corps, were so strong that he decided to run in opposition to Senator James F. Byrnes for the Democratic nomination to the U. S. Senate in South Carolina. Byrnes was one of the strongest supporters of the New Deal in the Congress.

Harllee had always considered public funds sacred, not to be squandered, and he had made his accomplishments with the utmost frugality—spending what would now be considered ridiculously little. He thought that was the way to handle the taxpayers' money and that the work could be done that way. He believed that what he considered the profligacy of the New Deal and the resulting ever increasing national debt would lead the nation into financial ruin. He felt that the people would be led to expect more and more from the government instead of from their families and communities and that there would eventually be no end to their expectations. He thought of what financial problems had done to the German Weimar Republic and to other governments which had lost control of their finances.

He also believed that far too much power was being unconstitutionally usurped by the federal government to the detriment of the people at the grass roots. He was concerned that these problems would destroy our form of government, which he believed was the best on earth.

His political stand was well expressed in the following excerpts from a short public statement he made in Dillon, South Carolina, on June 2, 1936:

> I stand upon the principles of Thomas Jefferson, the founder of our Democratic party, whose ideal of democratic government is summarized in these words:
>
> A wise and frugal government which shall restrain men from injuring one another and leave them otherwise free to regulate their own pursuits of industry and improvement and shall not take from the mouth of labor the bread it has earned. This is the sum of good government.
>
> I shall oppose every act repugnant to the democratic doctrine of "equal rights to all and special privileges to none."
> I shall oppose every act to lay tribute on all the people or any of them for the advantage of some of the people.
> I shall exert myself to return the federal government to the few functions granted it in the compact between the states by which it was formed and to prevent it from becoming an

instrument of dictatorial power to master and saddle upon the people who created it a regimented rule of despotic power operating through a bureaucracy beyond the control of the people.

I shall do my utmost to disband the host of federal bureaucrats which now infest our people and to make the federal government a frugal government, the only kind of government which will ever be an honest government.

I shall do my utmost to prevent the federal government from embarking on any enterprises not expressly assigned to it in the Constitution because I know that eventually every such enterprise undertaken by government will be operated, not in the interest of the people, but in the interest of politicians and their creatures, who do not become transformed into angels when invested with power.

He also inveighed against "Dollar Diplomacy" (armed intervention to protect our investments in smaller countries). He took a stand against war, which he believed was caused all too often by selfish interests which fooled the public with false propaganda. He believed that these interests included the munitions makers and financiers, and he believed that they had tremendous power and had black listed him. Nevertheless, he had no regrets. When asked for evidence for his beliefs he cited Santo Domingo and Haiti as well as his outspoken opposition to war. He specifically noted that he had publicly spoken against our entry in World War I—before we entered that war.

He denounced our action in keeping possession of the Philippines after 1899.

He assailed the actions of the European powers and Japan in China, although he felt our role in the Boxer Rebellion— that of rescuing our legation in Peking—was justifiable.

He claimed our second intervention in Cuba, in 1906, was brought about by the U. S. sugar barons.

He attacked our landing at Vera Cruz in 1914.

He spoke against our occupation of Haiti, where no American or foreigner of any kind had even been molested since the expulsion of the French in 1804, but where the Marines nevertheless occupied the country for 19 years beginning in 1915.

He was very unhappy about the nature of the Constitution of Haiti, written by Franklin D. Roosevelt. It contained such features as the appointment of a "Council of State" by the President of Haiti, and then the reelection of the President by that Council as well as the other objectionable features already mentioned in connection with his second tour in Haiti.

He claimed our occupation of the Dominican Republic was caused by the tenfold increase in cost of raw sugar in 1916. He said that was the reason agencies of a great American financial institution engaged in sugar production there. They encouraged "bandits" to depredate other sugar estates, thereby causing the United States government to occupy the country, set up a military government and keep the Marines there, thus freeing the bank from worry about a Dominican government for eight years.

With regard to World War I, he told the Women's Club in Mullins, S.C. on Nov. 12, 1935:

> The same kind of patriotism was invoked by profiteers who made billions from war munitions and would have lost much of it if our men had not been sent overseas to "make the world safe for democracy." You have seen just how safe the world was made for democracy.

One might ask how he reconciled these views with his own part in these wars. To this he replied in numerous speeches,

> Here let me remind you that the Marine Corps, in which it has been my great privilege to serve for many years, does not decide the policy of our nation. Gentlemen in the State Department get salaries for doing that. Marines do what they are ordered to do by the Commander-in-Chief, the President of the United States, through the Navy Department. Military bodies do not debate or question the propriety of the orders they receive. When a military body degenerates into a deliberative assembly it is time to disband it.

After he had matured enough to realize what was really going on in these wars in which he fought, he did, at considerable professional damage to himself, speak out against it in public speeches, to Senators and Congressmen, and in 1916 to a Senatorial Committee, with the caveat, as he expressed it;

> However, when our country entered a war the debate was over, and I did my best to help bring it to a speedy conclusion, victorious to our arms.

He had carried out his orders in the most humanitarian way possible—particularly in Mexico, Cuba, Santo Domingo and Haiti. There was not much of a way to do this in the Philippines and China, except for protecting non-combatants like Summer Crystal.

These were his positions on domestic and foreign issues.

The political campaigns in South Carolina afforded candidates for public office an unusually good opportunity to speak their pieces. So much objection had been raised in earlier years to the power of the press, which, of course, was under the influence of its owners and of money, that arrangements were made for all candidates for the Democratic nomination for statewide offices to speak together from each of the forty-six county seats under the auspices of the South Carolina State Democratic Committee. Other candidates spoke in the seats of the counties of their constituencies.

Will Harllee spent almost a year preparing for this speaking tour, which was to be held in the summer of 1936. He was able to get plenty of speaking engagements before Rotary, Kiwanis, Lion, Civitan, Ruritan and other service clubs; American Legion and V.F.W. posts; United Daughters of the Confederacy, D.A.R., and other women's clubs; and a potpourri of other organizations and events.

He called on all the newspaper and state and local magazine editors and got along famously with them. He had learned much of the newspaper game back in Chicago in 1907—the importance of deadlines, how stories were written, the value of carrying mats of speeches so that small newspapers wouldn't have to set type, the relationships between publishers, editors and reporters, and so forth. He had enjoyed many a drink and story at the National Press Club in Washington, and the gentlemen of the press liked him and he liked them. They gave him favorable publicity even if they liked the New Deal, which most of them did.

Harllee's first political speech, a year or so before the election, was quite an introduction for him. When he called on ex-U.S. Senator Cole Blease from South Carolina, he was asked,

"How would you like to talk at the big Jolly Street rally with Governor (of Georgia) Gene Talmadge and myself?"

Harllee replied,

"It would be quite an honor."

Blease continued,

"We're going to attack Franklin Roosevelt's New Deal, you know. The going may get rough."

The reply,

"Senator, I agree with your views. As far as rough going is concerned, remember I'm a U. S. Marine, even if retired. Once a Marine, always a Marine."

Then some of the newspapers reported that the crowd was not going to let the speakers denounce the New Deal and would hurl bad eggs and other objects at them if they attempted to do so. Blease and Talmadge were late, so Harllee had to make the first speech against the Administration. He expected some fireworks—but was amazed to get a good hand instead.

He worked up an organization in each county—ex-Marines, kinfolks, West Point, Citadel, and Chapel Hill classmates, and an assortment of other friends and sympathizers. He was absolutely confident that the people of the state agreed with him against the New Deal, and he exuded this confidence. He was so forceful that New Deal proponents generally did not argue with his powerfully stated views. He was heavily heckled a couple of times, but he gave back as good as he took. His health had broken, and he was going on mind and nerve. He was skin and bones, weighing 115 pounds at six feet tall at the time, but he didn't look that slight in his clothes. He dared the hecklers to try to toss him off the platform, which they had threatened to do. They didn't try, but anyone who had seen him stripped would have realized that physically he could have done little to stop them.

He was offered campaign contributions by mill owners and others, but he refused to accept a cent. If elected—and he expected to be elected—he was determined not to beholden one iota to anyone. He continued to get favorable newspaper publicity, particularly from the Charleston News and Courier, and to radiate confidence. "The tide is turning against the New Deal" was his favorite assertion.

But the tide was running strong, very strong for the New Deal.

TIME magazine gave the campaign—his good friend Tom Stoney, ex-mayor of Charleston was also running against Byrnes—six pages, quoting Will Harllee at length but accurately pointing out the great popularity of the New Deal.

Senator Jimmy Byrnes hammered away at the boast that he had raked off for South Carolina 242 million dollars from the federal government while only ten million were collected in federal taxes in the state. Nineteen thirty-six was still a depression year and the hope for even more "something for nothing" was irresistible. Byrnes won by a record majority.

Will Harllee wrote friends in jest that South Carolina should be grateful to him for the millions of extra dollars poured into the state by the federal government to ensure his defeat and Jimmy Byrnes' victory. Drew Pearson's and Robert S. Allen's "Washington Merry-Go-Round" reported on February 7, 1937:

> Not many except those close to the White House know how far the President has gone down the line for his old friend, Sen. Jimmy Byrnes of South Carolina. Extra appointments, PWA loans, WPA grants were all thrown in the Senator's lap.

More seriously, Will Harllee strongly felt that it was basically wrong to loot the national treasury. Such high civic morals have, of course, long since passed out of vogue. Senator Paul Douglas of Illinois, another ex-Marine, was practically the only Senator in modern times to oppose pork barrel projects for even his own state. It now appears to most people that the measure of success of a politician is how much he can get for his constituents, whether it is in the national interest, deserved or even badly needed. The expectations of so many people for the U. S. Treasury to be looted in their behalf is now exceeded in danger to the Republic only by the threat of nuclear war. It is not just the poor who batter at the gates of the Treasury; as George Will has pointed out it is now the middle class which gets the most. There is no question that those who need it should be helped, but many people believe Government aid has gone too far beyond this.

Theodore White in "America in Search of Itself" has expressed very well the case in and since 1936 (although before the time of the New Deal it was not so true):

> That was easy to understand if one understood the first rule of politics; Everyone, and every group, want more than they deserve, and demand more than they want. All congressmen and senators are sent to Washington to rip from the national government what their own voters want; but the people as a whole rely on the President to protect them from other people's congressmen.

Will Harllee did not complain. He had kept the faith as he saw it, that of Thomas Jefferson and the founding fathers, and had fought a good fight. Forty-four years later the voters of America would turn towards his point of view in electing their President.

Will Harllee's swan song in South Carolina politics was perhaps best sung by a piece reprinted in the Columbia, South Carolina State (then the state's biggest newspaper) on September 10, 1936:

> One candidate will wind up with only a few votes but with a good deal of respect. He is Col. William C. Harllee of Dillon, retired Marine officer in the United States Senate race, who had found in this first venture in politics that fighting for ballots can be a lot harder and much less satisfactory than fighting against bayonets and bullets. Harllee's platform of opposition to the New Deal was unpopular while the man against whom he was running, James F. Byrnes, has a popular platform and himself enjoys immense personal esteem and popularity, but Harllee battled on grimly and determinedly long after he realized that his own cause was hopeless—and he battled fairly. The fighting colonel will get few votes but we would like for him to know that he has the respect of thousands who today have voted against him.

XXXV
THE MAJESTY OF
MAN—JUSTICE FOR
ALL

*There is another, far greater side to
"The Colonel" than his driving power.
He has grown far beyond the indivi-
dualistic ego of his youth. If this were
not so, this history would not be worth
writing.*
—from "The Colonel" (an unpublished book) by
Albert H. Jenkins

Now that the story of his active life has been told, here is a
sampler of a few of Bill Harllee's views on religion and politics,
subjects understandably taboo for discussion in the Navy's
wardrooms and the Marine Corps officers' messes, but subjects
in which every human being has very big stakes indeed:

> The idea that all men have rights is a comparatively recent
> one. Aside from that doctrine preached by Jesus, which idea
> never took root politically, Rousseau and Jefferson and men of
> their school of thought revived that idea and it was considered
> novel and preposterous and denounced in the same fashion
> that men who now seek privilege denounce men like Upton
> Sinclair.

Sinclair's THE JUNGLE is a masterpiece of portrayal of people and conditions of the time it was written. It is a work of much literary merit, and will live as literature. It has been suppressed as much as possible and denounced by the great publicity agencies because it truthfully portrays features of our industrial servitude and exploitation of people.

Most men in all periods of history have been exploiters of as many other men as they could be. There are only a few exceptions. Jesus of Nazareth was the first to condemn that practice. Exploiters of men crucified him. Jean Jacques Rousseau was the next man to publish the doctrine of the majesty of all men; that is the reason why his EMIL and other writings are great works.

Tom Paine's three great books, COMMON SENSE, THE CRISIS, and AGE OF REASON should be read. He was a rough and rugged writer. He lacked the tact of Benjamin Franklin, who was his friend, but I think that Paine was a greater man. He was an intimate of Jefferson and a friend of Washington. When someone said where liberty shines is my country, Tom said where liberty does not shine is mine. He went from country to country and carried the torch of liberty.

No words more grand in religion and philosophy have ever been utttered than his words "the world is my country and to do good is my religion."

The French people thought so much of him that one of their arrondissements elected him to the French Assembly in Revolutionary times.

Jesus expounded the basic religious moral doctrine. Jefferson translated it into political terms. Henry George defines its practical application to social, political and economic affairs.

Yes, I subscribe to the doctrines of Henry George. I learned of them in the years from 1911 to 1914 when I was on duty aboard the U.S.S. Florida, then the largest battleship afloat. One of my shipmates was a "Single Taxer" and took me to a meeting of the Manhattan Single Tax Association where I met Louis F. Post (later Assistant Secretary of Labor during the Wilson Administration) and his wife, Alice Thatcher Post, who became my friends and through whom I have since met many good and worthwhile people, including all the living children of the great Henry George, whom I count as my friends.

When honest and intelligent people learn of the doctrines of that great philosopher of economics and politics, they want to do something about it and become missionaries and crusaders. That stage I was in just before The Great War, and I did crusade. I even became a "pacifist" and made speeches against our entering the war until war was finally declared. Then I did the best I could to help bring it to a speedy termination victorious to our arms.

With regard to Henry George, he opened Bill Harllee's eyes to an unknown world—a world far apart from the then artificial economic security of the peacetime military world—a world in which men and women strove even much more than now in fear to keep the wolf from the door.

He felt it was a world in which the fox so often fared better than the lion. A world in which so often the many did not get the bread they earned by the sweat of their brow—while the few added field to field and fortune to fortune. A world in which the good and merciful were driven to question whether goodness and mercy really paid.

And Henry George revealed to Bill Harllee's satisfaction the causes of this lost, strange world.

The Marine's spirit took fire at the new vision. He who was a leader became also a follower—one of that goodly company who fight the never-ending, thankless battle against ignorance and oppression. From him, in turn, some younger men with him caught the fire.

The big Marine asked all officers in his commands to read and report on the following five books:

Victor Hugo's "Les Miserables"—for the human sympathy and compassion for humanity it inspires.

Rousseau's "Emile"—for its conception of the majesty of all men.

General U.S. Grant's "Memoirs"—for his direct manner of thought and action—simple and effective—Southern Bill Harllee felt Grant was a rugged and determined typical American soldier.

Gen. Edward Porter Alexander's "Memoirs of a Confederate" which he felt was the classic of Civil War literature.

"The Seven Laws of Teaching"—mentioned earlier.

He was proud of being a Mason and a Shriner. He wrote:

I am a freemason, a life member of the lodge where my father and his father were raised to the sublime degree of master mason and which sprange from a lodge instituted by my great grandfather, Thomas Harllee, some time before 1819, the first

321

masonic lodge of the old Marion S. C. District. My mother's father was a freemason. I am a life member of Naval Chapter, Royal Arch Masons, Vallejo, California. I trod the "rough and rugged road" there in 1903. Then I went to Honolulu for duty and went in the Scottish Rite to the 32nd degree and "crossed the hot sands of the desert" to Aloha Temple of the Nobles of the Mystic Shrine.

XXXVI
THE SUNSET YEARS

Promoted to the rank of Brigadier General on the retired list, having been specially commended for the performance of duty in actual combat by the Secretary of the Navy.

During the last month of the South Carolina campaign, Will Harllee battled a severe case of what he called "grippe" which brought on a physical collapse including pneumonia immediately after the end of the campaign. He then spent four months at the Naval Hospital in Washington.

The fact is that his health was completely shattered. The long years of working too hard, of sacrificing everything to get the battles won all over the world, the marksmen made, the "dammed education" in effect, Kinfolks written, and the New Deal attacked, and of smoking too much and eating too little finally told on him. Like the one horse shay he broke down all of a sudden, but not until the fights were all over.

He stayed in his home in Washington after leaving the hospital. He quit smoking February 6, 1938. It had been one of his greatest pleasures since he was a boy.

September of 1938 was a big month. First he had a long talk with General Peyton C. March, who had been Chief of Staff of the U. S. Army and who had also been Harllee's battalion commander in the 33rd U. S. (Texas) Volunteer Infantry in the

Will Harllee explains the history of the Elliott Trophy at the Marine Barracks, Quantico, Virginia on May 24, 1939. First awarded in 1910, the Elliott Trophy is the oldest in Marine Corps competition, presented to the Winning Team. The Trophy bears the name of Maj. Gen. George F. Elliott, Commandant from 1903 to 1910, who was an early advocate of Marine Corps competitive marksmanship. The Lauchheimer Trophy is to Harllee's left.

Philippine Insurrection. Harllee was much pleased to hear General March say that the old 33rd in which he had done his first fighting had performed harder service and more of it than any other U. S. regiment in the Insurrection.

Still later that month General Thomas Holcomb, then Commandant of the Marine Corps, took his old team captain Bill Harllee and a galaxy of their old shooting friends including Colonel Holland M. Smith, later famous in World War II as General "Howling Mad" Smith, out to Camp Perry with him in a Marine transport plane to witness the National Matches. He was quartered in a tent, like old times, with two close friends. Unfortunately, the Infantry Team nosed out the Marine Team for first place by 4 points, but it was an exciting match to the last shot. At the banquet, Bill Harllee was designated by General Holcomb to respond for him if he should be called upon to make an after dinner speech.

On July 27, 1939, Rafael Leonidas Trujillo, President and Dictator of Santo Domingo, visited Washington and saw his old friend, Colonel Harllee. Trujillo had been assigned as a lieutenant to Harllee's command in the Eastern District in 1921 and 1922. He liked and admired the old Marine and on the 1939 visit asked him to come down to Santo Domingo as his personal chief of staff and military advisor. Although he had liked Trujillo as a lieutenant, he knew full well what kind of a dictator he had been and said thanks, but no. Senator Shipstead and Congressman Crosser and the big Marine had visited Trujillo in Santo Domingo from Haiti in 1927. They had been lavishly entertained, but a shrewd observer of Latin America like Bill Harllee could not be fooled about what was really going on in what was then the most ruthless dictatorship in the Western Hemisphere.

In September of 1939 General Holcomb sent his old friend to a reunion of the 33rd U. S. (Texas) Volunteer Regiment in Ohio in a Marine Corps plane. It was quite a sight to see the gaunt old Colonel lifted into the open cockpit by a couple of husky young sergeants and then put on his goggles, smile and wave.

One of Harllee's greatest sources of enjoyment aside from his family in his final years was his attendance at the weekly lunches of his West Point classmates at the Army and Navy Club in Washington. They had had interesting and varied careers and remained a close-knit class until the end.

Since he could no longer fight his private and unauthorized wars on the great and powerful, or the authorized wars either, he loved reunions, reflections and ruminations. He also maintained a keen interest in what was going on in the world and uniquely interpreted it through the prisms of his own viewpoint to numerous correspondents and visitors.

His pleasure in his family was exemplified in the following paragraphs from a letter about his only grandchild, then 19 months old:

Our grandson is perfectly at home with us—contented and

325

happy. He eats well and sleeps well and plays vigorously during his waking hours. He has shown no evidence of being displeased; in fact he appears to enjoy hugely his enterprising investigations of things within reach.

He likes his grandpa and to disport himself with me in my room. But he is a good boy and a little gentlemen, considerate of his grandfather, and not disobedient.

Last evening he went to sleep early—shortly after a big supper. About 3 o'clock in the morning he awakened, but he was not disagreeable. He chattered and sang and was in a merry humor until he went to sleep again and slept soundly until the time his grandmother usually gets up.

He is greatly interested in the operation of the typewriter as I type this. After pretending to bite my finger when I brushed him off he casually busied himself with other features of interest.

The active little grandson was not entirely reconciled at being brushed away from the typewriter. He did not utter any complaint, but retaliated by scattering the contents of the waste basket over the room. Everything reachable has now been placed high, beyond his reach, but just as I type this he has found his grandmother's hand mirror and brought it triumphantly to me. His grandmother has gone out for an hour or so and left him in my keeping.

On December 9, 1941, he personally and unconditionally offered his services to the Commandant of the Marine Corps for the duration, but the reply he received later expressed appreciation of his offer and cited the Marine Corps policy, strictly adhered to, of not calling to active duty any retired officer over 64 years of age (then the compulsory retirement age for all armed forces).

Although his son was at Pearl Harbor when the Japanese attacked, he later expressed the following views on our then enemies:

A professional officer should not let personal hatred of enemy antagonists soil his conduct. The Japanese are ruthless in war but they are brave and enterprising, and splendid discipline prevails among their forces. I learned much about them while serving in the allied army with them in China in 1900. If any of them should fall into American hands, they should be treated as honorable antagonists, rather than perhaps as Americans would expect to be treated in case they should fall into Japanese hands. Atrocities beget atrocities. Their hostile forces are not our personal enemies. The term "enemy" in war connotes national antagonists, and honorable officers do not commit indignities nor atrocities upon helpless men. I am curious to know what will be the attitude towards this war of the American born citizens of Japanese ancestry. I confess that I am unable to form a conjecture. I fear that unskillful handling of them may have unfortunate influence, and I hope that unskillful handling will be avoided.

This would sound strange to many citizen soldiers. However, twenty years later, General David M. Shoup, Commandant of the Marines Corps, publicly and repeatedly declared that the professionalism of the Corps could best do without anti-Communist indoctrination and that it is unnecessary and sometimes even disadvantageous to hate anyone, even enemies in action. He stated that the mission of the Corps was to fight anyone, anyplace, anytime, as ordered by the President or Congress and to do so with cool, efficient detachment.

On April 8, 1942, Will Harllee was advanced to the rank of Brigadier General on the retired list of the Marine Corps to rank from February 23, 1942, in accordance with a new law, having been specially commended by the Secretary of the Navy for the performance of duty in actual combat.

The rank meant little to him, of course, as had money, but he was content and happy in his closing years with the knowledge that he had made major and lasting contributions to the Marine Corps and to his very extended family. Although never a Rotarian, as was his son, he was a Christian and truly lived by the Rotary creed "Service Above Self".

In September of 1944 he received word that President Roosevelt had awarded the Presidential Unit Citation to Motor Torpedo Boat Squadron Twelve, commanded by his son, for six months action in the Southwest Pacific. Only one other PT boat squadron was ever so honored. Inasmuch as his son had listened well to the lessons of his father, this was a source of considerable satisfaction to him not too long before he died of a heart attack between 2 A.M. and 4 A.M. on November 21, 1944. He was interred with full military honors in the Arlington National Cemetery. Among those paying last respects were

Lieutenant General A. A. Vandegrift, Commandant of the Marine Corps.

He was buried in a beautiful site just below The Tomb of the Unknown Soldier, a spot overlooking all the glories of Washington.

Fearless as ever, he had faced death with equanimity. He believed:

There is no death; what seems so is transition
This life of mortal breath is but the suburb of life's elysium
The portals we call death.

BIBLIOGRAPHY

Bagot, Richard, "My Italian Year", Mills & Boon, London, 1911

Barde, Col. Robert E., "The History of Marine Corps Competitive Marksmanship", U.S. Marine Corps, 1961

Blount, James H., "The American Occupation of the Philippines 1898–1912", G. P. Putnam's Sons, New York and London, 1912

Bodin, Lynn E. (Text), Warner, Chris (Color Plate), "The Boxer Rebellion", Osprey Publishing, London, 1979

Catlin, Albertus W., "With the Help of God and a Few Marines", Doubleday, Page & Co., Garden City, N.Y., 1919

Clough, Shepard Bancroft, "A History of Modern Italy", Columbia University Press, New York City, 1968

de Mille, Wm. C., "Hollywood Saga", E. P. Dutton & Co., New York, 1939

Fleming, Thomas J., "West Point: The Men and Times of the United States Military Academy", Wm. Morrow & Co., New York, 1969

Grayson, Rear Admiral Cary T., "Woodrow Wilson—An Intimate Memoir", Holt, Rinehart, and Winston, New York, 1960

Fitch, George Hamlin, "The Critic From the Occident", P. Elder & Co., San Francisco, 1913

Forman, Sidney, "West Point—A History of the United States Military Academy", Columbia University Press, New York, 1950

Harllee, William C., "Kinfolks", Searcy and Pfaff, New Orleans, 1934

Harllee, William C., Personal Files

Harllee, William C., "U.S. Marine Corps Score Book and Rifleman's Instruction", International Printing Co., Philadelphia, Pa., Revised 1917

Hayden, J.R. and Burley, R.M., "A History of the University Divisions, Michigan Naval Militia", The Ann Arbor Press, Ann Arbor, Michigan, 1921

Heinl, Col. Robert D., Heinl, Nancy, "Written in Blood", Houghton-Mifflin Co., 1978

Heinl, Col. Robert D., "Soldiers of the Sea", U.S. Naval Institute, Annapolis, Md., 1962

Hill, Dean, "Football Through the Years", Gridiron Publishing Co., New York, 1940

Lala, Ramon Reyes, "The Philippine Islands", Continental Publishing Co., New York, 1898

Landor, A. Henry Savage, *"China and the Allies"*, Charles Scribner's Sons

MacCloskey, Monro, Brigadier General U.S.A.F. (Ret), *"Reilly's Battery"*, Richards Rosens Press, Inc., New York, 1969

Marine Corps Gazette, *February 1950 Issue*, U.S. Marine Corps, Quantico, Va. 22134

Metcalf, Clyde H., *"A History of the United States Marine Corps"*, G. P. Putnam's Sons, New York, 1939

Millett, Allan R., *"The Politics of Intervention"*, The Ohio State University Press, Columbus, Ohio, 1968

Millett, Allan R., *"Semper Fidelis"*, Macmillan Publishing Co., London 1980

Moskin, J. Robert, *"The Marine Corps Story"*, McGraw-Hill, New York, 1977

National Rifle Association, All Issues of *"Arms and the Man"* and *"The American Rifleman"*, Washington, D.C.

Navy Rifle Range, Newspapers and bulletins of World War I

O'Connor, Richard, *"The Spirit Soldiers"*, G. P. Putnam's Sons, New York, 1973

Raymond, Dora Neill, *"Captain Lee Hall of Texas"*, University of Oklahoma Press, Norman, 1940

Roth, Russell, *"Muddy Glory—America's Indian War in the Philippines"*, Christopher Publishing House, North Quincy, Mass., 1981

Serkin, James E., Editor and Trefethen, James B., Compiler, *"Americans and Their Guns"* (History of the NRA), Stackpole Books

Sullivan, Mark, *"Our Times"*, Charles Scribner's Sons, New York—London, 1933

Sweetman, Jack, *"The Landing at Vera Cruz: 1914"*, U.S. Naval Institute, Annapolis, Md., 1968

U.S. Marine Corps History and Museums Division (Stephen M. Fuller and Graham A. Cosmas), *"Marines in the Dominican Republic 1916–1924"*, 1975

U.S. Marine Corps History and Museums Division, (Oral histories as noted, including those of Lt. Gen. Edward A. Craig, U.S.M.C. (Ret) and Brig. Gen. L.A. Dessez, U.S.M.C. (Ret)

U.S. Military Academy Class of 1901, *"25th Anniversary Class Book"*, E.C. Tripp, Pasadena, California, 1926

U.S. Navy, *"Small Arms Firing Regulations 1917"*, Washington, D.C., Government Printing Office, 1916

Whyte, Arthur J.B., *"The Evolution of Modern Italy"*, Oxford-Blackwell, 1944

Winterblossom, Henry T., *"The Game of Draw Poker"*